JAPAN

THE WORLD IN COLOUR SERIES

ITALY

THE PARIS WE LOVE

THE PROVINCES OF FRANCE

SCANDINAVIA

SPAIN AND PORTUGAL

SOUTH AND CENTRAL AFRICA

NORTH AFRICA

GREECE

SWITZERLAND

GERMANY

JAPAN

In preparation

MEXICO AND CENTRAL AMERICA

THE WORLD IN COLOUR

JAPAN

EDITED BY
DORÉ OGRIZEK

McGRAW-HILL PUBLISHING COMPANY LTD
NEW YORK   LONDON   TORONTO

JAPAN

Copyright 1957

Printed in the Netherlands

The book has been prepared under the editorship of
DORÉ OGRIZEK

Text by
MADELEINE PAUL-DAVID — MARCEL GIUGLARIS
JEAN-PIERRE HAUCHECORNE — PAUL MOUSSET
RENÉ SIEFFERT — KIKOU YAMATA

Translation by
PADDY O'HANLON

Illustrations by
A. BRENET — JACQUEMOT — JACQUES LIOZU
BEUVILLE

The endpapers represent The Flower Festival at Yoshiwara,
a gouache painting by Utamaro

*The publishers would like to acknowledge with thanks the assistance
given to them by the Japanese Embassy in the preparation of this book*

KOREA
SEA OF JAPAN
TSUSHIMA
SHIMO-NO-SEKI
WAKAMATSU
MOJI
KOKURA
HAKATA
NOGATA
FUKUOKA
NAKATSU
KURUME
SAGA
SASEBO
Mc Butterfly
BEPPU
OMUDA
OITA
NAGASAKI
UNZEN
KUMAMOTO
SAEKI
M. ASO
AMAKUSA
TEA
NOBEOKA
KIRISHIMA
SENDAI
MIYAKO-NOJO
MIYAZAKI
KAGOSHIMA
SAKURAJIMA
YAKUSHIMA
TANEGASHIMA
130°
MITAJIRI
IWAKUNI
HAMA
HI
MIYAJIMA
YAWATA
UWAJIMA

JAPAN

HOKKAIDO

NOSHIRO

AOMORI

L. TOWADA

AKITA

HACHINOHE

SAKATA

U

MORIOKA

HANAMAKI

SHINJO

HIRAIZUMI

MIYAKO

YAMAGATA

ICHINOSEKI

YONE-
ZAWA

KAMAISHI

SENDAI

FUKUSHIMA

KORIYAMA

KINKASAN

TAIRA

MATSUSHIMA

JAPAN

CENTRAL

0   km   50

JACQUES LIOZU

OCEAN

JAPAN

NORTH

0 ——— km ——— 50

JACQUES LIOZU

·SURFACE

In 1944, the total surface of Japan was 147,700 square miles. But the present territory, less the Kuril Islands occupied by the U.S.S.R., and the Ryukyu Islands occupied by the U.S.A., is 142,300 square miles.

POPULATION

In the course of the 18th century, according to the census carried out at the command of the Shoguns, the total population of Japan wavered between 26 and 27 million inhabitants. It was at the end of the 19th century that the figures began to rise continuously: from 32 million in 1870, they increased to over 47 million in 1905. Since then, by a steady increment it may be seen that in fifty years the population of Japan has nearly doubled.

1871	32,876,000
1885	37,868,000
1920	55,391,000
1940	72,540,000
1945	71,998,000
1950	83,200,000
1955	89,300,000

The big cities have developed on a particularly large scale. Figures for the six most highly populated towns in 1953 were as follows:

Tokyo	7,664,000
	(1956—8,070,000)
Osaka	2,250,000
Nagoya	1,194,000
Kyoto	1,148,000
Yokohama	1,067,000
Kobe	871,000

CONTENTS

PREFACE by Georges Duhamel of the *Académie Française* 16

HISTORY by René Sieffert 19

LEGENDS by Kikou Yamata 33

RELIGIONS by Jean-Pierre Hauchecorne 47

   The Religious Scene in Japan Today 57

   Folkloric Festivals 62

ART by Madeleine Paul-David 71

LANGUAGE AND SCRIPT by René Sieffert 97

LITERATURE by René Sieffert 103

THEATRE by René Sieffert 119

   Noh 126

   Bunraku 137

   Kabuki 144

   Modern Drama 158

CINEMA by René Sieffert 163

THE REGIONS by Paul Mousset 169

   Tokyo 178

   On the Way to Kyoto 193

   Kyoto 213

   Round the Inland Sea 217

   Kyushu 223

   To the North 226

   Hokkaido 235

WAY OF LIFE 239

   The Japanese Character by Jean-Pierre Hauchecorne 241

   Social Structure by Jean-Pierre Hauchecorne 246

Survival of Ancient Customs and Traditions by Jean-Pierre Hauchecorne . . 254

Architecture by Jean-Pierre Hauchecorne 274

Floral Art by Kikou Yamata 289

Daily Fare by Jean-Pierre Hauchecorne 293

The Tea Ceremony by Kikou Yamata 304

Doctors and Healers by Jean-Pierre Hauchecorne 308

Women and Children by Jean-Pierre Hauchecorne 312

Trades and Crafts by René Sieffert 337

Sports by Jean-Pierre Hauchecorne 350

The Twilight of Life by Jean-Pierre Hauchecorne 357

MODERN JAPAN by Marcel Giuglaris 359

Information and Education Media 361

An Unsmiling Economy 372

IDIOSYNCRASIES OF JAPAN by René Sieffert 381

INDEX 397

PREFACE

THE Westerner who has not despaired of understanding even a parcel of the dramas now cleaving this world of ours will find sudden glimmers of enlightenment if he takes the trouble to scour seas and continents, from Alaska to the Philippines by way of Europe's tormented lands, from the Cape of Good Hope to Finland, and from Darkest Africa to the farthermost outposts of the human race on the shores of the frozen Ocean. To my mind, however, at the present time two countries in particular merit the traveller's attention. One is the centre of civilizing activities in the Far East, and the other, of all the States of the Near East, is the land most patently in the throes of evolution. Those who would benefit from a closer acquaintance with Japan and Turkey—the two countries I have in mind—but who are not in a position to undertake a journey there, may widen their knowledge of them by delving into carefully selected readings. To this end, as far as Japan is concerned, I have the impression that the present book should fulfil the wishes and satisfy the curiosity of the attentive reader.

Lafcadio Hearn, whose portrait may be seen in Nanzan University in Nagoya where he was a professor—that same Lafcadio Hearn who spent a great deal of his life in Japan and loved this land to such an extent that he became a naturalized citizen—remarked in one of his books that a traveller's first impressions were often the most valid, such impressions being illuminating and worthy of consideration. Were it not for this guarantee, on returning from Japan last year I should perhaps have hesitated to publish an account of my travels. But why, indeed? What my sedentary countrymen demand is now to burrow into deep and knowledgeable works, now to confront themselves with problems glimpsed and singled out by the observant passer-by. There are noticeable divergencies in certain of these problems, according to peoples, climates, and a thousand-and-one other reasons, whether historical, religious, economic, or biological in nature. Veteran expatriates themselves are often well advised to turn to the planetary pilgrim in quest of information to confirm or contradict their own observations. And thus it is that the casual globe-trotter may unite his voice—with due circumspection—with those of the specialists and experienced witnesses. And thus it is that, when invited to write a brief introduction to this book, I thought fit to acquiesce.

Moreover, I have had the good fortune to enjoy conversations, both in Japan and Paris, with several of the writers who evidence their competence in the following pages. It would be difficult, even in a large-scale work, to furnish an encyclopaedic description of Japan—to tackle in turn each of the countless chapters relating throughout the millenaries the life and activities of a remarkably intelligent people, blessed with the rarest of human virtues—and to produce *in fine* a synthesis thereof. Nevertheless, in my opinion, the chapters assembled in this volume give the essentials of what a cultivated Westerner should know.

In order to understand the scientific and technical revolution whereby Japan became what she now is—a great power—one must first know the history of this country which so long remained closed to travellers from distant continents. One must also know the legends, which are often more revealing than the history of historians. And the reader who wishes to acquire a true understanding of customs should likewise study the religions —the principal religions, at least, embracing the greatest number of worshippers. Literature, the dance, drama, and the plastic arts have shown themselves to be influenced by the attempt at Westernization Japan parades before us, and which is not restricted to science and technology alone. As far as the cinema is concerned, Japan was not obliged to choose—as in the other arts—between tradition and the future. In this sphere she has proven worthy of her teachers, and climbed to the top of the ladder.

Well may the geography of Japan fascinate the dream traveller, the armchair voyager. On these islands, only four of which cover an area of any significance, strives a population of over eighty-nine million. The demographers forecast that within the span of a few years this population may number as much as one hundred million. Unhappily Japanese soil is arable only in the regions of plains and valleys, which are rare. It is thus evident that the policy of expansion and conquest followed by the military until 1945 was dictated by the problems of food supply and over-population. How can such problems be overcome in future? Here is a major theme for the traveller to meditate upon.

And there is many another besides. Japan, industrialized of necessity, must find markets. On the other hand, the big industrial and commercial powers show no inclination to sacrifice clients that they have, on the contrary, snatched from one another openly and unconcernedly. One wonders how such problems may be settled in days to come.

A large proportion of this people would still appear to be deeply attached to their Emperor; nonetheless, youth is a-dreaming, and the type of education being lavished upon them shows no tendency to dissipate revolutionary ideas; Japanese youth is, in fact, suffering from a malady known in my country as *le mal du siècle*.

I stated that education was being lavished upon them. It is true; the traveller cannot but be astonished by the number of schools of every grade and the swarm of students everywhere. There, as in France, the onlooker anxiously asks himself: "What is to be done with this *élite*? Can they find employment? What influence will they exert on the people from whose depths we see them emerge?"

I trust that, having considered all these problems, our readers may find consolation from a closer acquaintanceship with a nation renowned for its politeness, its good taste, its high sense of discipline and its love of work. Gone are the days when the man of leisure sought fanciful escape in reading. Nowadays, on the contrary, it is fitting to honour fruitful knowledge, book in hand, and seek therein themes for hope.

GEORGES DUHAMEL
of the *Académie Française*

HISTORY

歷
史

W HAT an incredible number of fantastic theories has been devised to explain the remarkable continuity in the history of Japan, her immunity to invasion, her astonishing might—and the ensuing catastrophe! To what mysterious virtues of the race or the land, or what supernatural powers does she owe these privileges? The answer is simple: you have only to open a map, and it will strike you at a glance— Japan is an island!

If the Imperial dynasty has succeeded in enduring interruptedly since the outset, this is entirely due to Japan's insularity, and not to mystic considerations that date back only to the late 18th century, and owe their success solely to exploitation by official propaganda, ably abetted by Western writers who were either dupes or accomplices.

If, throughout her long history, the sole battles in which Japan was engaged were civil wars that had no serious effect on the development of her civilization, this again was due to her insular situation which sheltered her from large-scale invasion: the Mongolian sea that submerged the continent from Hungary to Korea was stemmed by typhoons rather than by the warriors of the Kamakura regents.

On two different occasions Japan opened her gates to Continental civilizations. A first time, during the Nara era (8th century), she embraced Chinese culture *in toto;* then, eleven centuries later, Western techniques were adopted. But her privileged position permitted her to do so freely; in both cases, having borrowed all she could, Japan was then able to pick and choose the acquisitions she wished to incorporate in her traditions, and thus build up an original civilization on these new bases. Although commonly described as her power of assimilation, this is hardly a fitting definition, since it is easy to assimilate something one has chosen of one's own free will. Nor is it true to call it a gift of imitating, for whilst the Japanese first copies in order to get his hand in, he then interprets his imitations and devises them anew in his own particular style.

Japan's political history was characterized by a succession of dynasties of regents parallel with the Imperial dynasty. The latter did not itself govern, leaving the power in the hands of the regents who gradually overstepped the mark and, after a century or two, fell beneath the onslaught of a new political power. In this way the Emperor's self-effacement periodically gave the youthful forces in the opposition a legal argument whereby they could precipitate the fall of a worn out power, by accusing the latter of usurping Imperial might, and pledging themselves to reinstate it. The Emperor then invested the new *de facto* power, to which he again delegated his indefeasible but theoretical rights.

THE ORIGINS—Until 1945, the fundamental dogma of official history was the foundation of the Empire by Jimmu-Tenno, the great-grandson of the Sun Goddess, on the 11th February in the year 660 B.C. This over-precise date was established by 18th-century philologists, as a result of scholarly calculations based on ancient chronicles (dating from the 8th century A.D.), the *Kojiki* and the *Nihonshoki*. No historian worthy of the name ever took this seriously.

As far as ancient times are concerned, Japanese archaeology is still in its infancy: rudimental prudence reduced Japanese scholars to silence, and even nowadays excavation of the Imperial towns is practically prohibited; moreover, bones and wooden objects are rapidly destroyed by the climate. One thing, however, would appear certain: there was no such thing as Japanese civilization prior to the second century of our era.

Anthropology is not much further advanced and it is difficult to specify where the Japanese originated. Although the people may appear homogeneous to Western eyes, in actual fact they consist of an extraordinary variety of physical types revealing an extremely varied influx in the days when the race was forming itself—Mongoloid, Korean, Northern and Southern Chinese, Malayan, and Polynesian—in short, Japan must have provided the last refuge for peoples from Asia or the Asian South-East fleeing from the waves of invasion that swept across the world in the first millenary B.C.

It is curious to note that one element is absent from this mixture: in appearance the Japanese bears no traces of Ainu, although the latter race allegedly occupied the entire archipelago. It would seem as if the Japanese had driven them back into the Island of Hokkaido without ever coming into contact with them other than on the battlefield; or rather, as if the Ainus had never ventured to leave the north of Honshu.

Be that as it may, by the time the Sun dynasty established its authority—probably limited at that stage to Yamato, the province of Nara—the population of the islands had apparently already assumed its present physiognomy. From then on Japan was to receive little other than Chinese or Korean political refugees, who made her the priceless gift of continental civilization. From the 2nd to the 7th century, the Empire gradually spread its domination to surrounding provinces. Traces of these endless battles

15th-century Courtier (Musée Guimet)

seem to have been preserved in the chronicles, but they are buried in a distant past. The most serious adversary—owing to its equally advanced civilization—would appear to have been the rival empire of Izumo on the Sea of Japan. The fact that the great Temple of Izumo is still the second major national shrine after Ise implies that the affair was settled by a compromise in favour of the sovereigns of Yamato.

The great god of Izumo was the grandson of Susa-no-o, the celestial boor

The Arrival of the Portuguese in J

Malotru, Amaterasu's brother. To this day on Cape Hi-no-misaki on the tip of Izumo, there is a temple to Susa-no-o which is unique in that it dominates a shrine to Amaterasu: a reparation of self-esteem.

Although still errant—the capital being moved at the advent of each new emperor—even in those early days the Yamato court was already in close contact with the Korean kingdoms. Thence came scribes who introduced Chinese script, doubtless at the beginning of the 5th century. This made it

16th century (Screen, Musée Guimet)

possible to constitute archives and form a bureaucratic government service, without which it is impossible to organize an empire of any consequence.

Finally, in 552, under the reign of the Emperor Kimmea, also from Korea, came Buddhism (a letter from the Korean king who sent the sacred texts to Japan stressed the magic of the new religion), and subsequently Chinese culture as a whole. The introduction of this universalist religion was a major event in that it determined the entire course of Japanese history far more decisively than the vague, incoherent beliefs that were to be assembled at a far later date under the name of Shinto. Art and literature, ethics and thought, all owe their stimulus and development to Buddhism.

Confucianist ideas, on the other hand, were to provide the State with its organic principles.

Thenceforth Japanese civilization possessed the elements of her evolution, which she subsequently cultivated in accordance with her own genius.

NARA (710–93)—From 604, in the seventeen articles of his ethical instructions, the Regent Shotoku-Taishi drew the political conclusions resulting from the adoption of Buddhism, in which Ethics and politics were closely associated. But for this first great Japanese statesman it was essential that religious unity strengthen political unity, and his conception took material form in temples built throughout the provinces.

Shortly after the edicts of the Taika era—the "Great Reformation" (645–49)—remodelled the empire on the pattern of the powerful T'ang State: creating a hierarchic government service, census, and fiscal reforms.

The capital was still shifting, but within an increasingly narrow radius. Nomadism was no longer compatible with the existence of a centralized civil service. This was the deciding factor in constructing an established capital, on the model of the Chinese metropolis of the T'ang dynasty. It was built on a quadrangular plan, comprising a vast, well laid-out city said to have numbered as many as 500,000 inhabitants. Such was Nara, and its structure has been preserved to this day, at least as far as toponymy is concerned.

There a brilliant society developed, cultivating the arts and the humanities, imbued with the superiority of things Chinese, yet capable of imperceptibly adapting foreign influences to her own canons. This society was, moreover, deeply steeped in Buddhism: neither before nor since has Japan ever experienced such religious ardour and so great a florescence of temples and statues in the most harmonious setting imaginable.

HEIAN · (794–1185)—In 784 the Court abandoned this prosperous city, but it remained the "Capital of the South". Another site twenty-five miles further north was selected, probably for political and governmental reasons, and in 794 Heian-Kyo, the "Capital of Peace"—in other words Kyoto—was established.

Heian was to witness the first version of a specifically Japanese culture, in a new and more refined atmosphere, and it is probably nostalgia for this period that explains why the *Tale of Genji*, translated into modern language, is still one of the most read books of national literature.

The Heian civilization, however, was essentially aristocratic. Amidst a Court increasingly divorced from political realities and increasingly effeminate in atmosphere, there reigned an emperor who had abdicated his powers to the powerful Fujiwara regents. Their authority was primarily based on a matrimonial policy that consisted of introducing their daughters into the imperial gynaeceum. In this way, as their grandsons or nephews, the emperors came completely under the thumb of their regents. Moreover, care was taken to ensure that they

Torii Kiyonobu
Scene from the Battle of Ichi-no-Tani (1184)

abdicated as soon as they reached an age where they might have been tempted to revolt.

At the outset one man foresaw the danger of this system—the minister Sugawara no Michizane (844–903)—and attempted to shake off the Fujiwara's yoke. But the weakness of the Emperor soon left him to the mercy of his enemies, who exiled him in Kyushu.

The Fujiwara themselves eventually fell victim to the languor of an over-easy life. By the late 11th and early 12th centuries, the regents were mere shadows, given to seraglio intrigue, whereby the outcast emperor-monks attempted to regain their power. For a while it looked as if one of them might succeed, but his efforts merely favoured the advent of the military Taira clan, in whose hands he was reduced to a plaything.

KAMAKURA—Taira no Kiyomori definitively put an end to Fujiwara domination, and in 1167 assumed the title of prime minister, a privilege the latter family had held for centuries. In placing his grandson Antoku on the throne in 1181, he thought his task was completed. Kiyomori died that same year. And the rival Minamoto clan, which he thought he had crushed, was already rearing its head again in the still barbaric East.

In the meantime the Taira had wrought hatred upon themselves for the severity of their regime. Within four years, with the powerful collaboration of his young brother Yoshitsune—a genial strategist—Minamoto no Yoritomo annihilated them. In 1185, the fleet, in which the remnants of the once all-powerful clan had taken refuge, was sunk in the naval battle of Dan-no-ura. The seven-year-old Emperor Antoku disappeared beneath the waves. The local crabs, whose shells resemble a warrior's breast-plate, are allegedly the spirits of the Taira, still haunting the scene of their defeat.

In Kamakura authoritative Yoritomo, abetted by his spirited wife Masako of the Hojo family, established the shogunate or military dictatorship that was to survive until 1868, despite various vicissitudes.

MUROMACHI—An emperor, once again, precipitated the fall of the Hojo, whose power was already on the wane. In 1333 they were crushed by the forces of the opposition that Go-Daigo-Tenno succeeded in remustering for a while. But in 1335 one of his generals, Ashikaga Takauji, proclaimed himself Shogun. Go-Daigo thereupon established his court in Yoshino, in a high valley south of Yamato, whilst Takauji set himself up as anti-emperor

HIROSHIGE—*The Forty-seven Ronin, The Night of Vengeance*

in the capital. Two lines thus continued to reign until the agreement of 1392 put an end to the schism.

Christianity was introduced into Japan in the 16th century and fostered by the troubled atmosphere. Recognizing the centralized authoritative religion of the Iberian missionaries as a political arm, the Daimyo of Kyushu encouraged the spreading of the gospel. Hideyoshi and Ieyasu in turn set about radically extirpating this dividing factor, and succeeded in the attempt. This explains the ferocity of the persecution, which the normally tolerant Japanese would never have applied to purely religious quarrels.

EDO—Ieyasu thenceforth devoted himself to organizing the empire. A new capital was built up from rock bottom round the citadel of Edo. From a handful of fishing villages north of Kamakura, Ieyasu and his successors developed a prosperous city that was soon to compete with the old capitals and eventually, under the name of Tokyo, become one of the metropoli of the modern world.

Under the Tokugawa, Japan was administered on the lines of a vast forti-fied camp commanded by the fortresses whose Daimyo were closely con-

Peace Conference at Shimonoseki at the end of the Sino-Japanese War (1895)

trolled by the central government. The Daimyo were frequently transferred (the most important fiefs were entrusted to the Matsudaira, a clan of which the Tokugawa merely formed a branch), and their authority was restricted to the powers granted to them by the Shogun. The latter retained them at his court for several months of the year, and the rest of the time they were obliged to leave their families there as hostages. This explains the paradox whereby throughout two centuries and a half of military government (from 1600 to 1868), the country enjoyed total peace.

Only the military class of the Bushi—of which the Samurai, or liegemen, formed the backbone—theoretically held certain rights. And even these rights were limited on the one hand by the brutal power of the Shogun, and on the other by a rigid code of honour. The system did not avoid clashes, as illustrated by the famous epic of the forty-seven Ronin who brilliantly avenged themselves on the man who insulted their sovereign, but for all that were condemned to disembowel themselves—an honourable death imposed on them by a government that shared the general admiration their deed had inspired, but could not tolerate indiscipline. The peasants, who victualled this army, were closely supervised and piteously exploited. On the other hand the despised but active merchant class quietly took advantage of peacetime conditions to build up a fortune which was later to serve them in good stead. As early as the Edo era, by becoming bankers to the Daimyo who were gradually being ruined, they guaranteed themselves an occult but genuine power. "When the merchant of Osaka knits his brows, the Daimyo trembles" says the proverb.

Meanwhile the great feudatories of Kyushu, who were less severely subjugated, were already preparing their revenge. When the power of the Tokugawa—who had until then entrenched themselves behind isolationism during the past two centuries throughout which Japan resolutely shut her doors to foreign influences—began to totter beneath pressure from Western powers, accentuated by people within the country who were anxious to restore Imperial might and study modern techniques, the Daimyo of the south raised the Imperial standard and crushed the last partisans of the Shogun.

MEIJI—Once again, a new feudal class made ready to establish itself under

Entry of the Japanese into Port Arthur (1904)

31

cover of an emperor, on the ruins of a fallen dynasty. But a surprise lay in store: this youthful emperor, Meiji-Tenno, proved to be a statesman. He succeeded in imposing his own authority, and above all in surrounding himself with trusty, intelligent men—Samurai and middle class—who changed the face of the country in the span of a few years. The southern clans revolted, but were conclusively crushed by a national army trained and equipped on Western lines.

We all know the sequel. A resolutely modernized Japan revealed herself to the surprised West in the guise of a great power. Intoxicated by easy military victories, beginning in 1931 in Manchuria and North China, she formed an exaggerated idea of her own power. Carried away by the naïve and enterprising new Shogun of plebeian origin, and fanaticized by imperialistic propaganda that made a mythical character of the Emperor and a dogma of universal domination by Japan, in flinging an insensate challenge at the mighty masters of the Pacific at Pearl Harbour in December 1941, she regarded herself as the lord of China. The Philippines and Indonesia fell, the citadels of Hong Kong and Singapore were stormed, and Indo-China occupied.

For all that, as early as 1943, even in Japan, lucid minds realized that their country was courting the worst disaster in her history. The bomb on Hiroshima in August 1945 simply precipitated the expected collapse. However, on the ruins of vanquished militarism the liberal opposition rapidly set the situation to rights, still in the name of the Emperor.

And the new constitution proclaimed what Japan's entire history had proven: that the Emperor was the symbol of the Empire in the name of which a *de facto* power wielded supreme authority.

LEGENDS

傳
說

MYTHOLOGY—The great Japanese legends are linked to the national cult, Shintoism, and the history of the country which situates them in the "Age of the Gods". The acts and deeds of the divinities, related in the first Annals of the Empire known as the *Kojiki*, originally constituted the repertoire of narrators who used to hand down traditions by word of mouth.

After citing the divinity as the centre of the universe, and the celestial genealogies, the *Kojiki* turns the limelight on a fraternal couple, the creators of the Nippon Isles.

In the words of the myth, Izanagi and Izanami encountered each other when circling round the pillar of the sky. "What a handsome man!" exclaimed the goddess. As she was the first to speak, their child was shapeless, gelatinous, unworthy of life, and therefore abandoned to the current of a river. The couple began to walk round the pillar again. This time the god was the first to speak, exclaiming: "What a beautiful woman!" As a result, their child was perfect in every way. A pair of wagtails fluttering round them set an example of love.

Izanagi and Izanami hovered in space, on the ethereal bridge above the waters. Izanagi dipped his lance in the foam of the sea, and the drops that trickled from it formed the Japanese islands.

When Izanami was burnt to death at the birth of fire, his wife set off in quest of him in the nether regions.

At this point, the legend coincides with that of Eurydice. The Nipponese god also failed to return. He succumbed to temptation, and then seeing how corrupted his companion was, he fled from her, terrified. In his flight his comb dropped out, and from its teeth the vegetable kingdom was born. Izanagi's eyes, mouth, and ears conceived myriads of gods, who invaded the heavens.

From these divinities emerged a luminous personality, Amaterasu, the Sun Goddess. She became the ancestress of the Imperial house, conferring on her great-grandson Jimmu, the first Emperor of Japan, the "government of the plains of bulrushes and heads of rice".

Amaterasu had a brother, Susa-no-o the Impetuous, the God of the Wind and Moon. The latter offended his sister by flinging the hide of a flayed horse at her loom.

Justly incensed, the Sun Goddess retired into a grotto, leaving the world plunged in darkness. In order to coax her out of hiding, the gods foregathered, decorated two evergreen shrubs—the sakaki—with mirrors and scarves, and planted them in front of the grotto. Naked to the waist and girt with fern, the young goddess Uzume danced between the shrubs, and the joyful gods created such a din that Amaterasu half opened her door. A stalwart god seized hold of her, and presented her with a mirror. Mistaking her own reflection for a rival, the goddess advanced a little further. Her companions then explained that the image she could see was none other than herself, and that she was the fairest of them all. In the end Amaterasu ceded to their coaxing, and the world recovered the light.

From this legend was derived the rite of the bouquet of sakaki, a religious offering in the form of a purifying bough.

LEGENDARY HISTORY—Jimmu-Tenno, the conqueror whose accession to the throne is celebrated in Japan on 11th February, first appeared in the year 660 B.C., according to Japanese historians, but some people date his advent from the first centuries of Christianity only. He was sent from heaven to conquer Japan. A golden kite settled on his bow and showed him the way. Could it have been the totem of a clan, as in Egypt? Be that as it may, kites hover in the sky all over Japan, filling the air with their cries. Jimmu founded the Imperial dynasty and drove the Ainus northwards. Several thousand survivors of this race still live in Hokkaido, where, as bear-worshippers, they represent an ethnographical curiosity.

From this divine epic, Japan has preserved the Three Treasures symbolizing Imperial might and legitimacy: Amaterasu's Mirror, and the Gem and the Spear that were concealed in a dragon's tail.

HIROSHIGE—*Ise no Saburo,*
Yoshitsune's Vassal

Contemporary history is reunited with those legendary days: in her sacred temples the Sun Goddess still receives the homage of her descendants. The Ministers of State and the Emperor himself visit her shrine to inform her officially of every national event.

In the 3rd century another legendary figure, that of the Empress Jingu, traced the character and the geography of this Empire looking out across the yellow continent. Leaving the Emperor in Japan, she set off, clad in a magnificent breastplate, to conquer Korea. Her child who, before coming into the world, urged her to undertake this expedition, was born only when the enterprise had succeeded. He became Emperor Ojin, and is honoured as the God of War, under the name of Hachiman. The pigeons fed in his temple are his messengers.

The heroes exalted by history are all associated with wonders. For instance, as a child General Yoshitsune (in the days of the Kamakura warriors, 12th century) was brought up in the mountains by the *tengu*—winged genii

37

with long noses who taught him to fence. Tales of his victories, his lives, and misfortunes are still sung of by errant monks, who accompany themselves on the biwa.

Shintoism, which also venerates the powers of Nature, is the source of countless local legends personifying mountains, rivers, old trees, and rocks. Each Spring for instance, Mount Fuji releases from its crater the goddess-who-makes-flowers-blossom. The two rocks linked by a cord in the Bay of Ise are husband and wife, and between them rises the sun, promising life.

BUDDHIST TRADITION—The sense of miracles, love of greatness, and intimacy between nature and the mind have taken hold of Japan not only in her national legend, but also in themes imported from overseas.

Buddhist legends have taken root there, together with legends of Tao. There is nothing confusing about this, as far as the Japanese are concerned. It nurtures their art by providing inspiration for their paintings, prints, ivories, and sabre-hilts.

By far the most popular Buddhist legend is that of Jizo, the guide to the nether regions. His statue is

UTAMARO—*Shoki, the Demon-conqueror*

to be found at many crossroads, beside a woodland path or country lane. His head is shaven, and long ear-lobes dangle on either side, whilst in his hand he holds a pilgrim's staff. This calm divinity personifies the earth. Women who have lost a child tie bibs round his neck and place their infant's cap on his head. They also bring him toys and pile pebbles on his shoulders, arms, or feet. So doing, they help their babies in limbo, and implore Jizo to guide them in the world beyond.

Kwannon, the Goddess of Mercy, once helped a poor fisherman by assuming the guise of his wife and going to sell his fish in the market. In recollection of this, sculptors represent her carrying a magnificent fish in a basket. She was also incarnated in the pious maiden who embroidered the reflection of the heavens on a tapestry—a treasure that is still on show in a temple in Japan.

THE BOYS' FESTIVAL—The dolls that decorate the shelves for the Boys' Festival on 5th May evoke several legends.

Kwannon (Buddhist Print)

One of the characters held up for the children to admire represents Shoki, the Chinese St Michael. This gigantic bearded figure drives the demons away with his lance. His head is so charged with magic fluid that the flaps of his hood stand up in the air. His powerful face is often depicted on kites.

The more elegant figure of the calligrapher Ono-no-Tofu appears beside him. Clad in a gauze tunic, he stands beneath a weeping willow contemplating a green frog jumping unwearyingly in an attempt to reach the branch of the willow gently swaying above its head. In the end, it succeeds. Although forty years of age, the man to whom it taught perseverance continued his exercises with the paintbrush and eventually became a renowned calligrapher.

ILLUSTRIOUS FAMILIES—Harp music was discovered by a pilgrim who sheltered in a village, lost on the mountainside. There he was granted hospitality by a household whose members all played the thirteen-stringed harp magnificently, and taught him their music.

On trying to return there to thank them he could find neither the village nor the house: the musicians had descended from heaven.

Certain legends are connected with illustrious families, such as that of the Saionji, whose leaders never dared to marry. According to tradition, they were the custodians of the secret lute music, and Benten, the Goddess of Beauty and Music, is so jealous that she never allowed them to take a legitimate wife. She inhabits the grottoes beside the waters. Men visiting her shrine always leave their wives outside and pay homage to her on their own: otherwise she would be offended.

FROM FABLES TO POETRY—Traces of Chinese legends adopted by Japan are to be found in her literature. The best-known relates that of the encounter between the stars, Vega the weaver and Altair the cowherd. The stars can meet only once a year, on the 7th July, provided it does not rain. They then traverse the Milky Way across a bridge formed by the outspread wings of magpies or crows. They were separated from each other because, being too deeply in love, in the heavens the one neglected her looms and the other his herds. This legend is so firmly established in Japanese customs that every year on the 7th July the children decorate two bamboo poles with poems and streamers in honour of the stars.

Then again, in the moon, the Japanese see a white rabbit pounding rice cakes on a mortar.

The maiden known as Kaguyahime, or Brilliant, born in a bamboo shoot where a woodman discovered her, grew up so reputed for her beauty that she was courted by countless ardent suitors, including the Emperor himself. Their rivalries form the subject of the first great legend to be retained in Japan's literary thesaurus, the *Taketori-Monogatari*.

Another celebrated beauty, the poetess Komachi, has survived in classical anthologies and noble lyric dramas of Noh. With her long tresses dangling down her back, and clad in a series of superimposed tunics of several hues and the billowing drawers fashionable at court, she triumphed in the poetical tourneys in the palace. A rival then accused her of plagiarism, claiming that the poem she presented had been copied from an old miscellany. Komachi demanded the anthology in question. On seeing her poem inscribed therein, she understood the trick that had been played on her. Hidden in her garden, her rival had doubtless overheard her reciting verses. Komachi then called for a bowl of water and washed the old anthology. The fresh ink became diluted, and the wicked poet was discomfited in the face of the Emperor himself.

But, intoxicated by her success, Komachi declined all her suitors. To His Majesty's favourite, General Fukakusa, she retorted: "I will receive you if you come to my door a hundred times in succession." He went there in all weathers, inscribing the number of nights on the shafts of his chariot. On the ninety-ninth visit, a snowstorm was raging. The general perished on the poetess's doorstep.

By way of punishment, she lived to the age of one hundred. She could be seen wandering through the cemetery where she was haunted by the avenging spirit of the man

HIROSHIGE—*Kaguyahime*

41

HOKUSAI—*Lantern with Ghost's Face*

she rejected. Who would have imagined that pitiful old woman begging by the wayside was once fair Komachi who, in time of drought, made the rain fall by addressing a poem to the Heavens?

When she died, her body was devoured in a field by a flight of carrion crows. In Buddhist ethics, Komachi has become symbolic of the vanity of the passions of this world.

By way of contrast, the legend of the Feather Dress provides one of the most beautiful lyric themes of the nature-loving Japanese. According to this myth, the beach at Miho was so tempting in the sunshine that an angel flew down from heaven to bathe there leaving her feather dress hanging on a pine tree. A fisherman seized it, and the daughter of heaven was unable to fly away. She entreated the fisherman, who consented to return her dress if she danced for him.

In fashionable wedding ceremonies, this legend of the Feather Dress, or that of the Pines of Takasago, are often enacted for the benefit of the guests. The Pines of Takasago celebrate the eternal fidelity of conjugal love. The Philemon and Baucis of Japan are a venerable old couple. Armed with a bamboo rake and a broom, they symbolize the love of two evergreen pines, from which they gather the needles. On their wedding day every Japanese couple inevitably receives a replica of this happy pair, in the form of a painting or sculpture, an ornament or a doll—accompanied by the centenary tortoise and the stork.

METAMORPHOSES—Animism has created other legends, some full of wit, others grotesque or terrifying. There is, for one, the fox, the messenger of the God of Rice and Riches, who transforms himself and lures travellers astray. Then again there is the vixen changed into a woman who may

well procreate human children with her husband, only to disappear one fine day. As for the badger who beats his stomach like a drum until the woods echo with the sound of the tomtom, he has a weakness for fritters. Consequently he is apt to follow people who buy fried food, and artfully snatch it away from them. He frequently disguises himself as an old bonze in order to hoodwink people more easily.

Animism also endows objects with life. A famous scene in classical drama represents a young fiancée being dragged away by the plumed helmet of white fur she is carrying to her Samurai hastening in battle.

TORII KIYOMASU
Watanabe no Tsuna's Battle

The wistaria or the peony painted on a panel detach themselves, assume human form and live a brief but passionate destiny. The iris becomes a woman in order to wed the poet Narihira, the prince of the plant kingdom, but alas, he is a Don Juan who gives his heart to all and sundry.

GHOSTS AND SORCERERS—More disturbing metamorphoses may spring upon you unawares in Japan. On the open road at night-time, never consent, even for a moment, to take a child from the arms of a tired traveller who implores your aid. You will find it is the ghost of a woman who died in labour, tormented by regret at leaving her child on earth. If you concede, you will feel your burden growing heavier and heavier, until a stone eventually falls at your feet.

Beware of the Lady of the Snows who rises in a flurry at night and waylays pilgrims visiting the temple of the God of Coughs and Colds in the first icy week of February. She will fade into mist in your arms.

Also beware of the beautiful demon who offers you a drink beneath the maples turned red by the onslaught of autumn. Never interrupt your hunt on her account, especially if she offers to dance for you. You will soon see her horns emerge, and fall under her spell.

HIROSHIGE
Urashima on the Turtle

Even beware of the old whimperers: never ask them for hospitality. They are ogresses who delight in human flesh. One of them actually succeeded in retrieving her arm from the good warrior Watanabe no Tsuna, who cut it off in an epic battle, and shut up his trophy in a stone coffer. An old woman came to him entreating: "I have heard tell of your doughty deed! Won't you just show me that witch's arm?" And as soon as the coffer was ajar, she snatched up her arm, stuck it on again, and flew off sneering.

FOLKLORE — On the other hand, Japanese folklore offers the most charming legends for children, with a moral. The most familiar by

HOKUSAI—*Momotaro and the Three Animals: the Dog, the Monkey, and the Pheasant*

far are the tales of the fisherman Urashima and that of Momotaro, the child born in a peach.

The background of Urashima is a beach flanked by thatched-roofed cottages. There the fisherman one day caught sight of some urchins tormenting a turtle on the sand. He offered them a small coin, liberated the turtle and threw it into the sea. One lovely afternoon steeped in sunshine, it reappeared and offered to take him on its back to the palace of the Dragon who rules over the seas. Urashima bestrode it and soon disappeared on the horizon in a frothing of waves. At the end of his travels, he discovered the wonderful coral palace of the Dragon-King of the Sea where, amidst dancing fish, he wed the princess, the Dragon's daughter.

The fisherman was happy with her, but one day, tenderly recollecting his parents, he requested his wife's permission to pay them a visit. The princess conceded to his desire, and handed him a coffer which he must never open if he wished to return to her. Borne on the turtle's back, Urashima landed on the shore and did not recognize a soul. He enquired: "Where is the house of Urashima the fisherman?"—"Urashima? His house disappeared long back. He is said to have left the village nearly two hundred years ago!" At these words, Urashima realized how long his happiness had endured. Terrified, he sought an explanation by opening the coffer. All that it enclosed was smoke that coiled into the air, whilst he grew wrinkled and white-haired, collapsed and died, an old man.

Momotaro carries us into the mountains beside the river, where an old woman washing her linen on the shore saw an enormous peach being swept along by the current. She snatched it out of the water and carried it to her cottage to share with her husband, the woodcutter. When he opened the peach, a beautiful child emerged. On reaching manhood, he set off to subjugate the Isle of Demons, together with the Dog, the Monkey, and the Pheasant he encountered on the way.

On returning, he brought back booty of gold, jewels, and silks for his old parents and the dazzled villagers.

Japanese children grow up in the midst of myths. The common people combine love of their native land, their heroes, and the spirits of their departed relations, in one and the same cult.

The dynamism of present-day Japan springs from these legendary sources: she is turned towards the Sun, the source of life.

RELIGIONS

宗教

THE religious panorama of Japan is one of the most extraordinary one could imagine in this 20th century of ours. Side by side with Buddhism and Christianity—both of relatively recent importation—there still exists a form of respect for the elemental forces of Nature mingled with the cult of deified beings or objects, a polytheistic religion as one of its Japanese exegetes affirms: in short, Shinto.

The origins of Shinto, or Kami-no-Michi—the Way of the Gods—is lost in the mists of time. They are as mysterious as the very beginnings of Japanese civilization. No written document on these two questions exists prior to the successive compilations known as *Kojiki* ("Notes on the Events of the Past") in 712, *Nihonshoki* ("Chronicles of Japan") in 720, *Kogoshui* ("Gleanings of Ancient Sayings") in 807, and lastly *Engishiki* ("Ceremonial of the Engi Era") in 927.

Some schools of thought have refused to recognize Shinto as a religion; others have qualified it purely and simply as animism or shamanism. However, one is obliged to admit that, for the average Japanese, Shinto assumes all the importance of a religion, and makes its presence felt in his every tradition and in the most trifling details of his daily life.

PRIMITIVE FORM OF SHINTO—Everything goes to prove that the cult of Uji-Kami—Gods of the Clan—was practised long ago by various groups scattered throughout the territory of primitive Japan. This cult was associated with respect for the spirits of the clan leader's ancestors, the gods of the clan becoming tutelary guardians of the locality and, in a wider sense, protectors of the harvests. In battles between clans, the gods of the vanquished were supplanted, or at least their importance was reduced, in favour of the gods of the victorious clans.

A first period may be distinguished, ending in about A.D. 550, throughout which the Japanese had no notion of religion as a separate institution. All that existed at that time was a collection of legends handed down by word of mouth, on the divine origin of the islands forming Japan, and of the Emperor himself as a direct descendant of the first sovereign Jimmu-Tenno, allegedly born in 711 and deceased in 585 B.C., and a mythical scion of the great Sun Goddess, Amaterasu-o-mi-kami, meaning literally "the August-Great-Goddess-who-illuminates-the-sky". In addition, the Shintoist pantheon contains eight hundred million gods, including the Uji-Kami whom we have already mentioned, and the majority of whom are personifications of the forces of Nature. In this respect, we should note that numerous outstanding figures in the history of the country have been deified throughout the course of the centuries. This explains why one of the most popular cults is that practised in the temples of Tenjin or Temmangu scattered throughout the empire and devoted to the memory of the great Prime Minister and poet of the 11th century, Sugawara no Michizane, who is regarded as the God of Calligraphy and Learning.

In those remote days, no distinction was made between the respect due to the living Emperor and that paid to the gods, who were in fact the ancestors of the sovereign and the defenders of the empire. The most widespread cults were those of

Buddhist Mendicant Monk

the Gods of the Wind, Fire, Epidemics, and Food. The people used to perform lustral ablutions to purify themselves from impure contacts, with corpses in particular. For all that, no precise moral code or coherent dogma was established.

INTRODUCTION OF BUDDHISM—From the 6th century, Buddhism began to infiltrate into Japan. To be precise, it was in 552 that the King of Kudara, one of the Korean kingdoms, sent Emperor Kimmei a statuette of Cakyamuni, Sutras, and other Buddhist objects. The impact of the new religion was so strong that Shinto lost all hope of evolution in a religious sense. The invention of the word Shinto, to designate the cult of specifically Japanese gods, dates from that time. Then came the introduction of Ryobu-Shinto— Shinto in dual form—based on an idea, skilfully propagated by Buddhist exegetes of that time, whereby behind each Shinto Kami a reincarnation of a Bodhisattva was concealed.

For centuries thereafter—until about 1700, in fact—Shinto underwent a long period of stagnation, and it became increasingly difficult to distinguish it from Buddhism. The two religions were so closely associated that certain Buddhist divinities were definitively incorporated in Shinto, and the majority of Shinto shrines housed bonzes who modified the architecture and performed their religious practices there freely.

In the beginning there were a number of sporadic attempts at resistance, but these were rapidly dispersed by the wind of reforms that swept right across Japan in the 7th and 8th centuries. Buddhism advanced, armed with a doctrine developed from the myriads of volumes of the *Tripitaka*. As for the rites and the wealth of statuary and other objects of worship, these inevitably exerted a power of attraction over the Japanese who, until that time, had no way of expressing their religious emotion other than communing with themselves in front of empty shrines, supposedly filled with invisible divinities. Apart from this, it should not be forgotten that Buddhism brought Japan the cream of the brilliant T'ang civilization, at a time when China was the most advanced and harmonious country in the world. The most important of these gifts was undoubtedly the means of expressing oneself in writing, thanks to Chinese characters.

In speaking of Buddhism in Japan, it is understood that we are not referring to Hinayana—or the lesser Vehicle—a cult widely practised in South-East Asia, whereby total extinction of passions and desires is the sole means

of attaining the blessed state of Buddha. We are referring to Mahayana—
the greater Vehicle—which progressed by way of the North, across China
and Korea, teaching a wider—and hence more international—development
of the basic idea of Buddha, that is, that salvation by supreme illumination
does not consist solely of the extinction of passions and desires shared by
beings endowed with feelings, but in the detachment of these beings from
their origin and their egoistic particularism, to permit them to attain a spirit
of universal fraternity.

CONFUCIANISM AND TAOISM—Two other intellectual and semi-religious
currents filtered from China into Japan at about the same time as Buddhism:
Confucianism and Taoism. The former made a profound impression on the
country, and its influence is still felt in more than one respect. Loyalty and
filial piety, in fact, form the basis of the fundamental Confucian virtues that
scrupulously control the five types of relationships between mankind: the
relationships between lord and vassal, parents and children, elders and
juniors, husband and wife (women being subordinated to men), and finally,
relations between friends.

The conception of Confucian life is crystallized in the idea of Heaven
(Tien, in Chinese), of which man is, as it were, the image or reflection. A
single order regulates all human institutions on earth as in heaven.

The achievement of this order in everyday life is the Way (Tao, in
Chinese), the moral norm of mankind. It is each individual's duty to live
and act in accordance with the statute that devolves upon him in the social
hierarchy. Heaven grants the sovereign a mandate to reign by seeking inspiration in the five celestial virtues: Wisdom, Benevolence, Justice, Might,
and Integrity.

It is easy to understand the importance of Confucianism's contribution
towards maintaining and developing Imperial power in Japan, and in
stratifying Japanese society; in fact innumerable traces of its influence are
still to be seen in 20th-century Japan. In the 18th century, Confucianism
manifested itself again in the origin of Bushido—the Way of the Warrior—
the rigid code of honour of the Samurai, the influence of which had its
repercussions on the social and moral system of the rest of the population.

As for Taoism, as outlined in the work of the Chinese philosopher Lao-
tseu, its Way (Tao) is not the same as that of Confucianism, but the "Way
of Nature", of which, once again, human life is a reflection. Freed of con-

One of the Ni-o guarding the Nitenmon Gateway at Nikko

SHINTO TEMPLE

A. *The "Holy of Holies"* (closed to the public). — B. *Haiden, the "Hall of Prayer".* — C. *Karashishi, "Lions of China".* — D. *Gateway to the Sacred Precincts.* — E. *The "Right-hand Minister" and the "Left-hand Minister" of the God.* — F. *Platform for the Kagura* (Sacred Dances). — G. *Offices, Priest's Dwelling, Sale of Votive Offerings and Amulets.* — H. *The "Pure Water" with which one Purifies one's Hands and Mouth before going further.* — I. *Stone Lanterns.* — J. *Torii.* — K. *Stele Bearing the Name of the Temple.*

ventions, the ideal man should commune to the full with Nature which has neither birth nor death; he should follow the natural Way, as freely as water flows and the wind blows. The perfect Taoist is a *hsien* in China (man of the mountains, or hermit) and a *sennin* in Japan. Another aspect of Taoism comprises a bundle of animistic beliefs, accompanied by the practice of witchcraft and magic, current not only in China but also in tribes in Mongolia, Manchuria, and Eastern Siberia. In Japan's semi-religious folklore, the sennin plays the role of sorcerer, mastering the powers of Nature.

There has never been an organized Taoist movement in Japan. The influence of Taoism is subtle in the extreme, and has never had occasion to come into direct conflict with any other system. On the other hand, because of its naturalism this religion is the reverse of Confucianism which insists on civic virtues and, because of its rigidity, is in turn the reverse of Buddhism, which is more tenderly human. However, through a curious phenomenon to which the particularly synthetic genius of the Japanese is not entirely foreign, it was Buddhism that bridged the gap between the two systems and consolidated their empire over Japanese life. Here we should mention the important penetration of the Zen form of Buddhism that took place in the 13th century.

Now it so happened that on the one hand Zen brought from China the rich and precious teachings of the Sung civilization, and the painting of this culture—impregnated with Taoist

BUDDHIST TEMPLE

A. *Hondo: Main Building.* — B. *Pagoda: Tiered Tower* (always an odd number of Tiers). — C. *Priest's Dwelling.* — D. *Belfry* (the bell being struck with a beam). — E. *Gateway* (where the Ni-o, or "Guardian-Kings" are generally to be found). — F. *Precincts of the Temple* (often a covered gallery). — G. *Monks' Dwellings.*

influence—was to be the point of departure of every form of Japanese aesthetic refinement, whether in painting itself or in landscape-gardening, the arrangement of flowers, the tea ceremony, poetry, or all the other forms of expression of artistic feeling. On the other hand, the Zen monasteries were the sole repositories of learning and teaching throughout the period of civil war and social upheavals that lasted from the 14th to the 15th century.

THE SIXTEENTH CENTURY OF CHRISTIANITY—When he set foot in Kago-shima on the southernmost tip of Kyushu on the 15th August, 1549, as far as his apostolate was concerned the Jesuit St Francis-Xavier could not have chosen a better time to visit Japan. After years of confusion, the whole

country was awaiting a new message. In two years, St Francis-Xavier himself christened several thousand Japanese, whom he used to call "the delights of my heart". The Catholic missionaries met with immediate success, and obtained a multitude of conversions. The maximum was evidently reached in about 1596, with 300,000 believers, an extraordinary achievement when one stops to think that Japan numbered no more than twenty-five million inhabitants at the time. Without in any way wishing to belittle the apostolic zeal of the first missionaries, it should however be pointed out that the large number of conversions was due in part to the fact that all the liegemen followed their lord when he embraced the Catholic faith. The country was all the more receptive to Christian doctrines in that Shinto and Buddhism had gradually developed towards a more monotheistic conception of religion—owing to the fact that the former accorded preponderance to Amaterasu, the Emperors' divine ancestress, and the latter to a certain representation of Buddha.

This fine start for Christianity was unhappily cut short by the edicts of persecution and interdiction set forth in 1597 and confirmed in 1614. For the next 250 years, Japan was to sever all relations with the outside world and develop in a closed circle, except for the tiny window opening on the Isle of Deshima in Nagasaki, where the Dutch established themselves in their outpost.

THE RELIGIOUS SCENE IN JAPAN TODAY

THE religious physiognomy of present-day Japan assumed its almost definitive character after the Restoration of the Empire in 1868, which strengthened respect for the Emperor and everything connected with him.

Entry to the Temple of Hachiman in Kamakura

Nowadays Shinto presents three aspects. First there is that of Emperor-worship, the rites and structure of which are, in a manner of speaking, closest to the origins of the religion; then there is that of the tens of thousands of shrines where priests, whose dignity is hereditary, safeguard the memory of the Uji-Kami—gods of clans or regions; and lastly, that of the 150 or so sects or sub-sects derived from Shintoist traditions in somewhat the same way that Protestant sects originated from Catholicism. One of the most remarkable is the syncretic sect known as Tenri-Kyo, a mixture of Shinto with elements derived from Buddhism and even Christianity.

Buddhism may also be divided into several groups. One of these would comprise three sects that originated during the early days of Buddhism in Japan and have since become more or less fossilized and devoid of influence, being reduced nowadays to barely 100,000 adepts in all. From the historic point of view, however, they are extremely important, since their temples contain priceless treasures of primitive art, both Buddhist and otherwise. We are referring to Horyuji south of Nara; Todaiji in Nara itself, containing the statue of the great Buddha in person and the unique Shoso-in collection; and lastly Tosho-daiji and Yakushi-ji near Nara.

A second group could be said to comprise the two sects of Shingon and Tendai, numbering respectively about ten and two million worshippers. These two sects, which influenced the entire civilization of the period known as Heian—former name of Kyoto—between the 9th and 12th centuries, are founded on practices of magic ritual that attracted a certain number of Japanese who were already receptive to the cult through Shintoist worship of the primeval forces of Nature.

The third group would consist of the most prevalent sects today, originating from a great reformation movement that took place throughout the 12th and 13th centuries. In this we might incorporate all the sects and sub-sects of the "Pure Land"—or Jodo—divided into two main groups, Jodo and Jodo-Shinshu, consisting of three million and a half and fourteen million followers respectively, mainly recruited from the peasant and humbler classes. Their doctrines, which are very similar, are simplified in the extreme, to make them accessible to the common people. The elaborate rites and mysticism of the preceding sects are relegated in favour of the dogma that entrance to the "Pure Land" is gained by sincere faith in the bounty of Buddha and fervent repetition of his name: "Namu-Amida-Butsu..." ("Glory to Amida Buddha!").

The Daibutsu of Nara

Nichiren-shu is an active sect retaining numerous traces of the aggressive character of its 13th-century founder, the bonze Nichiren "Sun Lotus": who spent his life battling incessantly with the other sects and the powers-that-be. Nichiren incited his disciples to emulate the battlesome qualities of the Bodhisattvas, who fight to attain the state of Buddha. In practice this consisted of beating in rhythm on a drum, whilst repeating emphatically and continuously the name of the Sutra that formed the basis of his teaching: "Namu-Myoho-Renge-Kyo...!" ("Glory to the Sutra of the Lotus of Truth!"). The fanaticism of Nichiren-shu attracted countless warriors, and subsequently extremist nationalists and militarists. This sect still has seven million followers, mainly plebeian—from the lower class districts of Tokyo in particular—since they find an outlet in the exacerbated excitation of the senses produced by the deafening din of monotonous invocations, to the rhythm of flat drums.

We have reserved for the end the Zen form of Buddhism (from the Sanskrit Dhyana, meaning meditation or contemplation), comprising nearly nine million worshippers. The altars of this sect are sparingly decorated, and often contain only one effigy of a meditating monk. The basic concept is that everyone can attain knowledge of the Law and Nature of Buddha by meditating about himself and progressively detaching himself from the various doctrines of Buddhism, some 84,000 in number! The technique of detachment is based on three elements: meditation in a kneeling position or sitting cross-legged; knowledge of a corpus of doctrines composed of anecdotes or "sayings"; and lastly, an active form of expression, developed by way of impromptu questions to which it is practically impossible to find an answer. The end in view is a kind of illumination (satori) completely divorced from logic and intellect. Meditation should tend towards detachment from every desire or passion. Whoever attains this state no longer needs to meditate; he lives in a natural state of contemplation, wherever he may be or whatever he may do.

When Japan opened her doors to the world in 1868, Christian missionaries once again flowed into the country; but the Catholics were no longer alone, and there were representatives of all the Protestant sects. Despite the multitude of zealots of Christ, the total number of Christians does not exceed 400,000, divided equally between the two groups, the favourable factors of the 16th century having disappeared for ever.

On the other hand, if we rely on statistics we are surprised to note that

Adepts of the Nichiren-shu Sect

the adepts of Shintoism exceed sixty million, and those of Buddhism forty million, for a population of approximately eighty-seven million! This paradox is easily explained, once we realize that every Japanese, whether he practises a religion or not, automatically falls under the influence of the eight hundred million Shinto gods, although this in no way prevents him from belonging to any one of the Buddhist sects. The same people may frequently be seen going from one shrine to another, according to the requirements of the moment. The same thing applies to the family altars in private homes, of which there are often two: one consists of a kind of shrine containing a Buddhist statuette or the family funerary tablets, and the other a Shinto altar for the household gods.

In short, the religious attitude of the average Japanese may be summed up as follows: he is born, marries, and respects the Emperor in accordance with Shinto; he dies as a Buddhist; meanwhile, throughout the course of his life he observes customs peculiar to both religions—mixed with a dash of Confucianism; lastly, he absorbs a little Christianity in studying the West and certain aspects of modern Japan.

FOLKLORIC FESTIVALS

FESTIVAL OF THE FOX GOD—The best way to realize fully the hold Shinto has on Japanese life is to mingle with the dense crowds that throng the temples on holidays, or matsuri. There is, for instance, the great festival of the "First Day of the Horse"—Hatsu-uma—according to the ancient calendar (that is to say, in February), in the large Temple to Inari on the outskirts of the southern suburbs of Kyoto. This temple is dedicated to the harvest-god, hence the God of Rice, as the etymology of his name indicates. Hundreds of thousands of worshippers flock there from all over the country, to invoke the gods' protection for their ventures. There you will see the backbone of the nation, from peasants and working-men to small tradesmen, merchants, and the middle class.

The crowd streams by, serried between two almost unbroken lines of street-stalls of all kinds, and flows beneath the first torii—the porticos that rise in front of every Shinto temple, consisting of two vertical shafts supporting two cross-bars. In this instance they are painted vermilion, the colour typical of temples to Inari. Here and there on either side of the road one finds effigies of foxes, the god's messengers, rising motionless, facing each other in pairs, with an enigmatic grin on their muzzles.

As one draws nearer the great shrine, the noise becomes more and more deafening, dominated by the clatter of wooden clogs on the flagstones. The worshippers' first act, accomplished with care, is to wash their hands and

Sacred Dance in the Kasuga Sanctuary, Nara

rinse their mouths with lustral water which they draw with a long wooden ladle from a large stone basin, the mitarashi, on the side of which are engraved two characters meaning "Heart" and "Purification". The visitors then go and pull the long cords that ring the suzu—enormous metal bells suspended from the eaves of the main shrine, or haiden. They cast their mite—whether a coin or a note—into the huge alms-box, or saisenbako; then, after clapping their palms several times and keeping their hands joined in front of their faces, they bow their heads and withdraw into themselves for a brief invocation.

The crowd winds in a dense stream round the annex where from hour to hour, on a platform open on three sides, the young miko attached to the service of the temple perform the sacred dances of kagura, a series of hieratic attitudes and slow evolutions to the rhythm of a religious orchestra. This is generally composed of an ancient koto or long horizontal harp with seven strings which the player strikes with ivory guards attached to the first three fingers of the right hand; a flageolet (hichiriki); a transverse flute (oteki); a kind of mouth-organ (sho); a drum shaped like a sand-glass (kakko); and lastly a large drum mounted on a base (taiko). In a temple of Inari, the dance building is on the same side as the haiden; elsewhere it is erected directly opposite.

On the other side, the temple's offices—shamusho—are wide open, and priests and acolytes are fully occupied in receiving gifts of silver and dispensing, in return for hard cash, post-cards, amulets, and good luck formulae corresponding to numbers that the supplicant himself draws out of a box.

Needless to say, on all sides we are surrounded by huge cords of woven straw—shimenawa—from which hang gohei, or strips of white paper cut out according to ritual, denoting the spots consecrated to the Shinto gods. On the other hand, in the temples of Inari there are far fewer lanterns than elsewhere. Since the 17th century these lanterns—which are also found in Buddhist temples—have become one of the principal decorative elements of Shinto.

But let us return to a temple of Inari. Following the stream of pilgrims, we make our way through a series of alleys that slope up and down beneath countless rows of red porticos, offered by the wealthier members of the congregation who have made sure to inscribe their name and address on them in large characters. We once counted over 4,000, leading to the maze of shrines dotted across three neighbouring hills, which take over two hours to tour on foot.

On all sides oblong stones have been erected, engraved with the names of divinities; the corresponding altars are once again preceded by innumerable little porticos, donated by humbler visitors. The visitors throw a few grains of rice on every one, without exception, or place food fried in oil, which the almighty fox adores. Countless reproductions of this divine messenger, big and small alike, and always in pairs, are placed in front of each altar. Acrid smoke curls up from cheap candles. Here and there the devout are kneeling, engrossed in their prayers and invocations. Occasionally a woman in a hysteric trance begins to stammer and groan supplications, having suddenly had a vision of "her" fox—a believer who prays sincerely being supposedly protected by an individual "spirit" that reveals itself to him alone; when this happens, one may ask the apparition for anything whatsoever, and the request is always granted.

The Fox of Inari

Further on, there is a group that has purchased the services of a kind of "medium", generally an old woman with a disquieting face, whose profession consists of evoking a sacred fox, naturally visible only to herself, and sending up prayers to him when she has reached a sufficient degree of exaltation to be able to communicate with the "divine spirit".

At nightfall, the sight becomes even more hallucinating. Belated pilgrims hasten homewards, and the noise of their wooden clogs echoes curiously amongst the myriads of porticos whilst the quivering light of the last candles suddenly seems to bring to life the stone foxes outlined against the sky.

FIRE FESTIVAL—Water and fire play an extremely important role in Shinto, as purifying elements. Temples are always situated near a spring or river, and consequently, often in the heart of the country. As for the fire festivals—hi-matsuri—they are naturally very numerous. One of the most picturesque takes place on 22nd October in the middle of the night, in the Kurama Mountain, in the heart of woods several miles north of Kyoto.

There a humble village lies in a narrow gorge, in the depths of which a foaming torrent roars by. In the solitary street, enormous pyres are lit, piled with gigantic roots—the remains of trees felled on the neighbouring slopes. For one evening, the whole village is placed beneath the sign of the sacred fire, and it is popularly believed that no accidents can take place on that particular night. To make assurance doubly sure it is the custom to seal carefully any house that has experienced an impure contact, such as a recent death.

Each household where there are boys in the family prepares one or more huge, long torches —tai-matsu—made of strips of wood bound together and lighted at the tip. The youths carry them all through the village on their shoulders, and even the children join in with torches made to measure.

It is an impressive sight and, in fact, an almost demoniacal one. Naked but for a kind of loincloth, straw sandals on their feet, and a narrow towel wound round their heads, the youths run though the streets, zigzagging and tottering not only because they have to weave in and out of the fires, but also because the effects of libations of *sake* eventually make themselves felt. Despite the sharp air of an autumn night, their bodies and faces stream with perspiration, some of the huge burning torches they carry weighing as much as a hundred pounds or more. Possessed by a kind of Dionysiac frenzy, they whirl round at random, occasionally plunging themselves right into the crowd that beats out the rhythm of their race with incessant cries of "Sairei! Sairyo!... Sairei! Sairyo!..." Spattered with sparks and fire-brands, the spectators scatter with roars of laughter, for this is the great night of purification when fire is welcome in every way, even in the form of burns!

But all this excitement is, so to speak, merely a series of interludes. The great ordeal comes after one o'clock in the morning, when two enormous

Fire Festival in Kurama

mikoshi—sacred palanquins draped with braid curtains and crested with a
phoenix, the divine emblem—are carried down on the men's backs, with
the help of long shafts. Prior to this, they had to be carried up to the main
shrine of the temple, perched high in the mountains. There, in the meantime,
two teams of stalwarts from the village have long been preparing themselves

with dances and songs, to the rhythm of clapping hands. Then suddenly comes the great departure. They seize one of the mikoshi, hoist it on to their shoulders, and the descent begins. The steps are steep, irregular, and slippery. Above the confused mass of bodies staggering under the weight, the palanquin pitches and rolls, reflecting the movements of the spirits of gods supposedly enclosed within it. Two long ropes are attached to the rear, to counteract the tendency to pitch forward. Straining on the ropes are rows of village maidens, with the sleeves of their kimonos rolled back as far as the shoulder, revealing arms as sturdy and sun-tanned as the boys'. The descent is accomplished slowly by fits and starts, to cries of "Sairei! Sairyo!" first uttered by the men and then repeated in chorus by the girls.

By the time we leave, after four o'clock in the morning, the two palanquins are ranged side by side in the building that is to shelter them until the following festival. The last pro-

The Visitors pull the Long Ropes

pitiatory dances have come to an end. At the bend in the steep road that leads us back to Kyoto, we cast a last glance behind us. The dark pine trees stand out like tall silhouettes in ink, outlined against the luminous mist that rises above the pyres, to battle with an immense moon hung in a lightening sky.

FLOWER FESTIVAL—There are thousands of matsuri: they are, in fact, as numerous as Shinto temples. Of the score or so of hana-matsuri (flower festivals) held in village after village throughout December and January, we shall select one that takes place in a mountainous region situated right in the heart of Japan, at the intersection of the prefectures of Aichi, Shizuoka, and Nagano.

In front of an extremely humble shrine, on a surface only a few yards square encroaching on the road itself, a light building has been erected, decorated with festoons of multicoloured papers. In the centre, a fire of huge logs is kept going beneath an enormous cauldron suspended from a tripod. Round this hearth, the dances are to take place.

The local priest is hardly distinguishable from the peasants; like his congregation, he cultivates his own plot of land, for in this remote district the religious cult requires comparatively little activity. Today he has donned a long white levite above the traditional ceremonial costume a black hakam or full pleated trousers forming a skirt above the kimono. He performs lengthy rites, invoking the protection of the gods. On the slope running down towards a torrent, a space has been marked out for the offerings, comprising grains of rice, beans, strips of dried octopus, bowls containing a little *sake*... and even sprigs of incense, adopted from Buddhism. The priest claps his hands and recites norito or Shinto invocations; then he purifies the four corners of the compass by thrice shaking a branch of the sacred sakaki tree. He subsequently repeats the same rites in front of the fire in the middle of the floor, in front of the rack containing the objects and masks for the dances, and then in front of the drum that beats the rhythm.

But the big drum—or taiko—has begun to resound; for the next twenty-four hours it will beat incessantly, with a drugging insistence, on two continuously repeated rhythms, slow then swift. In form the matsuri drum resembles a hogshead lying on its side, with oxhide stretched across either end; it is played with two short round drumsticks.

Four elders, in white levites—the guardians of the customs and masters of the ceremonies—open the dance with ritual evolutions accompanied by chants which they alone know, and in which the names of the gods particularly revered in the region constantly recur. Then the dancers follow each other, by twos and fours. The groups are composed of performers of the same age, to give a balanced aspect and symbolize the rhythm of the generations. As for the women, either they are mere spectators or else they busy themselves preparing snacks and warming the *sake* in pot-bellied stone bottles. According to the age or standing of the dancers, the accessories consist of fans, bells, sticks decorated with multicoloured paper streamers, and even swords. The costumes are both severe and colourful at the same time, the tight trousers and jackets of coarse dark blue cotton contrasting with their decorative motifs in the form of stylized phoenixes, tortoises, pine trees, plum trees, and bamboos, in sky-blue, brown, ochre, and pea-green.

The long winter's night is spangled with stars, suddenly effaced by squalls that send the snow whirling and make the trees groan on the neighbouring slopes. Around the steaming cauldron, straw sandals vigorously beat the ground.

Dawn rises on a rugged landscape, but the sun has to cross the sky from end to end before the festival terminates with the great dance of the lion, or shishi-mai. In actual fact, the lion looks more like some mythical monster. It is composed of two men who perform a dance, bent double within the long folds of the animal's body. The man in front manipulates the huge, square, heavy-jowled head, fleeced with a thick mane, and the wide muzzle split from ear to ear that opens and closes with a noisy click of the chops.

The gods are satisfied. After this communal outburst of exaltation, everyone returns home with the feeling of having accomplished his duty, and renewed courage to confront the monotonous tasks of the coming seasons.

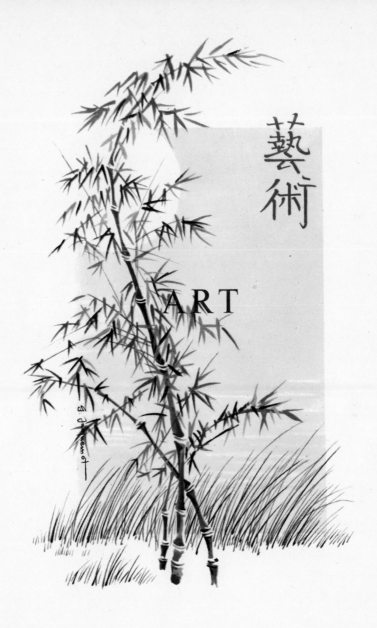

ART

藝術

J APANESE art, after that of China, represents one of the greatest chapters in the artistic history of the Far East. When, in about the 6th century A.D., the court of Yamato borrowed the art of writing from China, an entire culture, slowly elaborated throughout the course of the centuries, infiltrated into the country. In one fell swoop ancient Confucian and Taoist wisdom were introduced into Japan, together with Buddhism, which, though born in India, had already been radically changed by Chinese environment. And this acquisition was followed by many another, the cultivation of rice and bamboo, as well as the use of metals, being similarly introduced from the mainland. We should therefore not be surprised to encounter at each stage in the evolution of Japanese art that great master of civilization for the whole of East Asia—China—the purveyor of ideas, forms of government, methods of procedure, and techniques in general.

However, this art cannot be considered as a mere offshoot of Chinese art. The hazards of history conditioned their relationship with each other. Periods in which continental influence predominated were succeeded by others in which, left to her own devices, whilst drawing inspiration from ideas introduced in the past, Japan created original forms of culture. This elaboration of ideas implies selectivity, which is in itself indicative of personality. But the bases of the civilization were common to both countries, and love of nature, already latent in the Shinto religion, was revived by Taoism and Buddhism.

Above all, with the Chinese ideogram the art of the paintbrush—the symbol of scholar and painter—made its appearance in the Nipponese archi-

pelago. Paintbrush and ink are the main media of expression in the Far East: the expression of her way of thinking; the expression of her sensitivity as revealed in the harmony of the lines traced on silk or paper, and in the arrangement of the characters; and lastly, the expression of her visual image of the Universe, as interpreted by the artist in his peculiar treatment of forms. The primacy of writing—and thereby of painting—was, then, one of the main results of Chinese influence in Japan.

However, whilst the very structure of Chinese thought established itself in Japan, it was nonetheless adapted in conformity with Japanese genius. Chinese art aims at expressing essentials, and all it retains of a form is the most significant lines; it does not represent such and such a horse, but *the* horse. Being more instinctive by nature, the Japanese are sensitive to anecdotic and casual compositions; although equally synthetic, their forms thus became more individualized. Hence from one and the same culture, two different forms of art were born.

PREHISTORY AND PROTOHISTORY— The first vestiges of human activity discovered in Japan (1st millenary

Haniwa, 5th-6th century
(Musée Guimet)

B.C.) reveal the existence of a people who lived by hunting and fishing, but were as yet unversed in agriculture. They utilized implements of stone and shells, and produced handmade pottery known as jomon shiki (pottery imprinted with ropes or matting), in the form of funnel-shaped jars, decorated with engraved or inlaid patterns.

The discovery of pottery known as yayoi and lance heads with flat, foliaceous blades reveals respectively the use of the potter's wheel and that of bronze in Northern Kyushu at the dawn of the Christian era. These techniques, borrowed from nearby Korea, were adopted throughout south and central Honshu at the same time that bronze bells known as dotaku—decorated with a pattern of waves or animals in filleted relief—were introduced there.

It was also in Kyushu, in about the 3rd century A.D., that the first great sepultures known as ko-fun were erected, on the model of those in South Korea. The immense size of these tumuli, either round or oval in shape, is in itself an impressive sight. They may still be seen looming above Nara Plain (Honshu) where, according to tradition, the Imperial clan—worshippers of the Sun-Goddess Amaterasu—settled at a problematical date on immigrating from the south. The majority of these tombs, believed to be those of the first sovereigns of Japan, have not been excavated. Some, however, have yielded material inspired by that of Silla or Shiragi, a South Korean kingdom where Chinese influence first made itself felt. The treasures included arms of bronze and iron, tama (beads of various shapes, made of hard stones or jade), Chinese mirrors, or

Miroku—in Wood, 7th century
(Koryuji, near Kyoto)

copies thereof often rather clumsily produced. The most original finds were terracotta cylinders driven into the ground to support the banked-up earth of the ko-fun. These haniwa—as they are called—are often crested with statuettes of helmeted warriors, women decked in necklaces and ear-rings, musicians playing the kin (flat Chinese harp), animals (horses, cocks). Crude though the style may be, there is an expressive grandeur about these productions.

INTRODUCTION OF BUDDHIST ART (6th-8th centuries)—The conversion of the Prince Regent Shotoku to Buddhism in the late 6th century was to provoke an influx of Korean bonzes and artisans to the Japanese court. They introduced Chinese forms of civilization in vogue in their country, and built the great pious foundations to the devout Shotoku. The architectural style of the period has been handed down by the partially preserved Horyuji (*ji*: Buddhist temple) near Nara, the most ancient example of wooden architecture in the entire Far East. In this continental architecture adopted by the Japanese, the pre-eminence of the carpenter made itself felt. The wall was a mere filling-in; the only dominant features were the four-sectional roofs of carved tiles, supported by a system of consoles resting on columns painted red. The buildings were laid out according to rules of the strictest symmetry, and, with a few slight modifications this

Kudara Kwannon—in Wood, 7th century
(Horyuji, near Nara)

76

plan was followed for the countless monasteries founded in Japan throughout that period.

The numerous statuary was also inspired by that of China. From the pantheon of Buddhist divinities, the most frequently represented were Cakyamuni (the ancient Buddha), Kwannon (Avalokitecvara, Bodhisattva, or Bosatsu the Merciful), Miroku (Maitreya, the future Buddha), and the four kings who act as guardians of space. This well-known triad in gilded bronze sculptured in 623 by Tori, the descendant of a Chinese immigrant, depicts Buddha seated meditatively in front of a great aureole ornamented with flames; his gown falls in a complicated pattern of sharp pleats; two

Kichijoten (Goddess of Fortune)—
Painting in Colour on Silk, 8th century
(Yakushi-ji, on loan to Nara Museum)

richly adorned Bodhisattvas stand on either side of him. They are shorter in proportion, and their flat bodies, obeying a rule of strict frontality, disappear beneath draperies; their ovoid faces, with eyelids lowered in contemplation of an ineffable vision, are lit by a gentle smile. Everything about this 7th-century Japanese work evokes art inspired by Chinese mysticism of the 5th and 6th centuries, and this time lag is explained by the influence of Korea, which long remained faithful to the formulae of primitive Chinese Buddhist art. This same style recurs in the elegant statuettes of gilt bronze gracing the temples as well as the National Museum in Tokyo. But the masterpieces of the first sculptors are the great wooden figures: Kudara Kwannon, some six feet high, with a slightly relaxed body and a scarcely modelled torso ornamented with a wrought-gold pectoral; Yumedono Kwannon, a mysterious idol with a rough-hewn face crowned with a magnificent openwork diadem, draped with veils forming a succession of fins on either side of the flat body; Nyoirin Kwannon of Chuguji (women's convent near Horyuji), seated in a pose of royal meditation with one leg

tucked in, the other dangling, and her dainty head reclining on two of her slender fingers; not to mention the slim and graceful silhouette of the Miroku of Koryuji (near Kyoto). These statues, venerated throughout Japan, are worthy to rank with the finest sculptured creations of humanity.

However, new models arrived direct from China once the Yamato court established direct relations with that country in the mid-7th century. Embassies were sent to Tch'ang-ngan, the wonderful capital of the powerful T'ang

Head of Ni-o (Guardian-King of Space)—Dry Lacquer, gilded and high-lighted with Paint, 8th century (Musée Guimet)

78

dynasty (618-907), whose influence then extended throughout the whole of Asia. The plan of Nara, the first fixed capital of the Japanese sovereigns, was inspired by the checkerboard pattern of Tch'ang-ngan. In a further attempt to vie with the Chinese metropolis, Emperor Shomu had a bronze Buddha fifty feet high erected in the new monastery of the Todaiji, consecrated in 752. Fires and earthquakes had no mercy for this antique figure, symbolic of the nascent power of the Japanese Empire; all that remains is the lotus-shaped base which is now the pedestal for a 16th-century statue. Other works, less imposing though they may be, have survived to recall this immense statue. For instance, the great bronze triad of Yakushi Nyorai (Buddha the Healer) and his acolytes in Yakushi-ji, dating from the early 8th century, betrays the influence of T'ang art: the bodies are more massive and better modelled, but the faces begin to have a suspicion of heaviness about them. In addition to bronze and wood (often coated with gilt lacquer) new media included plaster and dried lacquer (superimposed in layers and modelled on a wooden frame). Progress in the art of modelling was evidenced in realistic, animated figures such as Hokkedo's Bonten (Brahma) in

plaster (Todaiji), clad in court attire of the T'ang era—the forerunner of the kimono—and with a serenely gentle expression on his face; the menacing figure of Kongo-Rikishi (the guardian of the gate) by the same artist—a statue whose energetic mask and sumptuously coloured armour are displayed to the public once a year; disciples of the Kofukuji Buddha; and portraits of bonzes, all highly individualized even at this stage.

Dance Mask—
Painted Wood, 8th century
(Musée Guimet)

Detail from the Kitano-tenjin engi—Makimono Painted in Colour on Paper, 8th century
(National Museum of Tokyo)

The art of painting also flourished to the full, but, being more fragile, these works have nearly all disappeared. The only ones to survive until 1948 were the Kondo (Temple of Gold) frescoes in Horyuji (beginning of the 8th century), providing precious examples of Chinese Buddhist painting. In these murals the divinities, harmoniously grouped round a central figure, appeared to be impregnated with a remote Indian influence, modified and adapted to Chinese taste in the countless Buddhist shrines of Central Asia. The supple bodies, outlined by the play of light and shade, were draped with brilliantly coloured scarves. Unhappily this marvellous collection was destroyed by fire.

In Nara Museum little Kichijoten, the Goddess of Fortune—the Far Eastern incarnation of the Indian divinity Sri-devi—is one of the rare vestiges of contemporary painting on silk. Clad in an elegant court gown, she is clasping a jewel, the symbol of wealth. Her round face evokes the Chinese beauties of the day. This characteristic of T'ang art was said to be inspired by Yang Kouei-fei, the renowned favourite of one of the sovereigns of Tch'ang-ngan.

All the cosmopolitan art of the T'ang, in which influences of India and Sassanid Iran are mingled, is to be found in Shoso-in, a small log cabin which, since the mid-8th century, has housed the collections of Emperor-Shomu, donated to the Todaiji by his widow. Each year, early in November, privileged visitors are authorized to admire these treasures, comprising masks of the dancers who celebrated the ceremony of opening the great Buddha's eyes, the musical instruments—enriched with mother-of-pearl or paintings—that accompanied them, mirrors of bronze, chased or encrusted with mother-of-pearl, and sumptuous silks. The majority are from China, Central Asia, and perhaps even from distant Iran; others might well be works from the Imperial studios, and the onlooker is amazed by the sight of so much skill allied with such a high degree of refinement.

HEIAN ERA (794-1185)—In 794 the Emperor established himself in a new capital, Heian-Kyo, present-day Kyoto. Court life then developed on a most brilliant scale, as reflected in the narratives of the period, written by aristocratic ladies. Life was one long series of refined entertainments such as competitions of poetry or painting, excursions to admire plum or cherry trees in bloom, and melancholic contemplation of the red foliage of autumn. It was then that the symbols (flowers, birds, insects, animals) marking the cycle of rebirth and decline were established.

Love of nature was also impregnated in architecture; the new esoteric sects known as Tendai and Shingon settled on the slopes of

Portrait of Uesugi no Shigefusa—in Wood,   *Kamakura Period (Kamakura Museum)*

Hiei-zan and Koya-san. Their plan harmonized with the surrounding landscape, and thenceforth any pretence at symmetry was excluded. At that time the first Chinese-style gardens were laid out, decorated with pavilions linked by galleries reflected in mirrors of water. The Hoodo of Byodo-in (Phoenix Pavilion) at Uji, south of Kyoto—a pleasure house subsequently converted into a Buddhist temple—is one of the first attempts to reproduce this style which was to prove so popular in Japan. The Shinto temples were not immune to such influences, and the Taira shrine on the Isle of Itsukushima (or Miyajima) rises in a delightful setting behind its famous torii surging up amidst the waters.

Sculpture revealed several trends. In the 9th century, vigorous works were hewn out of solid wood. The great Fudo of Toji (Kyoto), an austere incarnation of the spirit in search of truth or salvation, glowers threateningly as it brandishes the spear of wisdom and the rope destined to bind temptation of all kinds. It demonstrates the growing influence of the esoteric sects that stressed the terrible aspect of the divinities and multiplied their attributes (such as the statue of Kwannon with eleven heads and a thousand arms).

Despite its size, the immense gilt wood Amida of Byodo-in, by the sculptor Jocho, reveals the rather placid gentleness of the sculptures of the T'ang style in its decline. The frailer Kichijoten of Joruriji (near Kyoto) represents an elegant court lady bowing beneath the weight of her countless superimposed gowns.

By 890 official relations with China had come to an end. It was then that original forms came into being, especially in painting.

Buddhist painting is precious in more ways than one. Its complex iconography reflects the religious trends of the period, in the form of elegant Bosatsus (Bodhisattvas), painted with supple lines heightened and underscored by gold and other bright tones; the terrifying Fudo of the Shingon sect; and, towards the 11th and 12th centuries, the Raigos descending in the land of Amida to save souls in distress who invoked them in their last hour. The immense tenderness of the sect of the Pure Land (Jodo) is expressed in these processions of divinities decked in myriads of jewels, hastening across mountains and rice-fields towards the humblest cottages.

Buddhist Divinity—Colour Painting on Silk, Kamakura Period (Anrajuku-in, Kyoto)

But Japanese genius really came into its own in Yamato-e, or national painting. The style was of Chinese origin. The sacred texts of Buddhism were transcribed on long narrow scrolls illustrated by edifying scenes. Towards the 11th century, this technique was adapted to more profane ends. The most ancient example to have survived is the *Genji Monogatari*, comprising fragments of the famous story in which the chapters are divided by illustrations representing the most outstanding episodes. The form of these scrolls determined the composition of the pictures, which ran from the top

Sesshu Toyo (1420-1506)—Buffaloes, after Li T'ang—Ink Painting high-lighted with Colour, on Paper (Collection of Mr Asano Nagatake, Odawara)

Tan-an Chiden (16th century)—*Heron—Painting in Indian Ink, on Paper* (National Museum, Tokyo)

right-hand corner to the lower left-hand corner. Buildings and people were often presented in profile, and the roofs removed to reveal indoor scenes. The text soon disappeared, to be replaced by a continuous composition in which the various episodes were separated by clouds or linked by landscapes. The techniques were varied, comprising opaque paint, gouache, or line drawings in Chinese ink lightly underscored by paint. Above all, the extremely diverse themes—stories, *monogatari*, tales of the legendary origin of Shinto or Buddhist shrines, *engi*, representations of the inferno, calamities, and epidemics—gave the artists the opportunity to demonstrate their talent as narrators. They switched with ease from popular scenes, frequently of a caricatural nature, to the elegance of court life. Not only are these scrolls a delight to look at, but they also provide an inexhaustible source of information on the life of the times.

Kano Naganobu (1577-1654)—
Divertissement beneath Blossoming Cherry trees—
Painted Paper Screen
(Kunizo Hara Collection, Kanazawa)

KAMAKURA PERIOD (1186-1392)—The last years of the Heian era witnessed the terrible battles that brought to grips the enemy Taira and Minamoto factions. The victor, Minamoto no Yoritomo, settled in Kamakura where the first Zen temple, the Shariden (Pavilion of Relics) of the Engakuji, was constructed: a small building on sober lines enlivened by bays with lowered arches in a style borrowed from Chinese architecture of the Sung era (960-1278).

In a desire to affirm his might, Yoritomo erected in his new capital an immense bronze Buddha—the celebrated Daibutsu of Kamakura—a rather cold, stereotyped work. The two great sculptors of the period, Unkei and Kaikei, worked mainly in Nara where they are famed for the two monumental guardian-kings on the gateway to Todaiji, conceived in the purest classical tradition of the 7th and 8th centuries. Also in Nara, Unkei sculptured the Patriarchs of Kofukuji. In themselves, the faces of his models—emaciated or smiling as the case may be—form a wonderful portrait gallery. The great Daimyo of the period—austere disciples of Zen which taught them self-control and conferred on them the power of conquest—are represented in their black costume with billowing trousers, carved in dark wood or painted on silk.

86

In Buddhist painting, set themes crept in, lacking in novelty, whilst the lines became more arid. On the other hand, Yamato-e met with brilliant success. The Kosanji scrolls reveal the satiric verve of the bonzes in savoury representations of animals—monkeys, frogs, and foxes—copying human gestures. The *Kitano-tenjin engi* relates the origins of the cult consecrated to Sugawara no Michizane, a 9th-century poet and minister who was exiled from the court as a result of a rival's intrigues. He died of despair, but his innocence and his literary talent were both recognized when miracles took place after his death. He was thereafter deified under the name of Ten-jin (a celestial divinity), and became the patron of writers. A temple was erected to him at Kitano, near Kyoto. The battles between the Taira and the Minamoto are evoked in the *Heiji Monogatari*, where animated compositions alternate with immense voids, space thus becoming an element in the setting. This magnificent scroll, one of the glories of Boston Museum, recently inspired scenes in the film *Gate of Hell*.

MUROMACHI AND MOMOYAMA ERAS (1394-1572 and 1573-1614)—The As-

hikaga Shoguns returned to Kyoto and settled in the Muromachi district, which has lent its name to one of the most brilliant periods in the history of Japanese art. The traditions then established predominate to this day, despite modifications arising from Western influences.

The Zen sect, and through its intermedi-

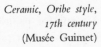

Ceramic, Oribe style,
17th century
(Musée Guimet)

87

ary the civilization and art of Sung China, played a primordial role in this evolution. The Shoguns began to surround themselves with aesthetes and artists, and practise Cha-no-yu (the tea ceremony). These ceremonies, centred round a painting and a bouquet of flowers, were performed in the Kinkakuji and Ginkakuji—the Gold and Silver Pavilions, or summer-houses in the midst of gardens. The Zen sect imported from China the "philosophical garden", where waters, trees, and stones evoked a universe in miniature, thus offering a theme for meditation.

Not being intended for strolls, these gardens were not particularly extensive; they were, in fact, specifically designed to be contemplated from the heights of a terrace or pavilion carefully placed to command a certain vista. The Ryuan-ji garden on the outskirts of Kyoto is composed of fifteen stones of various shapes—only fourteen of which may be seen at a time, protruding from soil covered with carefully raked granite—representing the worlds emerging from the waters.

Whilst the sculptors were carving Noh masks, some painters remained faithful to the formulae of Yamato-e which, under the name of the Tosa School, had set the style of Imperial Court painting. Unhappily it gradually lost its primitive freshness, contenting itself with repetition.

The Shoguns patronized the landscape painters Shubun, Sesshu, and their pupils, who sought inspiration in the great Chinese masters of the Sung era.

In China, the landscape had become a kind of language intimating the state of mind of the artist who, whether Taoist or Buddhist, interpreted his own conception of the world in his representation of mountains or waters. This was the heyday of monochrome painting—the major creation of Chinese artists—a process that consisted of diluting ink with water to a varying degree, and thereby obtaining a whole gamut of infinitely subtle shades in a succession of strokes.

Even as a child Sesshu was said to have revealed a gift for painting. Legend has it that one day in his early youth, when attached to a pillar

Has

...ohaku (1539-1610)—Plum tree in Blossom—Fusama Painted in Colour on Paper (Chishaku-in, Kyoto)

in punishment for some misdemeanour he drew mice in the dusty earth with his toes, to while away the time. His subjects were so vivid that they suddenly came to life, bit his cords, and set him free. As a pupil of Shubun, Sesshu went to the mainland to study the Chinese school. He painted immense landscapes in which steep mountains rose one behind another in the distance, lost in the mist, whilst in the foreground, beside a waterfall sheltered by a ragged pine tree, a hermit savoured the joys of solitude. If he occasionally copied the great painters of the Sung era, his own personality always came to the fore in a nervous, vibrant style.

The three dictators who strove to reinstate peace amongst the turbulent

Daimyo during the 16th century evinced less refined tastes than their predecessors. These luxury-loving warriors and upstarts ornamented their palaces with rich decorations by masters from the Kano School. Motonobu, the founder, succeeded in reconciling the Tosa taste for narrative with the tendencies of the artists who imitated Chinese styles. As a master of ink painting, he gave birth to a whole line of artists who remained the official painters of the Shoguns until 1868. His successors thus decorated the princely dwellings, ornamenting the fusuma with flowers, birds, tigers, and landscapes, on backgrounds of gold or silver, resplendent with colour.

Cha-no-yu, hitherto reserved for a small circle of initiates, then became a national institution. In the 16th century Senno Rikyu laid down the rules, the spirit of which was defined by the terms wabi and sabi, a mixture of simplicity and refinement as expressed in the cha-shitsu or tea-houses, where Japanese imagination was given full play in variations of detail on immutable themes. Asymmetry, search for unusual effects, and precious materials often evocative of natural phenomena define the taste of the cha-jin or tea-masters. Their empire soon extended over Japanese art as a whole; the

majority of the creative works of the period—from painting to floral arrangement, and from lacquers to ceramics—were destined for the tea ceremony.

Ceramic art had long been neglected in Japan, where wooden or lacquer utensils were employed in domestic life. In the Muromachi era, the potters of Seto manufactured bowls for sampling green tea and containers for fresh water or tea leaves. Soon after, under the impulse of the cha-jin, other types of ceramics became popular. These included Raku, characterized by rich black and russet glazing (named after the gold seal màrked Raku, the title of a summer-house belonging to Hideyoshi which the latter donated to Chojiro, a Kyoto potter); white Shinto and floral-patterned Oribe, the names of which evoke the memory of the celebrated tea-masters who, according to an ill-founded tradition, reputedly had a vested interest in their manufacture; Karatsu, painted with brown flowers under a grey glazing; and the heavy stoneware of Bizen. The Japanese proved to be masters in the art of baking ceramics, and their magnificent creations, discovered by our ceramists at the end of the 19th century were to transform the latter's art.

In 1545 St Francis-Xavier disembarked in Kyushu, and his Jesuits received a warm welcome in Japan. The Westerners intrigued the Japanese, who portrayed them in the famous namban byobu, "screens of the Barbarians from the South", also known as the screens of the Portuguese. The Musée Guimet in Paris contains a precious example representing the annual arrival of a ship from India laden with objects needed in the missionaries' daily life. The sumptuous costumes of the Westerners, faithfully reproduced, stand out against golden back-

Sotatsu (17th century)—
A Scene from Genji-Monogatari—Screen Painted in Colour against a Gold Background
(Seikado Collection, Tokyo)

grounds. Their prominent-nosed faces resemble caricatures, and to this day it would seem as if our features, so very different from their own, still look like this to the Japanese.

TOKUGAWA ERA (1614–1868)—The influence of Western ways of life was short-lived. Ieyasu, who acceded to the shogunate in 1614, took measures to assure the stability of Japan, devastated by battles between the great Daimyo. Driving out the Portuguese and Spanish settlers, he isolated his country from foreign contacts, apart from the Dutch to whom he left the monopoly of trade with the West. This was the time when Kyushu was beginning to manufacture porcelain, and the Dutch thus introduced

this new craft into Europe. Kakiemon and Imari china, decorated in rich and colourful patterns, became fashionable in the 18th century and was skilfully copied in Meissen, Delft, and Chantilly.

Ieyasu's descendants, the Tokugawa, perpetuated the architectural traditions of the Momoyama period with increasing luxury. Nijo, their residence in Kyoto,

Ogata Korin
(1663–1743)—Iris—
Screen
Painted in Colour
on Golden Background
(Nezu Museum,
Tokyo)

and more particularly Nikko, the mausoleum of the first Shoguns of that line, were ornamented with brilliant, overladen decorations, highly skilful but decadent in taste. Official art was no longer the source of revival. The late 17th century, when the economic power of the newly pacified country was at its height, saw the blossoming of a new school of decorators. Working outside the traditional schools, Koetsu, Sotatsu, Korin, and Kenzan became the most wonderful creative artists. In simplifying forms, they endowed each line with an extraordinarily evocative power, heightened by intense colours. A few branches sufficed to evoke a tree, a handful of iris in flower expressed all that springtime implies.

Lid of Inkstand, 16th–17th century—Lacquer Painted and Inlaid with Mother-of-Pearl
(Musée Guimet)

These painters also gave rein to their talent and imagination in the art of lacquer-work and ceramics. It is to them that we owe the repertoire of themes still encountered on women's kimonos, for instance, and other everyday objects expressing peonies and lions, bamboos and swallows, pine trees and cranes, does, and maple trees reddened by autumn.

Sharaku (late 18th century)—
Portrait of Actor in Female Role—Colour print
(Musée Guimet)

The works of the painters Ming and Ts'ing were made known throughout Japan by the Chinese who settled in Nagasaki, near the outpost reserved for the Dutch. They inspired the animal painters such as Maruyama Okyo and the adepts of the Naga School such as Gyokudo, who indulged in ink play dear to the eclectics of China.

The development of a mercantile class, fond of pleasure and not particularly cultured at that stage, had created a new clientele which traditional artistic forms failed to satisfy. This determined the success of the Ukiyo-e School —of "fashionable painting"—which, resuming the anecdotic traditions of the ancient Yamato-e, delighted in representing everyday life. The foundation of this school has been attributed to Iwasa Matabei (1578–1650).

By the end of the 17th century, wood block prints—a cheap substitute for paintings—made the style highly popular. The first prints were reproduced in black and white, but they were soon enhanced with vivid colours applied with a brush, in which yellow and orange tones dominated. The works of the primitives Moronobu, Kwaigetsudo, the Torii line —in great demand by the bijin (pretty women of Yoshiwara) or the Kabuki actors—have a frank and naïve vigour about them that still enchant us. Oku- mura Masanobu soon suc- ceeded in using several blocks and obtaining im- pressions first in two and then in several colours. This skilful technique (in which as many as seventy-eight blocks were used for a single print) was employed by the artisans who engraved the works of Harunobu, the painter of beautiful women, Utamaro, illustrator of *Green Houses*, and Sharaku, the wonderful portrait painter of the actors. And it should be admitted that these tal- ented engravers often suc- ceeded in transforming the works of second-rate artists into minor masterpieces.

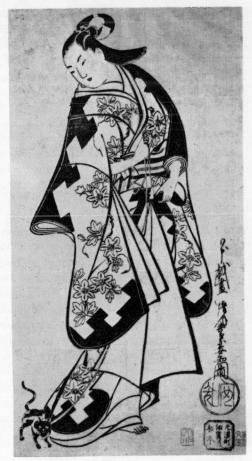

Kwaïgetsudo—Bijin (courtesan)—Black and White Print, 18th century (Musée Guimet)

In the early 19th century Hokusai, a nervous, prolific draughtsman, illustrated the works of Bakin, the novelist then in fashion. He also produced numerous albums in which he gave free play to his caricatural verve and his weakness for ghosts and monsters. His Mangwa, a startlingly imaginative collection of sketches needs no introduction. His other compositions designed for reproduction included the most beautiful sequences of land-scapes. The Mount Fuji series, the stations of the Tokaido (the road from Kyoto to Edo, present-day Tokyo), the Great Flowers, the Poets, and the Waterfalls reveal the extremely varied gifts of this artist who, at the end of his days, signed himself "the old man who dotes on drawing". Hiroshige also excelled in views of roads and cities, masterfully creating the atmos-phere of a rainy day, the sadness of snowclad roads. They were both discovered by Europe in about 1860, when they exerted an immense influence on the Impressionist movement which saw in their works a new conception of landscape-painting and an economy of colour.

MODERN JAPAN—When Japan emerged from her isolation in 1868, her art was completely decadent. Excellent craftsmen were repeating hackneyed themes to satiation point. Contact with Western arts took place too abruptly and introduced an element of confusion in artists' minds. But they recovered rapidly enough. Some, such as Kokei Kobayashi, Seison Maeda, and Gyoshu Hayami, faithful to ancestral methods, revived the classical styles of the Yamato-e and Korin with a depth of feeling not entirely exempt from the influence of European conceptions. They incarnated the true Oriental trend more genuinely than Fujita, the typical Montparnasse painter. Countless others resolutely opted for oil painting, passionately following the latest developments of our modern schools. Fauvism, cubism, and surrealism were the order of the day. Abstract art, or *avant-garde* as it is called in Japan, is now the rage, and the young painters go to Paris to become initiated in the most recent creations.

Bowl, Kakiemon Style, 18th century
(Guido Soro Collection, Paris)

LANGUAGE AND SCRIPT

CONTRARY to what one usually imagines, the Japanese language has nothing in common with Chinese, apart from the system of writing borrowed from China in the past, reshaped and adjusted to meet the needs of a language radically different in structure. It was about as logical to apply this system to Japanese as it would be to utilize it for the transcription of French or English.

The Japanese language possesses something that Chinese lacks—grammatical forms similar to conjugations or declensions. Thus, for instance, as far as conjugations are concerned there is nothing corresponding to tense or person. The idea of past alone is more or less clearly expressed: the past being hardly likely to change. But the present and the immediate future run into each other. Indeed, any action predicted for the future is necessarily vague, hence a series of forms which all imply this lack of precision and would signify: "it could be that....", "can one foretell if....", "maybe...."—all of which avoid making any firm commitments as to a future over which, after all, we have no control.

As for the person, it is indicated in an extraordinarily subtle way founded on the social categories of feudal times. According to the degree of respect with which you refer to him, you indicate the subject and at the same

お茶
Tea: o-cha

お米
Rice: o-kome

御飯
Meal: go-han

お風呂
Bath: o-furo

time classify him socially in relation to yourself. Such is the principle. In fact, for the Japanese the formulae that Westerners mechanically translate by "honourable", "humble", etc., and which are apt to sound ridiculous, are strictly equivalent in value to our personal pronouns.

Thus:

> *hon wo yomi-masu*—I read a book
>
> *go-hon wo yomi-masu*—I read your book (indicating respect for the owner of the book)
>
> *hon wo o-yomi ni nari-masu*—you read a book (indicating respect for the reader)

It is these particles *go* and *o*, indicating respect, that are so frequently translated as "honourable".

First of all, in speaking, all women and the majority of men nowadays have acquired the habit of putting *o*, and more rarely *go*, in front of terms designating objects of everyday use—things a woman uses or prepares in the household, i.e. articles relating to meals or baths—without the slightest implication of respect; women, in fact, especially in the lower classes, make such constant use of these particles that they have become almost a linguistic mannerism. However, without being considered effeminate a man can say: "*o-cha*—tea; *o-kome*—rice; *go-han*—meal; *o-yu*—hot water; *o-furo*—bath; *o-bon*—meal-tray".

To express the imperative, there is a whole host of forms, all of which can, however, find an equivalent in English:

> *yome*—read!
>
> *yonde kudasai*—read! (polite form)
>
> *o-yomi-nasai*—kindly read! (more polite)
>
> *o-yomi ni natte kudasai*—I beg you to be so kind as to read (even more polite)
>
> *o-yomi ni natte kudasaimase*—deign to read (politest)

The essence of picturesqueness, you will agree, is not the manner in which a language resolves such problems of expression.

The writing, on the other hand, is full of surprises: what would you do, supposing English did not boast a form of script and you were obliged to adapt Chinese characters? Such was the problem the Japanese had to solve for, let me repeat, neither the vocabulary nor the structure of these two languages has anything in common.

It took centuries to establish a system which, despite every effort, is still unwieldy and lopsided. And—which is more serious—this system has succeeded in completely disfiguring a language that was so beautiful in the days when the fair sex used to write it more or less purely, in the 10th century.

Two procedures were employed simultaneously. Let us return to the example of English. There is nothing to prevent us from writing the character 水 meaning water, and reading it as "water" rather than *suei* (the Chinese term); we could also decide to read it as *suei*, specifying that henceforth we would designate water by this Chinese name. The Japanese have done both: they generally read it as *mizu*, the Japanese name for water, but in compound words, as often as not borrowed as such from Chinese, they read *sui*. Hence *sui-do* 水道 water road—water main (*do*, a distortion of the Chinese *tao*, would, alone, read *michi*, the Japanese name for way).

So much for invariable nouns (the Japanese is unfamiliar with gender and number—details that are frequently unnecessary or perplexing). At this point, a difficulty arises: the function of the noun is indicated by "post-positions".

We have to write: "of" or "with" water, etc. Well

此の本を讀んで下さい

Kindly read this book

99

此の窓から富士山が見えます

*From this window
one can see
Mount Fuji*

then, all we need to do is to invent a phonetic script to transcribe these little words:

of 水　　　　　with 水

This is clear, and easy to read.

The Japanese thus invented *kana*, a phonetic system of fifty syllabic sounds composed of a single vowel or a consonant followed by a vowel:

水の　　　　　　水で

mizu no—water of　　*mizu de*—water with

Now for the verb. In Chinese, nothing could be simpler—it is invariable:

見—see, I see, etc.

the meaning being modified by other characters. In English, we should be perplexed: see, seeing, will see. What shall we do, then?—Why, it's simple: write 見 which indicates the idea of seeing, and add a phonetic complement sufficiently precise to determine the desired form without ambiguity—it is impossible to confuse

見, 見 ing, 見 n

In Japanese:

見る　　　*miru*—one sees, etc.
見て　　　*mite*—seeing
見たら　　*mitara*—if one sees

Thus, Japanese script utilizes simultaneously Chinese characters and *kana* just as, if one wished, one could utilize Chinese characters and add endings or entire words in English, which would result in something like this:

From 此 窓 one can 見 山 富士
From this window one can see Mount Fuji

which, in Japanese, is written as follows:

此の 窓 から富士山 が見えます
kono mado kara Fujisan ga miemasu
this window from Fuji Mount one can see

This would be extremely simple, were it not for the fact that thousands of Chinese words have infiltrated into the language—to such an extent that one often

100

hesitates before deciding how to read this or that character. Thus, the character 水 water, mentioned above, is sometimes read in Chinese, sometimes in Japanese.

A final, and particularly diabolical procedure—the picture puzzle—makes matters even worse. One writes in characters indicating the meaning, but having no relation to the pronunciation. One of the most common is:

煙草 — grass for smoking
and reads .... *tabako!*

Proper names—first names in particular—also present the thorniest problems, since everyone decides for himself how to read his name. It is as if you wrote your name Peter, and claimed to read it as Paul.

As far as celebrities are concerned, the public is inclined to refuse extravagant interpretations, and eventually imposes the most common one.

Friendship: yu-jo

House: ie

Newspaper:
shimbun

Inkstand

文學

LITERATURE

No national literature could be less well known than that of Japan. How many Westerners even so much as suspect that it exists? One may well be amazed that throughout its history a great civilization—one of the greatest in the world (there are relatively few)—could produce such a wealth and variety of original literary works, and that these works—which belong to the common patrimony of humanism by the same token as Greek or Latin classics—could be so generally overlooked.

But in actual fact this is not so astonishing when we consider that Japan voluntarily held herself aloof from the rest of humanity for centuries, until 1868, to be precise. And, since that date, has she not done all she could to reveal herself to the West in the falsest possible light, disclosing only facets resembling a caricature—a servile imitation—of the Occident, and concealing in her innermost depths everything that was original, all the most precious secrets she herself had elaborated? Japanese classical art did, of course, attract the attention of the European public, but in an extremely fragmentary fashion and often greatly misrepresented.

Literature entrenched itself behind the language barrier, a barrier that calls for intense obstinacy if one wants to cross it. A few translations have been published, but they have rarely fallen into the hands of the general public. Moreover, these translations are often extremely disappointing, especially those of contemporary works, which are frequently written specifically for that purpose and contribute to making Japan appear in the guise of a precarious westernization; in short, false and discouraging.

And yet Japanese literature—which is quite as abundant as any other as far as volume is concerned—contains treasures that should not be over-looked, comparable to the finest productions of the West. In this brief summary we can outline only the main tendencies of each era, mentioning the masterpieces—or at least some of them—that represent landmarks in the literary history of Japan.

THE ARCHAIC ERA, OR OFFICIAL LITERATURE — Even before the language had shaken off the shawls in which Chinese script—recently adopted and as yet ill-adapted to its needs—had swaddled it, by order of the Emperor, then resident in Nara, official historiographers sought to determine for future generations the origins of the Empire, still extremely limited in scope, and of the sovereigns themselves.

Two chronicles were to emerge as a result of their efforts: first *Kojiki* (712), or Notes on the Events of the Past, and then, in 720, *Nihonshoki*, Chronicles of Japan. The first, written partially in Japanese but transcribed in Chinese characters read phonetically, relates the mythical origins and contains precious information on the beliefs of the first Japanese. The second, in Chinese, notes the important events year by year in each reign, but the chronology is too whimsical to be accepted without reserve, apart from the years immediately preceding publication.

Such as they are, both works are precious for the historian. But from the purely literary point of view the most interesting work of all is the first great official anthology of Japanese poetry, *Manyoshu*, An Anthology of 10,000 Verses (*c.* 760), containing 4,496 poems that appeared worthy to be handed down to posterity. The assiduous reader of this compilation, consisting for the most part of extremely short poems (4,173 in number) —known as *tanka*, "brief poems" of thirty-one beats or *waka*, "Japanese poetry" proper as opposed to Chinese poems which were highly appreciated by intellectuals of the time—will note that it describes a rustic civilization, imbued even in those early days with an instinctive taste for things beautiful, as evinced in its naïve spontaneity. Even the works of emperors or courtiers reflect the simplicity of the Court which, despite the Chinese veneer it sought to acquire, was still close to nature.

HEIAN, OR THE PETTICOAT REIGN — Throughout the following reign when the capital was transferred to Heian-Kyo, present-day Kyoto, nature was still the fundamental theme of the second great official collection of poetry,

Kokin-waku-shu, An Anthology of Old and New Japanese Poems (905), compiled by the poet Ki no Tsurayuki (the brief introduction this writer placed at the beginning of his anthology is the first Japanese pretence at the "Art of Poetry"). However, descriptions of the beauties of nature were already beginning to show a tendency towards conventionalism which, unhappily, assumed wider proportions.

Heian gained first place in the great periods of literary production not so much through its poetry as by its tales and stories, and through notes on travellers' impressions, or everyday life. I shall not enter into details of *Taketori-monogatari*, Tale of the Bamboo Cutter, alleged to be the oldest work composed purely in Japanese prose, dating from the end of the 9th

KORIN—*The Assembly of the Thirty-six most Eminent Poets from the 7th to the 10th Century*

or beginning of the 10th century, relating how an old bamboo cutter gave hospitality to a princess from the moon, how she rejected her suitors, including even the Emperor himself, and then, one night when the moon was full, returned to her distant homeland.

We shall also bypass *Ise-monogatari*, The Story of Ise (*c.* 900), an anthology of legends each of which is merely a pretext and a framework for one or more *waka*.

Tosa-nikki, Diary of a Journey to Tosa, by Ki no Tsurayuki, the poet already referred to, deserves more than a brief mention. It is the recital of the author's journey back to the capital from the then remote province of Tosa in Shikoku, of which he had been Governor from 930 to 935. The memory of a little girl he had lost cast a veil of gentle, resigned melancholy over the pleasure of returning.

Let me also mention *Tsutsumi-chunagon-monogatari*, a delightful collection of tales overflowing with that never-failing Japanese humour, and *Konjaku-monogatari*, Stories of Yesterday and Today (late 11th century), an immense compilation of tales of all kinds and extremely varied origins.

But the two major works of the period, which many Japanese still consider the masterpieces in their literature, were written by Court ladies at the beginning of the 10th century.

Genji-monogatari, Tale of Genji, by Murasaki-Shikibu (completed in 1004) paints a vast fresco of Court life. It is, in fact, almost a saga (the English translation by Arthur Waley which was, and still is, a best-seller, consists of over 1,000 pages in close print), relating the amorous exploits of Prince Genji, an emperor's son. Although less cynical, he might well be compared with Don Juan. His adventures familiarize us from his birth to his death —and even after his death, the last part of the novel being devoted to his son, Prince Kaoru—with every walk of life in the capital, except for the lower classes who appear only in episodic fashion. Without being over-prudish, the author succeeded in safeguarding his reputation by casting an implacable light on the courtiers' effeminate, dissolute life.

If the renown of Lady Sei-Shonagon, who bequeathed to us *Makura-no-soshi*, The Story of a Cushion (written in about the year 1000) is subject to a certain amount of reserve, her work is interesting for all that.

Through her pen we live day by day the life of those same courtiers that Genji revealed to us from without, so to speak: an idle, futile life devoted to refined amusements such as poetry competitions, dancing, banquets, and love affairs—both courtly and free. All the episodes are slapped down haphazardly at the whim of the brush, without any semblance of order. Here and there brief notations appear as to things pleasant, things unpleasant, things to be avoided, etc.

KAMAKURA, OR THE EPIC AGE — Then came the reign of the warriors. Whilst the courtiers were leading a carefree life of pleasure in Kyoto, in the distant, barbaric East the way was being paved for the men of "bows and horses" to take over the reins. The war-leaders of Kamakura were preparing to seize the bridle from the hands of a weakened sovereign who had retained merely the nominal suzerainty of a do-nothing king. From the 12th to the 16th century the country was to echo to the clash of

HOKUSAI
*Abe no Nakamaro,
the Ambassador-poet, in China*

KORIN—*The Bridge with the Irises*
Ise-Monogatari relates that the eight bridges of the
village of Yatsuhashi inspired Narihira to write
a poem. Korin idealized the poet's vision

sabres, with only too rare periods of calm.

The Court continued to busy itself with poetry, and huge anthologies were still being compiled but, apart from *Shin-Kokin-waka-shu*, New Anthology of Old and New Japanese Poems, none of them is worthy of note. Even Kamakura witnessed the blossoming of delicate talent from the pen of Minamoto no Sanetomo, the son of ferocious Yoritomo. But this premature flower faded only too soon since this third Shogun (who was also general-in-chief and regent), was assassinated at the early age of twenty-six.

For all that, the style characteristic of this wild, austere period was still the ballad, or rather the epic tale. I shall mention only two of the many: *Heike-monogatari*, or Story of the Taira Clan, and *Gempei-Seisuki*, The Rise and Fall of the Taira and Minamoto (early 13th century), relating the exploits of the heroes of these two enemy clans that drenched the 12th century in bloodshed. After a brief interval of calm throughout which they cherished the illusion of being masters of the Empire, the Taira were definitively crushed by their rivals. One of their most outstanding enemies was Yoshitsune, brother of the Shogun Yoritomo. Shortly after his brilliant victories, followed by his faithful henchman

Benkei, this young general was compelled to flee from the jealousy of his elder brother, and died an obscure death in the north of Japan whilst still in his twenties. Yoshitsune, still almost a child, and the giant Benkei, are the favourite heroes of Japanese epic, and since their day literature and drama have turned their countless adventures to best—and worst— account. They are the first historical characters with which the young Japanese becomes familiar, and in every region travellers will find relics —authentic and otherwise—of their passage.

These tales—the authors of which have never been definitely determined—were handed down by blind monks. Like our medieval bards, they chanted them to the accompaniment of the biwa—a kind of four-stringed viola—in the countless castles that bristled all over the country in those troubled days, or in the villages where they were given hospitality.

Like every other in Japan, this tradition enjoyed long-lived success, and it has even been possible in our time to record the voice of the last of these bards.

It would be unjust to leave this era without at least a cursory reference to *Hojoki*, Notes on Seclusion (1212) by the monk Kamo no Chomei (1154–1216). After performing quite important functions at Court for many years, the author withdrew into the mountains to meditate on the misfortunes of the times and the instability of things human.

Episode from Genji-monogatari (Leaf from an Album of the Tosa School, 17th century)

MUROMACHI, THE GOLDEN AGE OF NOH — The reign (from the 14th to the 16th century) of the Ashikaga Shoguns, whose precarious power was soon to be contested, was also marked by the philosophic essays of a monk, Kenko (1283–1350), known under the title of *Tsure-zure-gusa*, On the Brink of Boredom (*c.* 1340). Prior to taking his vows, this writer, too, served for many years at Court. His work is a mixture of notations, anecdotes, and reflections, serious at times, amusing at others, never pedantic or fastidious.

However, the imperishable claim to glory of an age otherwise poor in literature was its conception of the noblest form of spectacle Japan—and probably the whole world—has ever known: the Noh play.

Whilst little is yet known about the origins of this art—which will be discussed at length in the chapter on drama—we do at least know that of the numerous actor-authors who contributed to its formation and development, two have outshone all the others and, so to speak, "made" Noh. They are the two Kanzes, the father Kanami (1354–1406) and the son

Zeami (1372–1455), who enjoyed the friendship and effective patronage of the third Ashikaga Shogun, Yoshimitsu. More than half the works in the present-day repertoire were created by these two artists, particularly the second. The specialists are still debating their respective roles in elaborating the Noh play. It is, in fact, probable that in many instances Zeami simply took up his father's ideas and developed them.

Episode from Genji-monogatari (Leaf from an Album of the Tosa School, 17th century)

HIROSHIGE—*Yoshitsune and Benkei*

Nevertheless, it is to him that we owe the most complete theory of his art, in the form of manuals intended for his descendants, handed down secretly in the Kanze family and published only in 1910.... These manuals—particularly the first, entitled *Kadensho*, or literally, Book of the Message of Flowers—often rise above discussions of technique as such, to general considerations on aesthetics extending far beyond the narrow framework of Noh. This work is considered—not without reason—as the acme of Japanese literary production. Of all the masterpieces of Nipponese literature, it is the one whose human and universal value is the least open to debate. I do not consider it detrimental to Aristotle to rank *Kadensho* in the same category as his *Poetica*.

EDO, OR BOURGEOIS LITERATURE — After centuries of civil wars, under the iron fist of the Tokugawa Japan was at last to experience what is probably the longest period of peace that history has ever recorded: an era extending from the early 17th to the late 19th century, throughout which there was neither civil war at home nor conflict abroad.

Under cover of the military dictatorship, the middle-class tradesmen—theoretically the last class in the State—were to build up a flourishing economy which permitted them to accede to political power, after the Meiji restoration.

In opposition to the courtiers, tirelessly repeating shadows of bygone gestures, and the ignorant, bellicose Samurai, the tradesmen of Osaka and Edo in turn created their own civilization. To be sure, it was crude and morally dubious at first, but in time it became more polished as contact with the culture and art of past ages gradually refined the new middle class.

Literature, which was originally the exclusive apanage of the Court, and later of the monks, was to find new life and vigour in the Tokugawa period. A new type of theatrical came into being, more dramatic and realistic in character than Noh which, aristocratically scorning contingencies, was now petrified, hieratic, and stereotyped.

A pleiad of novelists described the toils and trials, pleasures and pastimes of the merchant class.

HIROSHIGE—*The poet Saigyo Contemplating Fujisan*

114

HOKUSAI—*Women Reading*

The antique *waka* was at last dethroned by an even more concise poetic form, *haikai*, consisting of seventeen beats.

DRAMA — At this stage we shall speak of drama only in order to place it within the framework of the historical evolution of literature. The puppet theatre or Bunraku, as well as Kabuki — which are still alive to this day—will, in fact, be described in detail further on.

Bunraku owes its ascent to the rank of a classic mainly to the collaboration of the narrator Takemoto Gidayu (1651–1714), and the greatest Japanese dramatist of all time, Chikamatsu Monzaemon (1653–1724).

Chikamatsu had already written for Kabuki. The entire puppet repertoire was, moreover, to be adapted by this new form of art. The playwrights of the late 18th and the 19th century, on the other hand, devoted themselves exclusively to Kabuki. Above all, I should like to mention Tsuruya Namboku (1755–1829), renowned for his ghost stories, and more particularly Kawatake Mokuami (1816–93) who, in a more realistic and modern style, is quite worthy to rank with Chikamatsu.

THE NOVEL — The predominant novelist is Ihara Saikaku (1642–93). His prodigiously abundant output constitutes a mine of information on his period. It is useless to seek a moral of any kind in these stories, describing the dissolute life of the pleasure haunts, where we may witness the evolution of the gilded youth of the time amidst intriguing courtesans, in a series of amorous adventures of a sordid and often dubious nature. For all that, Saikaku never—or almost never—overstepped the mark.

One cannot say as much for the facile authors of *Ukiyo-zoshi*, Stories of the Drifting World, which were often sheer pornography accentuated by painters of prints who have proved elsewhere that they could do better. In this instance *Ukiyo*, a Buddhist expression designating the origin of the "Inconsistent World" or in other words "This Base World" assumed the specific meaning of "Pleasure Haunts".

The austere Tokugawa government took firm measures in regard to the authors and publishers of such literature, thus orienting the threatened writers towards healthier activities.

Ugetsu-monogatari, Tales of the Rainy Season, by Ueda Akinari, provide particularly fine examples of this reaction, conjuring up the echo of the great storytellers of Heian. The fantastic tale of the spectre of a woman who attempted to beguile a young craftsman, recently met with well-deserved success on the screen.

On the other hand, it is difficult for Westerners to understand the Japanese craze for Bakin's rambling novels (1767–1848). These interminable allegorical adventures of pallid heroes from tales of chivalry, are far too reminiscent of the soporific flow of certain 17th-century pastorals.

The picture would be incomplete if we omitted the comic novel, and especially *Hizakurige* (1802–22)—A Journey on Foot—relating the picaresque adventures of two gay companions—artful yet naïve, cowardly yet venturesome, braggart and waggish at one and the same time—on the Tokaido Road (from Edo to Kyoto). It brings to life a world of adventurers, thieves, innkeepers, maidens, soldiers, and pilgrims in all their native truculence, coloured by their local dialects and spicy jargon. The author, Jippensha Ikku (1765–1831) was himself an original character who carried

HIROSHIGE—*Gust of Wind on the Tokaido Road*

his craze for practical jokes to the extent of stuffing squibs into the gown in which he was to be cremated after his death.

POETRY — *Haikai*, which to this day every cultured Japanese should be able to improvise on any occasion, is to poetry as are to painting the pictures whereby with two or three strokes of the brush the artist conjured up in Indian ink not just a landscape, but a state of mind. Two poets who shone in this field were Matsuo Basho (1643–94) and Buson (1716–83).

CONTEMPORARY JAPAN — However, the evolution of Japanese literature was to be brutally interrupted and driven into a new trend by the opening up of the country to the West, in 1868. For many years the ancient forms were neglected. It was the heyday of translations, adaptations, or imitations of Western literature—mainly English and French, but also Russian and German. It was impossible for a real masterpiece to emerge from this period of transition, which was to last several decades. But over the past thirty years a reaction has set in: writers still seek inspiration in the West, but they have become more selective. This same period has also witnessed a return to national sources, more in line with the popular way of thought. In this way, equilibrium has gradually been restored, and a whole host of young writers thus came to the fore in the 1920's. Of the latter, I shall mention only Akutagawa Ryunosuke (1892–1927), the author of the short story on which the film *Rashomon* was based. This first generation has fully lived up to its promise, and since the end of the war in particular a new movement has been taking shape, predicting a brilliant future for Japanese literature. As far as variety and abundance are concerned, the latter can vie with any Western literature.

I should also point out that this national literature is supplemented by translations of many French and Anglo-American literary works, from Shakespeare to Jean-Paul Sartre and Ernest Hemingway. There is hardly a novel or play of any significance published in London, New York, or Paris that is not immediately translated into Japanese. Moreover, Japanese writers find that Western literature is an invaluable source of inspiration, which they turn to best advantage.

HIROSHIGE—*Scene from the Hizakurige*

演劇

THE THEATRE

IMAGINE for a moment that in England, medieval drama had been preserved intact to the present day, and the programme of amusements listed in your newspaper offered you the choice between a mystery, a drama by Shakespeare or Sheridan, or Christopher Fry's latest hit. Then suppose that all these plays include songs and dances with music, and you will have a notion of Japanese drama.

Its history may be schematically divided into three periods. The first, extending through the 14th and 15th centuries, saw the creation of Noh, a combination of court dances introduced in the past from China (and preserved to this day under the name of Bugaku), religious dances, and popular entertainment in the form of songs, dances, or farces. Noh, first performed in the open air, usually in a temple court before a vast public, was soon to become a refined and aristocratic form of amusement.

But meanwhile a second movement was already paving the way for the puppet play, Bunraku, and the even more important type of entertainment known as Kabuki, which came into being almost simultaneously. The puppet theatre recitative—Joruri—was merely a continuation of the epic poems, illustrated by marionette showmen. Towards the end of the 17th century, vocalists and dramatists transformed it into drama in the real sense of the word. At the outset Kabuki was a kind of fairground show. Nonetheless, uncouth though it may have been, it did prove that the repertoire of the marionette theatre, as well as of Noh and the farces, or Kyogen, that accompanied it, could be successfully adapted. Subsequently dance interludes were introduced, and in the 19th century came the more realistic dramas of Kawatake Mokuami.

The latter heralded the third period, that of contemporary theatre, characterized by the intrusion of Western drama. European influence was—and in fact still is—of considerable importance. The majority of European masterpieces have been translated and performed. Shakespeare, Ibsen, and, more recently, contemporary French plays have met with some success. Naturally, a number of Japanese authors have imitated their style,

Bugaku Dance in Nara

often in a rather servile manner. But on the whole the public is still faithful to Kabuki, and the new plays they most readily accept are those that take their roots in this favourite form of entertainment, and at the same time seek to rejuvenate it by incorporating Western techniques.

Needless to say, together with European music—of which they are passionately fond—the Japanese have introduced opera and music-hall.

For all that, whatever their importance, these types of amusement are essentially foreign and have no point of contact with tradition. Nonetheless, it is highly probable that here again Japanese artists will eventually find a source of inspiration in their own background, as they have done already in regard to the cinema.

Despite all these European influences, Kabuki is still by far the most popular type of theatre. For all that, in Osaka a large playhouse specializes in performances of Bunraku and Noh, and although on two occasions —towards the end of the 19th century, after Japan was reopened to the world, then again on the morrow of the last war—bewailing intellectuals predicted its disappearance in the near future, over the past few years Noh has taken on a new lease of life, and a growing number of increasingly youthful spectators flocks to see it.

COURT DANCES—Before following the movement and beginning our wanderings through the theatres, let us make a little excursion to the Temple of Kasuga in Nara. If we have picked the right day, we shall be able to see Bugaku dances there.

On a square platform, one or more dancers clad in ancient Chinese costume and wearing startling masks perform supple, majestic evolutions to the strains of music which at first strikes us as curious. The accompaniment is dominated by the flutes and the sho, or mouth organ, whilst two immense vertical drums—forming the background to the performance—beat the rhythm. First we are charmed and benumbed by the monotony of the melody; then we fall under the spell of the dancers' swaying movements and, once we have overcome our initial astonishment, we eventually distinguish subtle nuances woven on a musical and choreographic theme.

RELIGIOUS DANCES—Let us now visit a village on the day of the temple festival. On a fairly high covered platform, peasants attired in ancient costumes and masks—some of which may be rather uncouth whilst others, on the contrary, are extremely beautiful and often several centuries old— perform the kagura, the dance of their god. Although rudimentary on the whole, the dance is always expressive, representing elemental rites, sowing, exorcism, or pantomime of gods, demons, monsters, or heroes. The music is contrapuntal, comprising a flute melody punctuated by the beating of drums.

Noh Theatre: the Stage

Noh Play : the Actors

NOH

Now we are ready to undergo the experience of a session of Noh in which, if we follow carefully, we may still discern the original influence of those two trends, court dances and popular religious dances.

Since we want to recapture the atmosphere of classical Japan in which this art first flourished, we shall go to Kyoto where there is still a hint of that ancient environment in the air. And since we are determined not to miss anything, we shall select a day comprising a complete traditional programme of five plays, with three or four comic interludes, or Kyogen.

THE PLAYHOUSE AND THE AUDIENCE—In order to have the leisure in which to absorb everything, we shall take care to arrive a little ahead of time. At the end of an alley we glimpse the door of a house that does not stand out from its neighbours at all, apart from a signboard in Japanese indicating that we have not gone astray. We leave our shoes in the hands of a doorman, who puts them in the midst of the geta or zori belonging to the *habitués*.

Corridors with shining floors eventually lead us into the theatre proper. We have taken the precaution of booking in advance, to be sure of having good seats—in the middle, towards the back, preferably in a box where, in case we are afraid of remaining seated on the ground for eight hours at a stretch, there is a chair at our disposal. This gives us the added advantage of not being inconvenienced by the heads of the spectators in front of us.

The room is not very large: some fifty feet square, of which approximately a quarter is taken up by the stage. The section reserved for the spectators is covered with tatami, as they call those flexible mats that take the place of flooring in Japanese houses. The entire surface is divided by planks into squares measuring about four feet on either side, and completed with four cushions: the Japanese need very little room in order to be seated comfortably. The *habitués* arrive one after another, taking things leisurely, smiling, and exchanging an endless flow of polite greetings. Many a kimono is to be seen, even amongst the men. The young girls' dresses with their dazzling brocade belts form bright spots here and there, The more sober garb of the older women alternates with the black, grey. or dark brown suits of the men, the black uniform of the male students, and the sailor collars of their feminine counterparts. There are children too, of course, and even babies on their mothers' backs.

They have all brought the text so that they can follow the play, whilst music-lovers refer to the score to see how well such and such an actor of renown interprets this or that difficult passage. Some of them have also brought a meal, packed in a box wrapped in a large square of brightly coloured cotton or silk.

Aged Spectator

Everyone settles down, striking up animated conversations in criticism of the last play or discussing the comparative merits of the various actors.

From the wings waft the strains of flute and drums as the musicians tune in before taking their bow.

THE STAGE—Noh was originally an open-air show, the stage being erected in a temple court as often as not. From time to time Noh is still performed out of doors in the ancient style, on the occasion of a religious festival, for instance. But the most active stages, such as the one we have come to see, are to be found in theatres belonging to one or other of the five schools—or rather, families—of actors.

Stage architecture, on the other hand, has not changed. It still consists of an edifice roofed in Buddhist style, supported by four pillars forming a square three kens by three (the ken is a Japanese architectural gauge of about six feet). These pillars also serve as landmarks for the actors in their dances, their view being considerably hampered by their masks. Behind this square is a rectangular space three kens wide by one ken deep, reserved for the musicians and "supervisors". This rectangle is prolonged to the left by a "bridge" or kind of passage some thirty feet long, opening on to the auditorium, where part of the performance takes place. On the spectators' side this bridge is bordered by a balustrade beside which three small pine trees are planted at regular intervals, to serve as further landmarks for the actor.

The tip of the bridge is closed by a curtain with five vertical stripes of different

Dressing an Actor

colours, separating the wings. In front of the bridge there is a space about a yard wide, covered with gravel, another reminder of the temple courts. Finally, a stairway—no longer in use nowadays—runs down from the middle of the stage.

THE ORCHESTRA—But hush, a corner of the curtain is rising. In the gradually descending quiet, the musicians enter carrying their instruments: first the flute-player, who sits down slightly to the rear facing left, near the back right-hand pillar which is for this reason known as the "flute pillar". Then come the "small drum" and the "big drum" players. Both the latter bring

Feminine Character in a Noh Play

camp-stools on which they sit with their knees apart. The drums are shaped like two funnels linked at the mouth, with an ox-hide drawn over the opening, tautened by cords which the instrumentalist constantly tests, to verify the tension. The small drum should beat a muffled note, and the musician is therefore obliged to soften it continually with his breath. He plays the instrument by holding it on his right shoulder with his left hand, and striking it with the palm of his right hand. The big drum, on the other hand, should strike a short, sharp note; the hide is thus very dry,

129

The Bell of Dojoji

and it is beaten with the fingertips of the right hand protected by ivory shields, the left hand being used to steady the instrument on the left knee.

If the play is particularly lively —as, for instance, when the main character is a god or a demon— the orchestra is completed by another drum similar in shape to the Western variety, but here again covered with hide tautened by cords. This drum is placed on a small stand which holds it at a slight angle, to the far left of the orchestra, the musician himself sitting a little to the rear of the three others. He plays it with two drumsticks, raised alternately above his head and lowered again with an extremely majestic, sculptural gesture.

Simultaneously with the musicians, by way of a small door at the back of the stage, in the right-hand partition, enter the choir. This is generally composed of eight singers and two "supervisors", one of whom is often the head of the school. Their role is to make sure nothing is awry in the actor's costume, bring him accessories or relieve him of them, and criticize his acting after the play.

SCENERY—At this point, in the rare plays that make use of stage-sets, the scenery is brought in. It is schematic in the extreme, and usually symbolic: a pine branch on a stand represents a wood. A small platform about a ken long and half a ken wide, topped by a roof, is a cottage or a palace as the case may be. A bamboo frame covered with canvas indicates a mound, a tombstone, or a mountain, but bamboo framework on its own is a boat. Some of the accessories look more like children's toys, and most unrealistic toys at that. The only one of really normal size is the *Dojoji* bell, since the actor has to disappear under this bamboo and canvas dome suspended above the stage. Together with the

Noh Masks

majestic pine tree represented on the backcloth, and the bamboos painted on the right-hand screen, the musicians in the background and the choirs seated two deep on the right form the invariable setting in which all plays in the repertoire are enacted.

THE REPERTOIRE—Nowadays this repertoire, which differs slightly according to schools, comprises a total of approximately two hundred and forty plays. These are divided into five groups: introductory pieces, plays about warriors, plays about women, contemporary plays, and tales of demons. A complete classical programme consists of five works, one in each category, in the above order. A Kyogen is interspersed between two Noh; a full series thus comprises four such farces.

A Noh play is generally performed by only two actors; each of them may be followed by numerous "companions"; however, the latter have no distinct personality and, in short, are merely a continuation of their ringleader. One of the two main players is the *Waki*, or "the one in the corner" who introduces the drama but participates only as a spectator, seated at the foot of the right-hand pillar to the front of the stage, consequently known as the "Waki's pillar"; the second is the *Shite*, or "actor" —the one who sings and dances.

To be precise, the Noh is not a play as we understand it, i.e. a drama implying action. It is really a dramatized poem. This is particularly true of the standard works which embrace more than half the repertoire and, judged by our usual criteria, would appear dishearteningly monotonous and singularly lacking in imagination. As a general rule a monk (the Waki) travelling across the country arrives one evening in a spot made famous by literature or history. An old man or a young woman (the Shite) offers him hospitality and explains the local legend to him. This calls for a lyric dialogue crammed with quotations from ancient poems or epic tales. Then the Shite mysteriously disappears. Intrigued, the monk asks an inhabitant of the region for further explanations, and realizes he has been taken in by the ghost of the hero or heroine of the legend, or a god or demon who haunts the area. The Shite thereupon reappears, this time in his true guise, clad in a dazzling costume, and relives his past adventures by illustrating them in a series of dances. Through his prayers the monk either achieves repose for the ghost, exorcises the demon, or venerates the god.

In the introductory pieces where a god generally appears and utters words of good tidings for the Emperor's reign, the Waki is usually an Imperial messenger who comes to visit a famous temple. The god then makes his appearance, confirms that the messenger's prayers have not fallen on deaf ears, and promises long life for the Emperor and prosperity for his subjects.

In the plays about warriors or women, depicting the ghosts of famous characters whose earthly passions—whether warlike or amorous—prevent them from finding appeasement on the other side of the tomb, and in certain plays about gods or demons, the text and even the actors' comportment tend to transform this phantasmagoria into a dream of the Waki: a dream which at the end of the play—one can hardly call it a denouement since there can be no outcome in a drama devoid of action—"vanishes like the evening mist".

The example given below is a passage from the Noh play *Kanehira*.

The knight Kanehira, who fell in the Battle of Awazu on the banks of Lake Biwa, appears to a monk in the guise of an aged boatman. Then, in the second part of the play when the holy man has gradually prayed himself to sleep, the ghost reappears to him in his dreams, and the following dialogue takes place:

> The monk: Oh! wonder of wonders!
> You appear before me, armour-clad,
> near my pillow of grass in the fields of Awazu!
> Who, then, are you?
>
> The ghost: Oh! How vain a question!
> You came so far to pray here in my footsteps:
> Was not this your intent?
> I, Kanehira, am come to join you!
>
> The monk: Imai no Shiro Kanehira
> has departed from this world.
> Were this, then, but a dream?
>
> The ghost: In this, your dream,
> and in reality have you perceived me
> in the boat beside the wonted waters,
> rod in hand; could you so soon forget me? . . .

THE INSTRUMENTAL ACCOMPANIMENT—The chief actor's entry is always heralded by an instrumental overture, consisting of a high-pitched flute attack, immediately taken up by the drums. But the originality of the music lies in the modulated cries of the drummers themselves—exclamations, raucous howls, mewing, barking, long-drawn-out groans, and shrieks. At first hearing, these noises may seem barbaric, but in actual fact they are the outcome of long experience and, punctuated by the contrasting sharp and dull sounds of the two instruments, they contribute most effectively to creating the unreal atmosphere of pathos in which the play unfolds. The music drives the spectator into a state of nervous tension and hypnosis, bringing him to the pitch where he senses the strange beauty emanating from the scene. Notions of time and space disappear, and the supernatural comes to be accepted as a matter of course.

MASKS AND COSTUMES—This impression is completed by the mask worn

Noh Costume

by the Shite. The mask further accentuates the distance between the latter and the Waki, who appears all the more real in that his face is uncovered throughout. The masks themselves are masterpieces, jealously preserved in the schools for centuries. The finest are those of the 14th and 15th centuries, which become almost painfully alive on the actor's face. This is particularly true of the masks of old men, with that enigmatic smile heralding the approach of the last experience; and also of the young women, whose gentle features represent the purest form of beauty to the eyes of many Japanese. A slight nod of the head suffices to transform their expression completely.

The incredibly sumptuous costumes contrast with the barrenness of the stage, and help to concentrate the spectators' attention on the Shite. The Waki, on the other hand, wears the most inconspicuous clothes—especially when he represents a monk. The resultant contrast is also intended to emphasize the unreal character of the Shite. Some of these costumes are extremely ancient—five or six hundred years old—but the majority of those now in use date only from the 18th or even the 19th century.

In the so-called contemporary plays, the actor does not wear a mask, unless of course he is impersonating a woman. This group contains works more akin to drama in the usual sense of the word. The first phase of Kabuki sought inspiration in this form of histrionic art, in which both Shite and Waki belong to reality. The "companions" are often numerous, and the movement is far more rapid than in the standard type. But the true theatre-lover looks on this variety with a certain amount of scorn, since it is the one most far removed from the aesthetic principles of Noh, as defined by Zeami in his *Manuals*.

Mask of an Old Man

AESTHETIC PRINCIPLES—The fundamental principle of Noh is, in fact, *yugen*, that is to say a refined elegance, essentially esoteric in nature, which only an actor in complete possession of the secrets of his art can communicate to the spectator—provided the latter, through long training, in turn possesses the receptivity necessary to its understanding. Naturally, plays that content themselves with relating a real and often violent action are ill-adapted to express this elegance.

Elegance is the essential quality of the women's dances. Their interpretation serves as a yardstick for measuring the actor's talent. These dances are extremely slow, and it is difficult for the uninitiated to appreciate their beauty. They are accompanied by a very gentle air on the flute, whilst the long-drawn-out, modulated cries of the drummers help to create a melancholic atmosphere, the charm of which evokes the perfume of ancient loves, as befits plays about women. The dancer's evolutions bear the imprint of serene resignation, with never a violent movement. The step is an imperceptible glide.

The dances of warriors or demons are quite a different matter. The technical term by which they are designated, *hataraki*, implies violent effort, toiling, and physical strength. The heroic ghosts mime the last battle in which they met their death and which their ardent passions relentlessly compel them to relive unendingly. Throughout the dance, the chorus describes the battle to a rapid rhythm, now and then taken up by the unleashing of the orchestra. The movement becomes more and more lively, the drums beat out a terrifying din, then suddenly, with the last word of the chorus, total silence falls, casting an invisible veil over everything that went before. With the monk in the play, the spectator awakens from a dream. The actor has disappeared; or rather, the extremely slow motion with which he crosses the bridge to return to the wings makes one forget his mighty presence of a moment ago.

COMIC INTERLUDES—Noh puts the public's nerves to a severe test. It is therefore necessary to provoke a counter-shock and relieve the tension, failing which it would be impossible to appreciate, or even tolerate, another serious play. Hence the necessity for farces. The latter are based on comic themes, generally quite simple, similar to our medieval fables: conjugal strife, satires of lords or monks, escapades of valets, etc. Some time ago an adaptation of the famous French play *La Farce du Cuvier* was produced in Tokyo. With a little retouching to convert the characters into authentic Japanese, it was impossible to distinguish this European comedy from the most classic Kyogen.

Certain plays are parodies of Noh, over-exaggerating its sublime, emphatic style in an irresistible clown-like fashion. The masks sometimes worn by the actors in these skits—grotesque replicas of the Noh masks— are masterpieces of caricature.

But as often as not Kyogen is written in the popular jargon of the late Middle Ages, full of verve and spice, flavoured with ludicrous expressions. The comic effect is produced mainly by the contrast between the triviality of theme and text and the stylization—nay, dignity—of the acting, even in scenes of drunkenness or brawls. The entry of a drunkard, for instance, consists of an extravagant hesitation-dance, and the battles are acrobatic ballets necessitating severe training and uncommon suppleness on the part of the performers. Moreover, these actors are specialized, and they too are grouped in schools distinct from those of Noh.

BUNRAKU

Bunraku: Head of Articulated Puppet

FROM Kyoto, the ancient capital, now somewhat set in contemplation of her past, barely an hour's train ride takes us to Osaka. Although the citadel of modern industry, this city has succeeded in preserving a form of dramatic art unique in the world—the famous Bunraku, or puppet-play. A large European-style theatre, in a brick building that has nothing in common with the architecture of old Japan, shelters this art, which, in itself, is entirely free from foreign influence of any kind. The public, which has nothing picturesque about it these days—apart from the vivid kimonos of the geishas who go there to hear their singing-masters, the narrators— settles down demurely in rows of armchairs, rather too close together for European legs. A curtain, similar to theatre curtains all over the world, conceals the stage; on the right is a platform, on which the singers and musicians install themselves.

The curtain rises. The *décor* represents a house, the interior of a palace, or a panoramic landscape. A character clad in black from head to foot, and wearing a hood, comes to announce the play. The *samisen*, as the three-string Japanese guitar is called, strikes up the prelude. The deep voice of the singer breaks into the recital. After a seemingly interminable moment, the little actors of wood and rag appear, conjured up by the charm of the powerful voice. The recital gives way to dialogue, the puppets seem to become more and more animated, whilst voices and gestures merge into each other. Narrators and dolls transport us into an unreal universe, the world of drama, a universe surpassing humanity, and yet essentially human.

THE "ACTORS"—Unlike our marionettes, the Japanese puppet is not animated by a system of wires but by the manipulator himself, who holds it in front of him and, like his two assistants, is visible to the public. Each puppet necessitates three operators, first on account of its weight, secondly, and more particularly, because of its size, some being over four feet high. The puppet has no body, the clothes being supported by a simple bamboo frame. The head, made of carved and painted wood, is complete with genuine hair, carefully arranged. A shaft attached to the neck is fitted with levers which permit the chief manipulator to control the mechanism of the neck, eyes, eyebrows, and mouth. In order to animate the puppet, the operator puts his left arm through a slit in the back of its garments, to reach the mechanism of the head. With his right hand, which he slips into the puppet's sleeve, he manipulates

Scene from Bunraku

138

its right arm. The left arm is operated by an assistant, whilst a second assistant controls the feet; only male characters have real feet, the movements of women's feet being indicated by shifting the hems of their dresses. The hands are fully articulated, each finger-joint being movable.

Generally speaking, the two assistants wear black hoods over their heads, the main operator alone having his face uncovered. The most striking feature is the exact synchronism of the three animators' movements. And since these motions are transmitted from the man to the doll without any mechanical intermediary, they are perfectly continuous and supple, creating an extraordinary illusion of life. The dolls breathe, walk, and lie down; they turn round, bow, lift their heads, roll their eyes, close them, raise their eyebrows, and open their mouths. A play of shadows accentuates their expressions: they are sad, they weep and sob, become convulsed with grief or anger, or relax and light up their faces with a smile. And the entire

Bunraku : Narrator and Musician

action takes place with all the agility of life, a life that is transmitted to them by three impassive characters, clad in black; the gigantic shadows of the destiny that overrides them at the evocation of the narrator, a destiny from which they attempt to flee in quest of a life of their own, only to find it drives them back, inexorably, towards the dread finale.

The presence of animators on the stage in no way disturbs the emotional atmosphere. On the contrary, it sublimates the pathos of the play, imparting a profound meaning to the actions of the *dramatis personae*, a meaning to which they alone seem to remain indifferent. They belong to another universe, from which they are able to comprehend the functioning of the human world, yet impotent to change anything in it. It is, in fact, as if the superior powers of a spell constrained them to re-establish, by an imperceptible gesture, the order constantly threatened by man's enterprises. In this order, the manipulator appears as the mechanical executor of the unpredictable works of a fatality that he himself is incapable of averting. In face of this automatized man, the doll comes to life.

The types of character are extremely numerous, to meet the demands of a complex and varied repertoire. Certain of the dolls' heads are real masterpieces, especially those of old men. For over three centuries, artists have been carving these heads to fill the needs of the Osaka theatre. Unfortunately most of the ancient dolls have disappeared, either through age, or—more frequently—through destruction by fire which periodically devastated the town.

The garments are sumptuous, and in the course of a single play the same doll may appear in the most varied costumes. All that is required is to transfer the head from one garment to another; hence the most astoundingly rapid changes of costume.

THE PLAYS—All this technical perfection would be a mere curiosity were it not for the fact that Bunraku boasts a repertoire which, from both a literary and a theatrical point of view, forms the backbone of Japanese classical drama. Chikamatsu Monzaemon, the late-17th-century writer, and his 18th-century disciples and followers, bequeathed to us most of the great plays still performed to this day. Moreover, these same plays are still the most highly appreciated in *Kabuki* theatres as well.

The work of these dramatists was, and still is, enhanced by the high standard of the singers who declaim, or rather interpret the text. An extremely flexible voice is essential, since the narrator plays each role in turn, from the bellowing warrior to the shrill-voiced maiden. The changing expression of these chanters is a show in itself; they succeed in identifying themselves so sincerely with each successive character that they suffer with them, laugh, cry, yell, twist themselves into contortions, and finally withdraw, exhausted, after half-an-hour's performance.

The plays are exceedingly long. A complete drama would take an entire day of approximately twelve hours. Nowadays a performance seldom lasts more than ten hours or so, and programmes are generally composed of detached acts from various plays, to avoid wearying the spectator. Each act often forms a whole on its own, and even where this is not the case, the public knows the story by dint of seeing all the episodes bit by bit.

Kabuki: Shibaraku Ballet

However, the Osaka public is still patient enough to put up with an entire drama from time to time: *Chushingura*, the famous story of the vengeance of the forty-seven ronins, for instance, is still enacted in full to this day.

At another recent production, between ten and eleven in the morning during the first act one could see the villain assassinating an old man in order to rob him of a precious sword; then, after a series of tragi-comic adventures, the victim's two sons running the assassin to earth and avenging their father in a spectacular sword battle.... at about eleven o'clock at night! And two or three episodes too remote from the subject in hand had actually been omitted.... The spectators' interest never seemed to flag for an instant, and if some elderly person collapsed now and then, this was apparently due solely to the fatigue of having to remain seated in an armchair, a particularly uncomfortable position for a Japanese. Moreover, there is nothing to stop you stretching your legs during an act, or recuperating your strength by sampling the delicious grilled eels in the nearby restaurant, especially if you are an *habitué* and know the play by heart.

Then again, as in the Noh theatre, the authors have realized the necessity of amusing the audience by introducing comic interludes or those astounding puppet dances in which one is at a loss to know which to admire most—the skill of the operators or the virtuosity of the samisen players. On emerging from a show such as this, although overcome by fatigue, the spectator is bubbling over with enthusiasm and enriched by a stock of wonderful memories.

KABUKI

HOWEVER, Noh and Bunraku experienced a relatively brief period of activity, and the first-named has hardly changed over the past five centuries, nor the second in the last 150 years. More particularly, neither of them has renewed its repertoire: it is in fact just as if our own theatrical companies confined themselves to 17th-century plays. The only form of histrionic art to have moved continually with the times since the beginning of the 17th century is Kabuki, and this is explained by the fact that—at the outset at least—it took care not to encumber itself with literary or aesthetic pretensions. It was drama for the people. Kabuki was said to be derived from dances of religious inspiration, performed in Kyoto by a priestess named O-kuni, from the great Temple of Izumo. This is not entirely impossible, although as early as 1645 the government forbade women to go on the stage, because of the scandalous turn these shows had taken. It is since this date that female roles have always been played by men. However, by the beginning of the 18th century the puppet theatres had monopolized the public's interest, and Kabuki was able to regain a footing only once it had borrowed their repertoire of Joruri. Plays originally written for marionettes still hold a major place in present-day programmes, although at the end of the 18th century and throughout the 19th, a number of works had been written exclusively for Kabuki. The best are unquestionably those of Kawatake Mokuami who, following the lead of certain actors, also adapted part of the Noh and Kyogen repertoire, mainly as a pretext for dances. In addition, each programme nowadays includes at least one dance number, the theme of which is aimed solely at turning the limelight on the choreographic qualities of this or that idol of the public. Finally, almost every month some new play by a contemporary writer appears on the bills. Needless to say, some of them are inclined to be weak, but it is not unusual to see really first-rate productions worthy to rank with the classics. It should, however, be pointed out that these new plays are always in the ancient style, and invariably set in feudal Japan prior to the 1868 revolution.

THEATRE BUILDINGS—In order to contain the vast public that flocks to these shows, large modern theatres have been built in Tokyo. The most renowned is the Kabuki-Za, which holds approximately 1,500 spectators and was completely rebuilt after the war. If the exterior architecture is Japanese in inspiration, the interior is that of a European theatre, complete with stalls, balconies, and galleries. Nothing is lacking, not even the "gods" which, like everywhere else, is frequented by the most enthusiastic fraction of the public. There is, however, one difference, in the form of a bridge running right through the auditorium on the left. This extension of the stage is utilized for spectacular entrances or exits; it also gives depth to processions or battle scenes, for instance.

The stage itself, some eighty feet in width, is relatively deep, and equipped with a revolving platform to permit rapid—hence frequent—changes of scenery. Trap doors are devised in various spots throughout

Kabuki : Stage-hands

the platform and even the bridge. Their main use is for the entrance of ghosts, who boast an extensive repertoire—especially in summer, as they have a reputation for casting a chill! A highly complex and perfectly regulated machinery shifts the various elements of the scenery vertically or horizontally, in accordance with requirements. During the intervals, a whole army of stage-hands busies itself behind the curtain in a bustle of activity. The dexterity and precision with which they transform into a stormy sea a scene that an instant before was the interior of a palace is a magnificent and refreshing sight in itself. It should be added that one of the most interesting features of Kabuki is the realistic effect and the

technical perfection of the scenery, frequently designed by painters of renown. Not only is it unimaginably vast in scope, but also remarkably precise in detail. Whenever a historical play is enacted, everything materially connected with the characters is scrupulously reproduced. The actors' technique—handed down from generation to generation—transforms certain traditional episodes into living archaeological documents. By the same token, wherever a scene takes place in a celebrated setting, the latter is faithfully represented. The very composition of the set is a work of art regulated by classical principles: contrast and balance are always meticulously studied and, however numerous they may be, the actors take constant care to place themselves in such a way that at every instant they form a perfect tableau with the background, in conformity with the canons of painting.

THE WINGS—From the stage a maze of corridors and subterranean passages, inextricable for anyone other than an *habitué*, leads to the players' dressing-rooms. These vary in size according to the importance of the actor. They consist of small rooms in Japanese style, complete with reed mats, mobile paper screens, and a nook in which to hang a painting or calligraphy, invariably decorated with a bouquet of fresh flowers, frequently renewed. Needless to say there are no chairs, except perhaps a low armchair for the odd foreign visitor. The actor kneels in front of a mirror to make up. He begins by covering his face with a thick layer of ceruse. Then, with the help of a brush, he delicately outlines the features which gradually give him that fantastic appearance we in Europe have learnt to know from 18th-century prints; these, in fact, were actually portraits intended for fans, depicting the actors in their favourite roles. A few moments ago we were confronted by an amiable, courteous old gentleman nostalgically recalling his memories of a trip to Paris in the days of his youth, and lo and behold, without interrupting the conversation, by a strange, imperceptible metamorphosis he has transformed himself into one of those fearsome arrogant-mouthed warriors, quick to draw the sword. The addition of a wig completes the illusion and terminates

Actor's Dressing-room

147

the work of the brush. The sumptuous costume carries one unerringly into another era, in the ageless Japan of the theatrical world.

Even more astonishing is the way in which a middle-aged, bespectacled gentleman on the portly side, and rather unobtrusive manner, turns into a timid maiden or an elegant, *blasé* courtesan. In this case, however, it is sometimes better not to have a close-up view, since the hardness of the features scarcely creates an illusion at less than ten paces. Seen from the auditorium, on the other hand, the player's gait makes one forget the deception so remarkably well that the geishas have come to consider these actors as masters of deportment and models of feminine grace. We should add that, for the Japanese, a woman's charm has always lain in her bearing rather than in her face.

THE ORCHESTRA–The curtain is about to rise. Musicians and singers are taking up their positions. The puppet theatre tradition has been retained in the classical plays: a narrator tells a story which the actors illustrate by their gestures, but they themselves make their own rejoinders. The reciter and his accompanist on the samisen are installed in a small box to the right, above the stage, concealed by a curtain. A second orchestra is established on the left, flush with the stage, also hidden by a partition per-

Kabuki: Characters in the Ballet Kanjincho

forated with vertical slits. The main role of this latter orchestra, comprising a samisen, flutes, drums, or various other instruments according to requirements, is to produce "noises off". An animated passage, a battle scene, or the wrath of the hero which petrifies him in a sculptural pose, with his eyes hardening into an incredible squint, are underlined by a rolling of drums in crescendo. If the scene represents the sea, one hears the lapping of the waves or the billowing surf. Moonlight is underscored by a melancholy air on the flute, and so on. Occasionally the orchestra also plays a kind of prelude—sung, of course, for Japanese music without a vocal accompaniment is almost inconceivable. In short, the orchestra is intended to indicate the prevailing atmosphere at each instant throughout the play, without ever monopolizing the spectator's attention or diverting him in any way. Moreover, it is highly successful in the attempt, and you have to be wide awake if you want to observe its discreet yet effective role. Moments of intense emotion are often stressed by still another noise: on such occasions, enter an assistant clad in black who crouches on the far right of the stage and with two pieces of wood, strikes a small plank lying on the ground, to an ever-quickening tempo and with ever-increasing force.

FIRST SCENE—Everything is in order, the musicians have settled in their box and the actors on the stage; the curtain rises on a grand tableau. A programme generally comprises an extract from a so-called "period" play, highly spectacular and rich in colour, with dazzling costumes and glittering scenery to set off heroic and violent action. Then, in variable order, come a dance, a new play or a revival of a recent one, and finally a "realist" play—as often as not one of Chikamatsu Monzaemon's "bourgeois" dramas, or a play by Kawatake Mokuami.

The "period" play supplies the initial tableau, on a spectacular scale, grouping as many as twenty or thirty actors simultaneously on the stage, reminiscent of a review number. For the Japanese, Kabuki takes the place of music-hall, ballet, opera, and classical drama at one and the same time. Nearly all the historical plays have been borrowed from the puppet theatre repertoire. Scenes that were not entirely improbable in the puppet world become over-exaggerated on the Kabuki stage, and ring false. But in these plays we are not in quest of truth. Above all, we are seeking aesthetic emotion. The means employed are crude, to be sure, and the wires are only too conspicuous—excessive showiness, forced attitude on the part of the actors, pathos in music and singing, and voice-deforming declamation. Everything, in fact, is opposed to the principles of Noh; but for a "popular" show, Kabuki maintains a standard many a Western stage might envy.

For a spectator who does not understand the language, this opening scene is liable to be wanting in interest once the first flush of wonder is

Kabuki Dance in Honour of the New Year

past, the action being very slow as a general rule, to allow the onlookers to appreciate the overall effect at length and to the full. The interminable dialogue is full of refinements, and a real pleasure for the initiated.

I recollect one particularly appreciated scene entitled *Daitokuji*, from the name of a temple in Kyoto. The setting represents the interior of the

temple, where the vassals of the Shogun Oda Nobunaga are gathered to hold a funeral service for their recently assassinated lord. In an order strictly regulated by feudal hierarchy, each of them advances in turn to drop a pinch of incense into the perfume-brazier in the centre. Two sons of the deceased are in the first row, the elder born of a concubine, the younger a legitimate son. The problem is to decide who shall step forward first, and thus be recognized by all and sundry as his father's successor. Each has his partisans. A discussion breaks out between the great vassals, lasting fully an hour—a subtle, crafty discussion, full of legal references and veiled threats. For a moment it looks as if the action is about to develop as the most violent of the speakers leaps up, half-drawing his sword. His most ardent enemy does likewise, and one has the impression that they are about to come to grips. But at this precise moment Hideyoshi, the most dreaded of the late Shogun's generals—and the one who is, in fact, to replace him a little later—intervenes. He has found a solution, by bringing in Nobunaga's grandson, the son of the Shogun's first-born who was assassinated at the same time as his father. The affair is settled; one after another they all go to burn incense. This last scene is particularly beautiful, for the actor can give full scope to his talent in the glances the enemies exchange; glances more murderous than sword thrusts, heralding the bloody outcome of the drama.

Dance of the Lions (Renjishi)

For a foreigner, the whole interest of a scene such as this lies in the splendour of the tableau and the strangeness of the setting which transports him into that fearsome, legendary land of Japan that Loti and his emulators, blinded by their own littleness, did not even dream of. For an *habitué*, on the other hand, these elements are merely a familiar but necessary frame, setting off to best advantage the subtlety of the text and the skill with which the author—in this case Mokuami—weaves the tissue of juridical cavilling that never really touches upon the issue at stake: the succession is, in fact, not once specified in as many words. I have dwelt at length on this example since it is characteristic of the use of symbolic forms of expression in drama as well as literature, and even in real life.

MODERN KABUKI—In contrast, the modern plays are apt to appear lack-lustre at first sight. Their subjects are generally more down-to-earth, more human, more dramatic even—for, whilst one may admire the magnificence and the subtlety of the classical dramas, one can hardly take the plot seriously. The characters are closer to mankind as a whole; even when a historic hero is depicted, the accent is on his human rather than his heroic side. The role played by music and singing is reduced, if not entirely suppressed. Even the actors' diction is more natural, and their voices do not rise to that extraordinary pitch which rings so strangely in the ear of the layman. The women alone retain the falsetto tone of the conventional voice which is no more like a woman's voice than a man's, and which, for all that, creates an illusion, once the subconscious has accepted this convention. In short, plays such as these would not even qualify for the title of Kabuki, if one followed to the letter the classical but possibly erroneous etymology whereby the term would signify: "the art of song and dance".

Certain intransigeant theatre-fans profess to scorn this novel form of histrionics, but they are disavowed by the warm reception which these plays generally receive—when they are good, of course. Surely the best way in which an art can prove its vitality is through constantly seeking to renew itself, and it should again be stressed that this very characteristic fundamentally distinguished Kabuki from the other classical types, both of which are set in their unchanging repertoire, and one of which—Noh—could find new life only by attempting to recapture the more rapid rhythm of its origins.

In fact, these modern plays are really still Kabuki. Not the least of their charms lies in the talent of the actors, some of whom are truly amazing. A secular tradition has gradually condensed their technique into reliable, proven principles, assimilated throughout a long apprenticeship, the profession of actor being transmitted from father to son, with training beginning at a tender age. Moreover, their perfect knowledge of the classical repertoire enables them to make the most of any text, whether old or new. A background such as this gives them complete mastery of every situation. Then, of course, there is the talent of the playwrights, whose dramatic

Dance of the Young Girl with the Wistaria (Odori)

sense is seldom dimmed by preoccupation with literary style, as is so often the case with ourselves. Last, but not least, there is the infallible artistic sense of the producers and designers. In this respect, as mentioned above, the most famous painters in present-day Japan do not consider it beneath their dignity to turn their brushes to composing a setting, in which the most audacious researches of modern painting are far from neglected. In short, the intelligent and sensitive cooperation of author, artist, and actor —who is often his own producer—continues to promise modern Kabuki masterpieces worthy of comparison with the great classics of bygone centuries.

BOURGEOIS DRAMAS—Chikamatsu's bourgeois plays, adapted from the puppet-theatre repertoire, are still very popular. They stage the merchants of Osaka in love dramas frequently terminating in the dual suicide of the heroes. From the literary point of view, these plays are the finest the Japanese theatre has produced. Whilst they are less spectacular than the historical dramas, their documentary and human value is inestimable.

In their transition from the puppet-theatre, they have retained musical and vocal accompaniments which are often extremely beautiful. The tragic scenes are separated by comic passages, giving an interesting insight into the life of the common people of Osaka at the beginning of the 18th century.

REALIST DRAMA—Mokuami's "contemporary" plays, depicting the population of Edo (Tokyo) in the middle of last century, are in the same vein. They portray a whole world of middle-class citizens—tradesmen, craftsmen, roisterers, courtesans, and robbers, lifelike in the extreme, talking a picturesque patter that has almost disappeared nowadays—a free, truculent universe of people who spring to life beneath our eyes, with all their qualities and defects, virtues and vices, braggart, bantering, somewhat lax in morals perhaps, but extremely likeable and colourful for all that. Plays of this nature are difficult for foreigners to understand, since half their interest lies in the snappy dialogue, but the vivid, impassioned acting is in itself a delight for the spectators, even if they are unable to follow the text.

DANCES—No picture of the Japanese theatre would be complete without a section on the dance. To accompany it, an imposing orchestra—composed of samisen, drums, tambourines, flutes, and vocalists—takes up its position on a small dais at the back of the stage. There is no theme, or a rudimentary one at most outlined in song, or rather, a long poem set to music. The dancer himself is often supported by a veritable *corps-de-ballet*. This is where one becomes fully aware of the extent to which song, dance, and music hang together in Japan, forming interdependent elements of dramatic art. One might say that since Noh was first conceived, the theatre has unerringly continued to set the tone for music and dancing. Noh assimilated and codified the classical dances that preceded it. Since then, the themes of Noh dances have been constantly revived. For its part, by replacing the biwa—a kind of viola that set the rhythm of the epic recitative—with the samisen, Joruri introduced a more complex type of musical accompaniment which was in turn adopted and modified by Kabuki. Thus were born modern dances, almost all of which are inspired by Kabuki dances, from which they continually derive both themes and music. The Kabuki actors might be described as the dancing masters of modern Japan, and the samisen-players as her music teachers.

Kabuki dances may be classified into several clearly defined categories. First there are the adaptations of Noh or Kyogen. These are extremely interesting and often very beautiful, but disappointing for devotees of the earnest, concentrated style of the pure Noh dance. In its adaptations, Kabuki sacrifices far too much to its fondness for padding, and is all too apt to become affected; with Kyogen in particular losing all its comic force. By the same token, the adaptations of choreographic interludes from the puppet theatre are inclined to appear insipid compared with the virtuosity of the artists from the Osaka theatre.

There remain Kabuki dances proper. Some are purely aesthetic, such as that of the Young Girl with the Wistaria. This is where the specialists of female roles really come into their own, and where one realizes to the full the unexpected consequences of excluding women, a measure laid down by an outside authority. What could be more unnatural than to have a maiden of sixteen portrayed by a somewhat portly actor of forty odd? And yet, if you go and see the same dance performed by Kyoto geishas, you will find it is they who seem unnatural! The mere weight of the costume prescribed by the choreography calls for uncommon vigour. Moreover, a long study of typically feminine bearing enables these actors to be even more feminine than the fair sex, if I may be so bold as to say so.

Ultra-rapid changes of costume—as many as eleven in a forty-minute performance—add to the attractions. The music, one of the greatest successes in Japanese music as a whole, is also unforgettable. Consequently, for foreigners these dances are often their finest memory of Kabuki.

Some of them are based on mythical themes, such as the Dance of the Lions, which demand considerable strength and suppleness on the part of the actor. As for the comic or grotesque interludes, they are veritable circus acts, complete with clowning and acrobatics, to remind us that Kabuki was originally a fairground show.

Kabuki thus offers a wide range of performances, and as a result it is indisputably the most popular form of dramatic art in Japan. In 1950, 37 % of the performances given in Tokyo, Kyoto, and Osaka were Kabuki (against 8 % for the puppet theatre). The theatres are always full, and the box-offices sold out. In fact, after the first few days of the month it is extremely difficult to find tickets and these are sold at ransom price in the black market, right in front of the theatre. Apart from the Kabuki-za mentioned above, two other big theatres—Shimbashi-embujo and Meiji-za —are equipped to stage Kabuki. The programmes, which change every month, consist of two parts (lasting five hours each) per day, at noon and 5.00 p.m. respectively.

MODERN DRAMA

THE same theatres occasionally produce Shimpa, or the "new (theatrical) movement", a form of dramatic art derived from Kabuki, from which it has borrowed its techniques and in particular the interpretation of feminine roles by men. This type of drama, born at the end of the last century, responded to moralizing and political considerations. The main aim was to make the Japanese of the period appreciate the necessity and advantages of modernizing the country. With the disappearance of the needs that give birth to it, Shimpa has gradually lost its vitality. A few plays, however, have become classics; but even the best of them are inevitably boring in the long run, owing to the eternally sermonizing tone of the text. The youth of today has little liking for this form of entertainment, but in a picturesque way it may give foreigners a glimpse of Japan as she was in the age of great changes, in all her naïve ardour and quaintness. The performances are the same length as Kabuki and have the same caste, but the theatres are never full.

The Shingeki, or "new theatre" was more interesting. This movement was aimed at creating a new type of histrionic art inspired by the West. To this end the initiator of the movement, Tsubouchi Shoyo, began by translating Shakespeare's works. His translations—which were excellent— gave rise to a series of performances which, according to the critics of the day, were followed with curiosity, not to say passion, yet failed to produce the revolutionary effect he had counted on. As much may be said of the translations of Ibsen. They were, in fact, straight translations, performed by actors in European dress, as yet unfamiliar with the ways of the West, in entirely European and often somewhat fantastic settings. They could therefore meet with success only as curiosities, and being too far removed from Japanese conceptions of drama, they astonished the public without making any deep impression. Moreover, these plays were all performed in small theatres whose financial situation was precarious. French authors —Molière in particular—were also translated. Two French plays did, in fact, meet with more than mild success—*Le Cid*, produced in the Kabuki theatre, and *Cyrano de Bergerac*— because both of them were adapted rather than translated. A Frenchman would have had difficulty in recognizing Rodrigue or Cyrano disguised as Samurai, but Corneille's emphatic style and Cyrano's swashbuckling ways were much closer to Japanese conceptions than Shakespeare or Ibsen.

Scene from a Modern Play

DRAMA AND MUSIC—Western music, on the other hand, has definitely taken root. In Tokyo and the provinces alike one has only to see the enthusiastic crowds that throng to the recitals of foreign musicians on tour in Japan. And Japan herself has produced—and will produce more and more—virtuosi, whose matchless sensibility and suppleness will conquer the whole world. It has reached the point where Japanese classical music is relegated almost exclusively to the theatre and popular songs, and the latter are greatly influenced by Western techniques. This is mainly due to the difference in scale and rhythm, which more or less compels the Japanese to make a choice, if he is at all sensitive to music. Added to this, Japanese music has scarcely enriched itself over the past century, contenting itself with extremely limited and relatively simple types. The thirteen-, seventeen-, or nineteen-stringed harp known as the *koto* is the sole instrument that could be adapted to create a new aesthetic form, by reason of its wide register, reminiscent of our harpsichord.

Opera met with only relative success, mainly due to the fact that Japan lacks singers. Recently Japanese composers have made extremely interesting attempts to create a form of art based on opera and Kabuki at one and the same time. Any forecast of success is premature as yet. Nonetheless, the great dramatic event of the postwar years was the performance in 1951 of a play of this type, *Yuzuru* by Kinoshita Junji, on a theme borrowed from Japanese folklore.

VARIETY PERFORMANCES—In about 1910, a cocktail of operetta, review, and Kabuki produced a form of entertainment which has since met with considerable success—the "girls' lyric theatre". The best-known is Takarazuka, named after a small town situated between Osaka and Kobe, from which it spread to all the big towns throughout Japan. In these plays, whether inspired by European works or based purely on Japanese tradition, all the roles are filled by actresses. Whatever one may say, men interpreting female roles are more convincing than women in male roles. However, as it is merely light entertainment, this is not serious, and the performance is often good. It is better, at any rate, than the music-halls which content themselves with pallid imitations of Montmartre or, worse still, Broadway, as they imagine them. For the tourist's information, I should point out that as a general rule these entertainments have retained the tradition of long sessions lasting five hours, with different programmes at noon and at

5.00 p.m. Generally speaking, the best are those of the "Imperial Theatre" or Teigeki.

POPULAR ENTERTAINMENTS—In the popular pleasure districts of Asakusa, near the ancient site of the famous Yoshiwara area, an extraordinary mixture of all the influences is to be found. The countless theatres large and small in this corner of ancient Edo, miraculously preserved, or rather rebuilt, after each cataclysm, offer a choice of a variety of shows, ranging from a kind of Kabuki abounding in swordplay—often performed by worthy actors, or first-rate fencers if nothing else—to the most vulgar "strip-tease".

SCHEDULES—We should add, for the information of the tourist, that the best time to go to a show is the beginning of the afternoon, all the theatres being full by four o'clock.

And whilst on the subject of schedules, I should like to point out the best way to see the puppet theatre or a Noh play, two shows that a tourist worthy of the name should be sure not to miss.

Koto-player

As already mentioned, there is only one marionette theatre in existence: the Bunraku-za in Osaka. In principle the programme changes every month. Lasting ten to twelve hours, it begins either at 10.00 or 11.00 a.m., or—less frequently—at noon. But in July—and of recent years in December also—the whole company goes to Tokyo, where it stages a two-week run in the Shimbashi-embujo Theatre. During the course of the year, it also goes on tour in the provinces from time to time. It is therefore advisable to make inquiries at the Tourist Bureau before undertaking a trip to Osaka.

As for the Noh play, the best place to see this is Tokyo, where performances are relatively frequent. At present there are five Noh theatres in the capital: of the eighteen prewar playhouses, one alone was spared. Performances take place every Sunday, often on Saturday, and occasionally —as an exceptional measure—on holidays that fall during the week. Only two theatres are easily accessible to strangers, the other three being either remote from the centre or very hard to find. The most frequent representations are held in the Suidobashi Theatre, the larger of the two, a kind of glass palace with uncomfortable seats, icy-cold in winter and scorching-hot in summer. The programmes consist of two to four plays, and the time of the performance varies. In Suidobashi, the curtain usually rises at noon or one o'clock, whilst in Somei (the other theatre) the show begins earlier in the morning. The English-language newspapers rarely indicate Noh programmes. I am thus obliged once more to refer the unfortunate visitor to the Tourist Bureau where, with a little luck and a lot of patience, he will occasionally obtain a more or less accurate piece of information. As for the hotel-doormen, Noh usually lies beyond their scope, wide though this may be.

映画

THE CINEMA

THE award of the Grand Prix to a Japanese film at the 1951 Festival of Venice caused a considerable stir in the West, and an even greater stir in Japan. Why should Europe take an interest in a film which, for the Japanese, was a rather mediocre adaptation of one of Akutagawa Ryunosuke's short stories? This particular picture had passed almost unnoticed in Japan. The fact that it was selected in Venice simply revealed the judges' astonishment at discovering a hitherto unknown cinemaland.

An unknown territory maybe, but not a wasteland by any means. UNESCO statistics inform us that in 1952 Japan already held third place amongst the world's first producers, as runner-up to the United States and India. More than 750 reels, including 258 full-length films, were produced in Japanese studios strictly for domestic consumption. Indeed, apart from the two or three films sent each year to international film competitions, this entire output is intended for a single national market—extremely vast, to be sure, with 3,000 cinemas to feed.

Needless to say, Japan imports foreign films, and as usual Hollywood has the lion's share. But provincial spectators in particular are not very keen on these American stories which are too remote from their normal way of life. Outstanding British successes include *The Conquest of Everest*, *The Dam Busters*, and, above all, *A Queen is Crowned;* the last attracted long queues for many weeks. As for French and Italian productions, they enjoy snob value, having been publicized as strictly cultural. All the cinemas bill five-hour programmes, including two main films. The foreign film is thus invariably accompanied by a Japanese production.

"Rashomon

For all that, the Japanese are primarily interested in their own national productions. To satisfy the never-ending demand, the film companies concentrate on cheap and rapid turnover. The public incessantly clamours for novelty; they are no more exacting than Western cinema fans, but they pay relatively lower prices, and producers cannot rely on export. The answer is to shoot as many outdoor scenes as possible. Every day, in town and country alike, one comes across film units at work, using make-shift devices characteristic of Japanese ingenuity. Interiors, too, require a minimum of expense, the very principle of the Japanese house excluding any costly decoration. The result is quite astonishing. The production as a whole may be sketchy, but the photography is always perfect. The second-rate film invariably strikes you at one point by some unexpected artistic effect, often without any bearing on the subject in hand.

As in the theatre, motion pictures are usually divided into two types: "historic" films (*jidaimono*, or literally, "period" pieces), and "contemporary" films which are usually pallid imitations of American comedies, or sparkling, sentimental trifles. However a few producers occasionally venture to tackle social themes or topical problems, such as *Children of Hiroshima*. And in the near future we shall probably see more films depicting the everyday life of the Japanese, which is so fascinating to Western eyes. A meal, a stroll through a shopping quarter, an encounter in a picturesque suburb, may hold for us the charm of a travelogue. It was, in fact, realistic details of this nature that set the tone of certain passages in *Children of Hiroshima*, introducing a disconcertingly incongruous note in this modern tragedy.

The central theme of "period" films is provided by what is known as *Chambara*, or sword-fencing. The story, invariably set in the Tokugawa era, is neither subtle nor complex on the whole. It is, in fact, a mere pretext leading up to a battle—an extraordinary ballet in which the hero, run to bay and beset by countless enemies, always gains the whip hand after a general massacre. Generally it is centred round a sombre and often obtuse tale of vengeance. Gloomy though the tale may be, it raises many a laugh since, in contrast to cowboy films which it replaces, it is never taken seriously and invariably guyed often to the point of ludicrousness.

Cinemaland in Tokyo

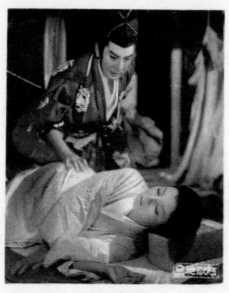

"*Gate of Hell*"

Under the heading of "period" films the Japanese also place a more classical type, and in fact most of the productions that carry off international awards each year fall into this category. After the unhoped-for success of *Rashomon*, the producers have sought to exploit this vein by tailoring their competition films. On the other hand, they have by no means relied on exoticism as an easy way out. To be convinced of this, one has only to read the list of prizewinners: *Genji-Monogatari*, grand prix for photography at Cannes, 1952; *Ugetsu-monogatari*, adapted from two tales by Ueda Akinari, first prize in Venice, 1953; then the grand prize in Cannes, 1954, *Gate of Hell*, enhanced by wonderful colour. Finally, there is the 1954 prizewinner in Venice, *The Seven Samurai*.

The success of these productions is to a great extent due to the acting —and above all to the delicate and sensitive interpretations of the lovely leading lady Kyo Machiko. Each producer has a style of his own, and as a result the cinematographic art is instilled with new life. The centring, the contrast of black, grey, and white, and the poetic settings and poses make each still a beautiful print. The cutting and mounting—not to mention the actors' interpretation—vary the pace of the anecdote which, whether unfolding at lightning speed or crawling along at a snail's pace, is at all times extremely curious to our eyes. *Gate of Hell* was a revelation in colour photography. It comes as a dual surprise to Westerners to see the ever-moving beauty of old Japan's dazzling costumes combined with the craftsmanship of young Japan's technicians, whose remarkable utilization of ultra-modern processes makes them worthy to rank with the kings of Hollywood.

地方

THE REGIONS

WHATEVER picture the Westerner conjures up of Japan, reality far surpasses his dreams; not that the country truly satisfies reason, for the very essence of her charm defies description. Foreigners are invariably stunned at first sight of her landscapes, but this initial shock is rapidly eased by her subtle grace. And in no time, all that remains is this impression of grace against a background of grandeur. In seeking to reveal the secret of her charm, for want of sufficiently diaphanous words, the writer is inevitably ill-equipped to compete with the painter. How could he dare to vie with the woodcuts of those Japanese magicians whose exquisite lines and skilful hues speak the only language the soul comprehends? A stay of any length of time in Japan confuses accepted ideas to such an extent that, after a few months in the archipelago, one is at a loss to decide whether the emotion created by the wonders of the natural surroundings springs from the fact that the painters themselves have achieved perfection in the play of shadows, pine trees, mountains, and sea, or whether this countryside, these skies, shores, towns, and villages seemingly strive to improve on the discoveries and simplifications of the artist . . . .

Two days by aeroplane separate London from Tokyo nowadays. This rapidity is disconcerting rather than vexing. An endless source of delight for the eye and mind alike, and better known throughout the world than any other Asiatic country, Japan should be "gained" by small stages. Three or four weeks by boat make her seem remote, without doubt. The recompense is all the more enjoyable, and the excitement all the more intense. How can I ever forget that December morning, several years before the last war, when at the end of a fifteen days' sail across the Pacific we were welcomed by the very emblem of the Nipponese Empire: the perfectly round, completely red disc of a sun about to pierce through the fog. In the roads of Yokohama, hundreds and thousands of jellyfish turned the sea to silk. Clad in black uniforms, with toylike swords dangling at their hips, police and Customs officials clambered aboard. Shortly after, the city revealed herself, ill-recovered as yet from one of her devastating earthquakes. But since she is dead, crushed by months and months of bombing that burst her towns asunder and sent them up in flames, we shall say nothing about the Japan of that period when, deceiving the Emperor and deluding themselves, the military leaders of Tokyo were preparing a conquest—and a defeat—unparalleled in history. Another Japan has emerged from the barely tepid cinders. At heart, she closely resembles the land of long ago, and of course, the general topography of the isles has remained unchanged . . . .

THE COUNTRYSIDE—One has only to look at the map. Between the 30th and the 45th parallels—the Japanese who have never renounced their territorial integrity say "between the 29th and 46th"—east of Manchuria and Korea, between the Pacific, the Sea of Okhotsk, the Sea of Japan, and the Yellow Sea, extends an archipelago 1,250 miles long, that has often been compared with an arch but in which we prefer to see the stylized silhouette of a Japanese lady, complete with kimono and obi. All these islands, so the legend runs, were born of drops of water that trickled straight from the lance the god Izanagi once plunged into the ocean. Leaving aside the Ryukyu Islands resembling stones in a ford between Kyushu and Formosa, and the twofold island network of Sakhalin and the Kurils (respectively restored or donated to the U.S.S.R.), this Japanese archipelago is basically composed of four large islands: Kyushu, Shikoku, Honshu, and Hokkaido. "Asia", in the words of Lavisse, "reflected and condensed as in a mirror."

At this stage, let us make amends . . . . The aeroplane, whose advantage we deplored only a while ago, suddenly reveals itself to be indispensable, It alone enables us to understand to the full the fabric of this countrys

HIROSHIGE—*The Tokaido at Hodogaya*

where the descendants of Mongols and Malays multiply at a somewhat alarming rate and attempt to snatch nourishment from 16 % of arable soil. With their mania for statistics, the Japanese specify that on 0.28 % of the world's territory, their population represents 3.6 % of the total inhabitants of the earth. It is only through flying by day and night over those four islands, from south to north and east to west, that one realizes the extent of overpopulation and the problems this presents for the Japanese; and only from the air does one really thrill to the beauty of the landscapes, rugged, frail, and majestic each in turn.

THE MOUNTAINS—On a territory less restricted than most Americans imagine—being inclined to regard Japan as a "miniature country" in comparison with the almost boundless spaces to which they are accustomed —on an area exceeding that of the United Kingdom by approximately 50,000 square miles, one looks down on a seething tangle of mountains, brilliant green or dazzling white according to season, in chalk, crystalline schist, or granite, now worn down by erosion, now abrupt and bristling, swamped by a network of narrow valleys and gorges. This geologist's paradise was born of flexures colliding and thwarting each other and by subsidences near certain coastlines producing ocean basins as much as 26,000 feet deep. The layman, like the Japanese, simply observes that "wherever one goes in Japan, there's always a mountain close at hand".

There are mountains everywhere, of various shapes and heights. Trees both strange and familiar cling to the slopes, scattered pines crest barren summits. Seen from above, Japan resembles a rippling sea. Here and there are plains (Tokyo, Nagoya, and Sendai), unfurling as if in repentance.

THE VOLCANOES—The rift valley running from Tokyo to the Tsugaru Channel north of Honshu seems to reveal a zone of lesser resistance on the earth's crust, where volcanoes surge up like a row of enormous boils. Another cluster punctuates the north plateau between the Sea of Japan and the Inland Sea, whilst a third prolongs the coast of Kyushu in a series of peninsulas. These volcanoes (representing 27 % of the total surface) form an integral part of Japan, and their eruptions are terrifying. When that of Sakura, in the Bay of Kagoshima, erupted in 1913, it could have buried a town such as Tokyo beneath a layer of cinders and lava 100 feet thick . . . .

On our way back from Korea many is the time we have flown over craters bubbling with the scarlet and yellow sulphur of melting lava. Some emerged from the waves; others loomed up on the hinterland like giant bumps. Then, as if the relief could no longer tolerate these cones of lava sprouting from peneplains almost level with the sea, the

HIROSHIGE—*Mountain Landscape*

174

mountains again came into their own, intersected by valleys of varying widths. From the torrents glittering in their depths, miniature canals branched off to irrigate the fields, pale green or dark, light brown or buff, covering the only-too-rare plots of land tilled, sown, and planted with all the care of a horticulturist. Rising perseveringly one above another, the rice plantations carved giant steps up the mountainside. But inevitably there came a time when they too were compelled to retreat.

THE COASTS—But mountains, volcanoes, valleys, and sparse acres are not the beginning and end of our bird's-eye glimpse of Japan. We have yet to see the pride of the countryside: the shores of these islands, with their 800 ports, claim to be one of the most jagged coastlines on this planet

especially those of the Inland Sea, commonly regarded as the epitome of Japan. There, with a precision almost too close to a reproduction to be believed, we find those subjects of prints and kakemonos which, over the past century, have revealed to Europe the supreme originality of Asia: "the land of silver beaches and emerald pines".

Half-emerging from water as calm as mercury, myriads of islands loom up, downy with groves and thickets, arching their backs, now dispersed, now grouped in herds like peaceful manatees or other aquatic monsters. Countless creeks shelter tiny havens surrounded by rows of houses as spick and span as bamboo toys. Hundreds and thousands of boats and fishing-smacks ride at anchor. Here and there the ark-like roof of a temple stands out. Though man-made, not created by the gods, the setting respects the ideal scale of proportions to the tiniest detail. Harmony reigns on all sides. Whilst it is no surprise to find ships and dwellings proportionate to their inhabitants, one is astonished to see that even the nearby islands in no way clash with the perspective, forming a natural continuation of the hills that run down into the gentle beaches, losing themselves in the sand and rocks in which gnarled pine trees dig their clutching roots.

The very profile of the trees is significant. In Japan serenity (a mere guise) masks the ardent passions of human-beings and the devastating powers of earth and sea. In this land of typhoons and cataclysms, the soil suddenly quivers, cracks, and gapes. Houses collapse, fires rage. The sea batters against the shore in a furious onslaught of seething waves recoiling like a bishop's crook. Once the outburst is over, the sky smiles down on the disaster. Fishermen in medieval breeches and canvas jerkins repair the damage beside peasants swathed in cloaks of straw, stooping over the rice fields, pick in hand.

THE TOWNS—Poverty, unhappily almost general, combined with the anger of wind, sea, and underground fire, explains the light, precarious structure of most Japanese dwellings. With the exception of a few castles, it was not until the 20th century and the advent of Frank Lloyd Wright —who introduced the art of construction on sliding foundations—that Japan ventured to produce buildings of any consequence.

With their ridge-line, so much shorter than that to which we are accustomed, and their projecting eaves, the roofs of those low houses —usually one storey high—look particularly strange from above. And if the thought of the countless lives seething in those overpopulated cities sets one's head awhirl, it is nothing compared with the vision of districts covering hundreds of acres where the dwellings are welded to one another on either side of streets that wind in spirals like a snail's shell, branch off in multitudinous forks and blind alleys, dig their teeth into an avenue and then desert it, until you wonder how on earth to find someone in this maze when you know only their address. The answer is simple: you won't find him—or at least if you do, it will be only by trial and error. Whilst in theory Japanese streets have names and the houses numbers, they take great care not to be consecutive. The police alone possess a plan of each district. They alone can efficiently direct a foreigner or even a Japanese searching for a friend, a business contact, or a craftsman as the case may be. There is a non-stop performance of men and women, clad in kimonos or European fashion, accosting each other with endless polite formalities to inquire as to the whereabouts of a certain street and, once they have miraculously discovered it, the probable location of Mr So-and-So's house, or the site of Such-and-Such an inn. There are, of course, open spaces here and there. Vast parks extend round lakes and ponds. Long and relatively wide arteries unfurl for miles beneath a serried network of tram cables (fully availing herself of her waterfalls, of all the countries in Asia Japan is by far the most highly electrified). Although this description applies mainly to Tokyo, it holds good for the majority of large towns. And even smaller cities and villages reveal similar labyrinths of streets and alleys whose primary purpose would seem to be that of preserving the inmates from all attempts at invading their privacy.

"I live in a delightful spot,"—a Japanese once said to us—"so hidden away that only people who have been there often will ever find me!"

TOKYO

"Short of a fire in Tokyo, there is no hope of rejuvenating the town," the Marquis Okuma Shigenobu long ago declared. The Japanese have certainly had their share of fires, but for all that the general appearance of Tokyo has hardly changed. Other causes than the desire to live as far out of reach as possible from the powers-that-be doubtless explain the extraordinary, inextricable disorder of Japanese cities and the anarchical development of the urban areas. Yet anyone who arrives in Haneda, the airport of Tokyo, and continues by car to the centre of the capital, would tend to believe throughout his half-hour drive that the town had been laid out according to a definite plan. In summertime the most propitious moment for this excursion is shortly after sunrise. At this hour the heat is still dry, and in the wide, straight, dusty avenues there are as yet few, if any, cyclists—a permanent menace in Japan. To the right and left are buildings of wood or brick, occasionally crested with a terrace, and ornamented with inscriptions in Chinese characters which are surprisingly decorative although they merely advertise laundries, grocers' stores, carpenters' workshops, electricians' or radio repairers' booths. Above many of the doorways hang lanterns of paper and bamboo, red, green, or orange in colour, shaped like gourds, melons, or pumpkins as the case may be. But despite the apparently strict observance of alignment, this façade is merely a decoy behind which thousands of houses (if such is the word) huddle together in a chaos that defies all description. Then, almost without transition, "real" buildings of stone suddenly loom up, six, seven, or eight storeys high, in blocks intersected by temples, sportsgrounds and parks (of which there are 215 in Tokyo, big and small alike). Unhappily what the architecture loses in quaintness is by no means gained in beauty. At a crossroads carefully guarded by a policeman—the absolute dictator of traffic—the sun gently dances on the roofs of the Imperial Palace. There beats the heart of this city, capital of the Empire since 1868 only.

Two or three hours later, once the morning shade has vanished, crowds clad in light colours stream across the pavements. At the same time, in a peculiarly Asiatic cacophony of hooters, bells, and horns, the streets begin to overflow with trams, cars, trucks, tricars, motorcycles, and bicycles. The disdain which they show for their neighbours as they speed by is the most striking—not to say the only—form of individualism that comes to the surface in Japan.

In a few paragraphs one can sketch only the salient features of this town of eight million inhabitants which, though restricted within its bay, has practically annexed Yokohama and is ruthlessly clambering over the hills dotted all round the city. The distances to be covered are exhausting (some 6,300 miles of arteries of all sorts). A journey from one point to another beginning in "the

Tokyo in the Morning Mist

centre of the city" turns out to be a real excursion, and many an ancient Tokyo taxi jibs at climbing up to the "residential" districts. For all that, it is true—as the propaganda leaflets from the Japanese tourist bureaux proclaim—that in Tokyo East and West live side by side. However, it is a Japanese form of the West, restricted to a few dozen tall air-conditioned blocks in American style such as the brand new Nikkatsu Building, and a certain number of avenues which, in contrast to the famous Ginza, are hardly more select than Oxford Street, and certainly not fit to rank with Regent Street. As elsewhere, the dilapidated state of the streets is perilous for the ankles (and one is tempted to believe that the honourable corporation of wooden and straw sandal-makers really did protest at the rebuilding of roads, as harmful to their trade!), but for the first few days at least, the tourist's attention is so firmly riveted on the long publicity streamers dancing in the sky above like captive balloons, that he rarely drops his eyes to complain about disjointed paving-stones or gaping holes in the

Ramparts of the Imperial Palace

pavement. And he is quite right. This town whose soil dissolves into mud at the first rainfall and scatters in dust after two or three days' drought —and which, to her merit, never claims to be an aesthetic masterpiece— possesses a charm that is not entirely due to the exotic fascination of her bazaars and motley crowds. The Imperial Palace—one of the wonders of that huge urban area—would alone justify the journey.

THE IMPERIAL PALACE—On leaving the maze of alleys leading to one or other of the 5,824 bridges on which Tokyo prides herself—streets so narrow that even the smallest car would not venture there—one stumbles upon a remarkable avenue. Without the slightest warning, the ramparts of the palace, which had almost slipped our minds since we arrived, suddenly tower above the willows beside a moat full of water. However did we fail to catch sight of it immediately? It is so thoroughly represent-ative of everything the newcomer to Japan expects! Planted opposite that broad walk which—for want of a better name, and to be sure of recognizing it—the Americans named "Avenue A", it haughtily looks down on the Marunouchi district of evil-smelling canals and baby skyscrapers housing the head offices of the large trusts, banks, and insurance companies now restored to their owners after sheltering the G.H.Q. of the Far East Supreme Command. But these are recent memories, and those of the past will lose no time in supplanting them.

Beyond those wide moats, the pine-crested ramparts are peopled with the colourful, bellicose shadows of soldiers in helmets of horn and wing-shaped breastplates who have been holding the fort with their lances, bows, or harquebuses ever since they were first garrisoned there in the 5th year of Keicho (A.D. 1600). The admiration aroused by the builders of the Pyramids may well be compared with that inspired by the mastery with which the specialists of the period heaped one upon another those millions of enormous blocks, all different from each other, yet superimposed to form a solid mass without a trace of cement. The upward curve of the walls is so pure and ethereal that when the onlooker at last succeeds in wresting his mind from contemplation of the corner arrises, he feels spiritually inclined to treat a simple straight line as barbarism. This peculiarly Asiatic curve of roofs, and sometimes even of walls, that look as if they were striving to reach the sky, recurs throughout Japan in temples

Entrance to the Imperial Palace

and other buildings as well, lifting them above their vulgar purpose. Certain experts claim that the style is reminiscent of the flaps of primitive tents when raised during the day. In their more prosaic way, modern architects assert that the ramparts are so shaped in order to resist earthquakes. This collection of posterns and ramparts encloses the most banal-looking buildings, but the exterior is extremely impressive. The Imperial castle of Chiyoda was destroyed by fire four years after the Emperor Meiji transferred his capital from Kyoto to Edo (present-day Tokyo), rebuilt on the original plan, damaged anew during the last war, and not yet repaired. With its white walls and grey-blue roofs dominating evergreen foliage, it bore little resemblance to the castle built in the 17th century by the first Shogun, Tokugawa Ieyasu, and still less to that of Ota Dokan, the 15th-century soldier whose passion turned him into a poet. "An avenue of pines", he wrote, "links my dwelling to the sea, and from my attic I glimpse Fujisan." The trees have now vanished, as far as the shore at least, but the view of Mount Fuji is unchanged. However, whether Japanese or foreign, only a privileged few are admitted inside the palace. The approaches and precincts,  sentry posts, tall gateways, and ramparts, faithful to the period, confer an air of tranquil pride on this imposing estate of nearly 100 acres; patches of greensward and pine growing out of the grey stone soften the contours here and there, whilst squadrons of ducks circling on the moats introduce

The Ginza

a pathetic note. And what of the bridges leading to the buildings reserved for the Emperor and his family? The most famous is the twin bridge known as Niju-bashi, in the depths of which recent excavations brought to light a dozen skeletons, mostly buried in a standing position. By voluntarily

TOKYO

1—Imperial Palace. 2—Niju-
bashi. 3—Palace of the Diet.
4—Asakusa Park. 5—Ueno
Park. 6—Zoological Gardens.
7—Nihon-bashi. 8—National
Museum. 9—Korakuen Gar-
dens. 10—British Embassy.
11—Yasukuni-Jinja. 12—Aka-
saka Palace. 13—Aoyama
Palace. 14—Aoyama Ceme-
tery. 15—Ginza. 16—Stadium.
17—The Port. 18—Meiji Sanctuary. 19—Arisugawa Park.
20—Shiba Park. 21—Temple
of Fukagawa Fudo. 22—
Kiyosumi Park. 23—Kabuki
Theatre. 24—Central Station.
25—Central Post Office. 26—
Hibiya Park. 27—Kameido
Temple. 28—University. 29—
Shinjuku Park. 30—Hamacho
Park. 31—American Embassy.

SUMIDA-KU

CHUO-KU

R. SUMIDA

KOTO-KU

JACQUES LIOZU

sacrificing themselves in this way, the Japanese of long ago hoped to win the gods' favour for the new building.

But we must know where to draw the line. Otherwise we should never stop raving over this palace from which modern Japan sprang forth less than a century ago, complete with her industry, her army, her suicide-airmen, and her navy, and from which in 1945, after stigmatizing the treachery of his councillors in 1940, the Emperor pledged his country to a new way of life. Moreover, the Chiyoda Palace is not the whole of Tokyo: far from it. Nonetheless, before changing the subject we should

first like to relate an anecdote that we heard from one of the academicians of the old school who had remained faithful to the national costume. Needless to say, his version was duly punctuated by the countless nods and sighs that add weight to a speech. To cut a long story short, we were coming down from Hanzomon on foot, hugging one of the most inaccessible sides of the ramparts when, carried away by enthusiasm, our learned companion stopped short, indicated with a nod of the head a patch of grass between two pine trees, and droned: "This is where—when he was French Ambassador—the great writer—Monsieur Paul Claudel—of the Académie Française—had a rendezvous with inspiration.... Thus was conceived his *Coup d'Œil sur l'âme japonaise*." This detail probably has but the remotest connexion with reality. But at least it proves the esteem in which the Japanese book-reading public—which is legion—holds French literature: an esteem which French writers have repaid to Japan, with interest. This is just another instance in which, for some inexplicable reason, the extraordinary graciousness of these Asiatics (in peacetime), their charming concern for detail, and their ant-like life, awakens the gentlest of feelings in a white brother.

Let us wander at nightfall in the districts round Ginza. What people other than this would have dreamt of lighting otherwise characterless streets with that multitude of globes and little bells, grouped in bunches and illuminated inside, in imitation of lilies-of-the-valley? Beneath their light, these pleasure haunts with their bazaars displaying silks, tortoise-shell, dolls (real works of art, and at ransom prices!), lacquers, and ivories, become as fascinating as those mysterious blind alleys from which emerges—complete with kimono and shaven head—the double of Sessue Hayakawa, eternally branded by the film *Forfeiture*. But it were wiser to drag oneself away from

HIROSHIGE—*White Rain on the Nihon-bashi at Edo*

the temptations of Tokyo by night. Even though he resists the painted charms of the bawds and wantons in ravishing kimonos, rapid ruin threatens the tourist "who already envisages how, in his house or flat back home, he will employ . . . ." the fascinating obis, rich in colour and texture. It is high time to return to Ginza, fleeing the neon lights of the cinemas, the big dailies, and the bars, hastening past the shop (closed at this hour, needless to say) of the late pearl king Mikimoto Kokichi (we shall return to him later apropos of his diving girls), and, as tramcars, taxis, and motor-cars dwindle in number, slowly make our way towards one of the most highly reputed spots in Tokyo: the Nihon-bashi Bridge.

NIHON-BASHI—What is it that makes this particular bridge so renowned? The answer is: History. In Japan, history has so strong a hold that a handful of coarse earth fetched a considerable sum simply because it had belonged to an empress. Nothing is of real value there unless it has an authentic pedigree. In this respect the Nihon-bashi Bridge has everything that could be desired, meticulous engravings of it—or its remotest ancestor—having been preserved since 1603.

Whether its name is derived from that of Japan *(Nihon)*, or whether its four syllables signify that from this bridge better than anywhere else one may "see the sun rising on the eastern sea" is still a subject of controversy for the erudite. Having been demolished, rebuilt, and subsequently overthrown by the 1923 earthquake, the present bridge is the thirteenth of the name. Nowadays unromantic department stores loom up between its parapets and the round hills that used to limit its horizon, but for all that the Nihon-bashi does not appear to have lost any of its renown.

Its first claim to fame is the fact that the great Shogun Tokugawa selected the middle of this particular bridge as the point from which all distances, not only in Tokyo but throughout the Empire, should be measured (calculated in *ri* of 36 *cho*—about 365 feet each).

In the realm of anecdotes, it was popularized by one of the most curious upstarts Japan has ever known—Kinokuniya Bunzaemon. Having distinguished himself by poisoning a shark that harassed the fishermen in his native village, this local hero subsequently earned such an immense sum of money that, whilst still in his youth, he was able to build a sumptuous dwelling beside the Nihon-bashi Bridge and throw gold coins from his windows to the mob below. Morality was saved by the fact that after a

Tokyo by Night

life of dissipation, he died poor and unknown. Shall we confess the third reason that endears this bridge to us? It overlooks a small bar called "Villon", in memory of the famous French poet. Inside, verses from the *Ballade à la Grosse Margot* decorate the mirrors. One would be hard put to estimate the worth of its teaching as far as the *habitués* are concerned since, although they are never loth to drink a thimbleful of cognac to France, few of them have any inkling of the language . . . .

A conscientious description should undoubtedly include directions as to which streets lead to the goals one sets oneself in Tokyo. But details of this nature are no use at all. And at this point, a word of advice: wherever you want to go, never be content with an address even transcribed in kata-kana, but have a plan drawn—an accurate plan with careful indications of landmarks—and make sure the driver takes it in. Even this will not prevent him from straying a little, unless of course he simply has to drive the uninitiated to spots so well known that he cannot pretend to be unfamiliar with them. These include:

EMPEROR MEIJI's SHRINE—Since sentiment plays a primordial role for the Japanese, they are inordinately proud of this cenotaph. For all that, foreigners should be sure to visit the site even if they are more attached to ancient Japan and her remains than to the Emperor who fostered her integration in the modern world. To tell the truth, all that has survived the allied air raids is the shade of a kind of basilica preceded by three gigantic porticos and surrounded by literally hundreds and thousands of trees, offered by all the local governors throughout the archipelago. Devastated though it may be, this spot is still a place of national pilgrimage. It is best seen at the iris season, when the truly patriotic Japanese have the immense honour of meditating in the presence of the spirits of their illustrious leader and his imperial spouse (whose bodies are buried in Kyoto). This homage to a great reformer may fittingly be concluded by a visit to the museum in the gardens, containing paintings of the glorious hours of a brilliant reign.

Having accomplished this pious duty, on the way back we shall merely cast a passing glance at the Palace of the Diet, or Parliament, a recent building dating only from 1936, unscathed by the war. This massive, Germanic-looking edifice seems to typify the period when a number of Japanese envisaged an alliance with the Axis.

But anyone who, on returning to Tokyo, had no desire to see any more of the town than her daily sights and the squat outline of the Imperial Hotel, seemingly sculptured in lava, would later regret not having visited some of her numerous temples nestling on all sides. By some curious deformation, despite their deep-rooted tradition which links them constantly with the past, in talking to foreigners the Japanese feign to attach little importance to the monuments of their great history, whilst they rave over statues of admirals and generals in the purest 1900 style, or buildings on the lines of the Diet. Thus, though we may hear its praises sung, we shall overlook the temple known as Nishi Honganji which was so frequently destroyed by fire in the course of the centuries that the last architects rebuilt it in stone, in imitation of a Hindu model.

On the other hand, if an unexpected detour leads the traveller to Anjin-Cho (Pilot Street), he may stop in front of a chapel built to the memory of William Adams, the Englishman whose ship—*Charity*—ran aground in Japan in 1600. Although at first imprisoned, he later became adviser to the first Shogun Tokugawa, to whom he taught ballistics, geography, and mathematics. He married a Japa-nese and died in Tokyo in 1620, at the age of forty-five.

The pleasantest way for the stroller is to lose himself—an easy matter in Tokyo—and leave his taxi or car as the spirit moves him, to admire the torii (which, according to a rather fanciful interpretation, are large-scale

Yasukuni-Jinja Ceremony

191

reproductions of perches of sacred chickens) in front of each temple. But there is one spot where one should be sure to meditate: in the shade of the Shinto pantheon, or Yasukuni Memorial, adorned by a black and gilt porch, on Kudan Hill not far from the War Ministry.

YASUKUNI-JINJA—Majesty and simplicity are allied in this monument dedicated by Emperor Meiji himself, in 1869, to the souls of the soldiers killed during the battles for his Reformation, and subsequently to the victims of the Russo-Japanese War. The conflict with China and the Second World War added to the number of ceremonies held in this temple, and the present Emperor has paid many a visit there in his capacity as supreme pontiff of Shintoism. Nothing could be more moving than the very sobriety of the tablets, also black and gold, on which are inscribed the names of all the soldiers who, in dying for their homeland with the Emperor's name on their lips, thereby became gods.

Yet, in spite of lofty spots such as this, or the tomb of the Forty-seven Ronin—the knights errant who committed harakiri after avenging their master in 1703—despite the profusion of parks and the charm of the changing seasons of plum trees, peach blossom, cherries, irises, peonies, or chrysanthemums, and although, in addition to fine museums and famous theatres, Tokyo offers other intellectual resources, and other sources of entertainment of all kinds, we must admit it is without great regret that we leave this administrative capital, port, industrial and business town, to travel southwards.

The Port of Yokohama

ON THE WAY TO KYOTO

THE TOKAIDO—If we followed our fancy, we should have no hesitation in selecting our route—the Tokaido (the East Sea Road)—that ancient flagstoned track linking Tokyo to Kyoto, and one of the eight Imperial roads that crossed the archipelago in times gone by. The pines along the wayside, grouped in verdant arbours here and there, have witnessed most of the mighty feats of the feudal age. The 350 miles separating Tokyo from Kyoto used to comprise fifty-three stages in the form of inns and post-houses immortalized by Hiroshige's brush. But, whereas the train now covers the distance in seven hours, it is reckoned that the pedestrian of the past used to take two weeks. As for the great lords or Daimyo who were obliged to sojourn in Edo each year at the Shogun's command, they travelled even more slowly, at the rate of ten miles per day on the average. What a storehouse of folklore was built by this incessant migration along a road that has hugged the Bays of Tokyo, Suruga, and Atsuta since the 8th century! What a wealth of themes, tragic and comic, Japanese literature has derived as a result! Even today after the devastation of war, within this land of artists and artisans in Kyoto one may still unearth dioramas of sculptured and painted bamboo, depicting a Daimyo on horseback with his escort of Samurai, soldiers, bearers of demi-johns of *sake* or boxes of rice, gaily advancing in step between the pines and cryptomerias of the Tokaido. When one thinks that the last voyage in the ancient manner was that of Meiji in 1869, behind the gauze curtains of a lacquered palanquin borne by four men of the same stature stepping out in rhythm on their journey from Kyoto, where the emperors had resided for the past eleven centuries, one has a clearer idea of the close confinement in which this country lived until the 19th century, since when it has been progressing at double quick time.

But the historic scruples that deterred us from adopting this itinerary a little while ago fail to stand up to closer examination. What does it matter, after all, if a number of towns now popularized by tourism were not included in Hiroshige's fifty-three paintings? Whether by car or train, the detours involved are so insignificant that a few digressions on the eastern beaches can only enhance our pleasure. From there, after hailing Fujisan and before visiting Kyoto and Nara, we shall turn towards Nagoya, Osaka, and Kobe, reaching the Inland Sea by way of the two large islands of Shikoku and Kyushu. Returning to Nikko by way of the west and then heading northwards, we shall end our excursion in Hokkaido.

YOKOHAMA—Though they may submit the springs of one's car to severe trials, there is no shortage of roads in Japan, where wide, clear stretches alternate with twists and turns between the pine trees and bamboos. The road we are now taking, flanked by houses, extends untrammelled as far as Yokohama, a simple fishing village at the time the Empire of the Rising Sun opened its gates to commerce with the West in 1859, and now an immense trading port. However, the million inhabitants of Yokohama, her 500-year-old pagoda in the Sankeien Gardens, her cherry trees and lotus, have no more hold on the tourist in search of the picturesque than has the cemetery beside the sea, where the foreigners who contributed to the development of the city sleep their last sleep.

Not being botanists ourselves, we shall reserve for another occasion the nursery garden where peerless lilies grow beside artificially dwarfed trees.

The nautically minded will be unable to resist the desire to visit the naval base and dockyards of Yokosuka (built in the 19th century by a French engineer Émile Bertin) on the southern tip of the peninsula. Those who are keen on sidelights in history will pore over the stele erected in Kurihama to commemorate the appearance of Commodore Perry's four ships—*Kuro-fune*—on the 8th July, 1853. For our part, we are in a hurry to go down into the Bay of Sagami, to enjoy the ideal climate and the beach of fine sand at Kamakura.

Hiroshige—*The Tokaido at the Utsunomiya Pass in Okaba*

KAMAKURA—History in the real sense of the word—at least, the type of history in which we are interested—summons us there. In Kamakura in 1185, the first of all the Shoguns, Minamoto no Yoritomo—who had hitherto held the sinecure of "generalissimo victor of the Barbarians"— seized the reins of government from the Emperor. There followed a period of strict discipline and religious austerity. It was also a period of great aspirations, as evidenced by that enormous yet harmonious bronze Buddha 50 feet high—the Daibutsu—cast in 1252. Deep in a dream, with his eyelids half lowered over eyes of pure gold, he now sits in the open air amidst a collection of temples, monasteries, and museums full of objects from the period which itself goes by the name of "Kamakura". There an immense court once lived in the lap of luxury. Time, fires, and typhoons have vanquished the buildings, monuments, and men. All that remains is the Buddha....

ENOSHIMA—That is why the Japanese, who never tire of prostrating themselves in front of

The Daibutsu of Kamakura

Enoshima Bridge

him in groups, or paying homage to the imposing gilt Kwannon, the Goddess of Mercy in the nearby Hase temple, or to Hachiman, the God of War in his shrine to the north of the town, rarely leave Kamakura without first making another pilgrimage-cum-excursion to Enoshima, facing the coast nearby.

Enoshima .... the name rings a bell for many an expert in French literature. He turns it over in his mind, delves into his memory, ar d then the penny suddenly drops and he recollects "Enoshima .... *l'Honorable Partie de Campagne!*" To be sure, this is where Thomas Raucat set the adventures of his heart-stirring heroines. An exceedingly long concrete bridge now joins the island to the coast. But low tide reveals the debris of a footbridge nearby. Could it be the very one that collapsed beneath the weight of an overladen car? The new bridge, at any rate, is open only to foot traffic, on payment of a toll. And from dawn until dusk the island resounds with the ceaseless clatter of wooden sandals as pilgrims wander from a torii of bronze to another of scarlet wood, climb innumerable steps to the temples, restaurants, and hotels nestling in the foliage, the zoological gardens, and the refreshment parlours where loudspeakers broadcast Wagner to a thirsty crowd. Thence, after recuperating their strength (and breath), they descend towards the sea and plunge into a jumble of caves in the depths of which piety enjoins them to offer the smoke from a handful of sticks of incense to the spirits of legendary serpents and dragons. Enoshima is a curious mixture of Lourdes and Luna Park that tourists should be sure to visit.

Another experience they should not miss is a stay in a strictly Japanese hotel in one of the nearby resorts dotted along the coastline, such as Atami, the "Japanese Riviera", or Numazu, the "Naples of the Orient", with its unforgettable panorama of Fujisan looming up in all its proud splendour behind the successive screens of mountains.

THE HAKONE DISTRICT—In the heyday of the Tokaido, at the exit from a pass hollowed out of the basalt rock (between Hakone-Machi and Moto-Hakone, two prosperous towns of the period), there was once a barrier flanked by a control post. Whether heading north or south, after an exhausting march across the mountains travellers were compelled to halt there and show their credentials. The check-up was severe, the Shogun's agents being as anxious to prevent the flight of certain hostages to Kyoto as the entry of spies into the capital of the Tokugawa. A woman who attempted to force the barrier was hanged on the spot. In our times, now that tourism is the order of the day, several roads and railways give access to the district of Hakone (extending far beyond the small town of this name), a region close to the sea and yet in the heart of the mountains.

The spas such as Gora, Sengokuhara, and, above all, Miyanoshita, the main resort, owe their origin to hot sulphur springs. Being subject to rheumatism, the Japanese make prolonged stays there to take the waters, and the hotels are full all the year round. In summertime when the coastal region is stifling, the air in the Hakone district is particularly agreeable, and the scenery even more enchanting: at first sight the vista is ever the same, and yet it is ever changing. From forest-clad mountainsides (pine

trees are scarcer here: they were said to have been torn up after a princess had pricked her foot on a pine needle), pathways lead down beneath a succession of torii towards a lake in which Fujisan is reflected on clear days. With its sense of gradation, which is perhaps the secret of the Japanese landscapes, the Hakone region and its natural wonders merely form a transition between the beaches, the coasts, and the mountain of mountains, which the people in their fervent admiration were not afraid to deify.

FUJISAN—What a magnificent country is Japan, where a simple detail in

Fujisan, from Lake Hakone

the landscape imposes itself on the mind to the point where it relegates all the other beauty spots to the background, and finally becomes confused with the country as a whole, by engulfing it completely! Fuji is Japan, and Japan Fuji. One may retain the sweetest and most vibrant recollections of a journey through the archipelago. But the memory of Fujisan dominates —nay overwhelms—them all: not on account of its altitude of 12,395 feet, but because of the reactions its majesty provokes. Is it conceivable that a geographic feature could influence, model, and create a national psychology? In Japan Mount Fuji has played—and is still playing—such a role. Its name is one of the first that a Japanese baby hears, and utters; its outline is one of the first that children learn to trace in three strokes of the brush. In the mental pictures they form of life and the world, "Fuji" is early associated

with the concepts of purity, greatness, might, eternity, and nobility. And this education is subsequently completed by a thousand and one legends, innumerable poems in verse and prose, myriads of paintings, engravings, or photos inspired by this volcano which, so tradition runs, brutally rent the soil one night in June 286 B.C., at the same time that Lake Biwa scooped out its basin nearly 200 miles away. At dawn the next day it revealed to the horror-stricken peasants of the neighbourhood an almost perfect cone, notched at the summit by two blows of an axe, whilst the base—at present over sixty miles in circumference—extended over the provinces of Kai, Suruga, and Sagami. Hence the qualification "the largest mountain in three lands". (For the Japanese this is a standing joke, since to their minds it implies Japan, China, and India . . . .)

For 2,000 years its dread voice continued to thunder until that memorable day in December 1707 when, after a last terrible eruption that left its mark on history, it agreed to subside. Since then, with its flanks slightly marred by a rise to the west, and the gigantic *névé* cresting its peak, it looks as though it were compelled to personify "that which never changes".

Once again, this is a mere guise, as Hiroshige—whom we cannot avoid mentioning once more—and Hokusai clearly demonstrated in their albums. In reality, no mountain could be more varied in aspect, or more capricious in mood. Without the slightest warning, turn and turn about it cloaks itself in the clouds or dances in the sun. And if one ventures to climb to the summit, when the air is sufficiently damp it is reflected upside down in the atmosphere. But if, in the words of the proverb, it is as foolish never to have attempted to climb Mount Fuji (a feat that anyone can accomplish) as to attempt to conquer it twice in a lifetime, it is nonetheless advisable to keep to the beaten track and never venture without a guide beyond the paths which swarm throughout July and August each year with tens of thousands of pilgrims who journey to Fuji in the same spirit as Moslems visit Mecca, jingling bells and chanting: "May our feelings be pure and the weather fine on the honourable mountain."

Since the day several hundred years ago when the bonze En-no-Gyoja first ventured on its slopes, certain forest-clad areas, said to be haunted by bears and other wild beasts, have remained unexplored, and numerous mountaineers who had too much faith in their instinct have vanished for ever. But, whilst the privilege of seeing the sun rise from the summit of Mount Fuji confers great merits on those who have braved the cold of a night in a stone refuge, this should be completed by the incomparable experience of wandering round the mountain from village to village, from dawn to dusk, from the instant when the *névé* glows pink, blanches, sparkles, and reflects all the hues of the rainbow until the moment when the entire mountain stands out against a crimson sunset . . . .

Westerners are apt to speak of the "obsessing presence of Mount Fuji", and this is no idle description, for the obsession really does exist. In fact, it manifests itself to such an extent that even beyond the twenty-two Japanese administrative districts from which the volcano may be seen, it is impossible to drive it out of one's memory. And, as if destined to renew the charm that emanates from the sacred volcano and makes its solitude more moving still, a series of five lakes is dotted around the mountainside dominating the plains that border its base. Situated many thousand feet above sea level, these lakes vary in colour from pale green to jade, according to depth. Could they have formed a single lake in ancient times, as legend would have it? Geology would seem to support the hypothesis, and three of them at least (Seiko, Shoji, and Motosu) evidently communicate beneath the earth, since any diminution or increase in the volume of water in one invariably incurs a similar modification in the level of the other two. Fishermen in canvas smocks, protected from the sun by mushrooms of straw that serve as hats, crowd together in the villages on the shores of the lakes, protected at the rear by virgin forests. In the valley below flows a river, the Fuji-Kawa, intersected by rapids that the mariners descend on long, flat boats steered with poles, ever at the mercy of a shipwreck. On nearing the sea, the river slows its pace, and Fujisan reappears on the horizon.

NAGOYA—Remarkable as the Hakone district may be, centred round

Mount Fuji and prolonged by the pleasant Izu peninsula, the real touristic hub of Central Japan lies further south in Nagoya, five hours from Tokyo by express train. Well may we wonder whether this port and great industrial town, the third in the archipelago, with her 1,200,000 inhabitants, is simply—as in the eyes of Europe and America—the city of *cloisonnés*, lacquers and ceramics, chemical products and textiles, large-scale construction of locomotives,

Ricefield at the Foot of Fujisan

railway carriages, bicycles, and the manufacture of plastic goods.

When questioned on the subject, many a Japanese relapses into silence, their jealousy of this important administrative centre being matched only by their prejudice against it. The prejudice is inspired not by the smoothness of the local way of speaking—which, by common consent, is acknowledged to be the sweetest language of love—but by the high esteem in which the people of Nagoya hold their town and themselves alike.

And one must admit that, compared with the rest of the country where the struggle for life is evidenced at every turn, Nagoya would seem to be abnormally favoured by the gods. Situated as she is like a turntable, the city has no communication problems to face, whether by land or sea. Her soil, which lends itself to farming as much as to pottery, provides an abundance of vegetables. Besides this, being the hub of intercommunications both at home and abroad, the town is a great pleasure haunt, a fact that visiting businessmen never fail to appreciate.

Fishing with Cormorants in Gifu

How could a city such as this fail to regard herself as a capital? "Like all women who meet with success all too readily," say the envious, "Nagoya has a past." And indeed, the sole past to which she admits is a source of pride for the town, since it was in Nagoya that the feudal system finally took root. To be convinced of the force of this regime which held the Mikados aloof up to the time of the Meiji reformation in the 19th century, until quite recently one had only to raise one's eyes towards the castle, one of the most beautiful castles built in the early 17th century by a half-score of Daimyo at the command of the Shogun Tokugawa Ieyasu. Kato Kiyomasa, a mighty lord who distinguished himself during the Japanese invasion of Korea in 1597, made himself personally responsible for the construction of the keep—a keep in Nipponese style comprising five storeys, each slightly smaller than the one below and crested with a roof curving back at the rim. Not a single stone of this citadel touched the ground in its journey from the quarry to the unloading point (thus, according to tradition, are stormproof castles built). Two dolphins in pure gold, 6 feet high, crowned the upper roof as talismans against fire. But alas, the magic of dolphins—even of gold—is powerless against thousand-pounder bombs, as has been demonstrated. All that now remains of this former splendour is a rather melancholy collection in the Tokugawa Museum, comprising ancient paintings and furniture that used to decorate the interior of the fortress.

At least the ravages of war spared the cherry trees which, in springtime, cast a snowy mantle of petals over the several parks, each of which seems prettier than its neighbour. Despite their great age, none of these parks can lay claim to glory as can the Temple of Atsuta, just beyond the boundaries of Nagoya, where the famous double-edged sword—one of the symbols of Imperial power—is preserved.

But let us not permit this weapon (jealously protected from prying eyes) to detract us from that typically Japanese pastime of fishing with cormorants—which takes place by torchlight every moonlight night at Gifu on the River Nagara—or a sail down the Kiso, the Japanese "Rhine". May it, on the other hand, incite us reverently to undertake another pilgrimage to the great national park of Ise-Shima at Uji-Yamada, in the prefecture of Mie on the other side of the Bay of Atsuta.

Ise—There rise two temples, the oldest in Japan. In these severe wooden buildings—reconstructed every twenty years—almost every celebrity in the country has come to pray at one time or another, on the eve of some major decision or prior to undertaking a long journey. By the same token, in the 13th century a people threatened by a Sino-Mongol armada thronged before this shrine, imploring the goddess Amaterasu ("who had already blessed the Nipponese race with sagacity, the spirit of justice, and courage") to prevent the barbarians from invading the archipelago. The goddess' reply was a typhoon (kami-kaze—literally "divine wind") that destroyed the enemy fleet. Just as she manifested herself that fateful day, so would she still seem to respond to all who come to consult her in this temple. Hidden away amongst the cryptomerias, it has no need of the

Girl Pearl-Diver

two bridges and three walls built to defend it. Primitive though it may be, the wooden shack is a goddess's home in every way. So many prayers have been offered there that the very planks and beams—which, though they betray the influence of Chinese architecture of the Six dynasties, look crude in the extreme—are for all that permeated with disturbing fluids. The music and dances, especially the colourful dance of the butterflies whereby the faithful hoped—and still hope—to win the goddess's favour, are believed to date back 1,200 years, having been imported from China by way of Korea.

It is wiser not to watch the dancers' evolutions too long, nor to accustom one's ears to rhythms and tones Europe cannot yet comprehend. In this atmosphere, steeped in captious waves, a Christian would be tempted to lose his faith. And what advice could one give him then, other than to find escape in this formula: should the Westerner see no more of Japan's curiosities than Mount Fuji and the Ise Shrine, surely they alone would suffice? For indeed, both of them appeal to something deeper than sensibility

Fishermen in the Bay of Ise

206

The Keep of Osaka Fortress

alone. By heeding their message, we may learn more about a civilization and a people than a dozen books could teach us.

But, as if to help break the spell, by good fortune the prefecture of Mie offers a light diversion in the Bays of Goshako, Ago, Hasama, Hikimoto, and Kata, where we find the pearl oyster beds of the late Mr Mikimoto who died in 1954 at the ripe old age of nearly one hundred years. Complete with kimono, hooded cloak, wooden clogs, and bowler hat, his picturesque figure was part and parcel of the quaintness of Japan. For twenty years the whole world followed the accounts of his struggles, his disappointments, and his triumph when he at last succeeded in producing perfectly round orient pearls by introducing a foreign body into the shell of a live oyster. To tell the truth, his pearls and even the memory of the oyster king himself are overshadowed by his diving girls—a band of sturdy, laughing women with beautiful naked breasts—highly skilled in their craft and proof against the hardest trials. It is only natural one should wish to linger in their company. But why, despite their dazzling teeth and athletic bodies, do they seem to live solely for the sea and for pearl oysters?—"What," they exclaim whenever anyone attempts to switch to another subject, "You don't know Kyoto? Then what are you doing here? Kyoto's the place you should be visiting"—concluding, with artful charm: "As for pearls, you can find them anywhere in Japan . . . ."

OSAKA—Underpaid though they may be (but then, who isn't, in Japan?), these nymphs know what they are talking about. At this stage, the voice of logic, combined with the railway and the road, demands that we travel up to Kyoto. For all that, after a last thrust towards the south of the prefecture where the cliffs hurl themselves into an ever-angry sea (Kyoto being even more difficult to reach than Japan herself), we cut diagonally across the isthmus stretching between the gulfs of Atsuta and Osaka, to reach the first of the two large ports—Osaka and Kobe—guarding the entrance to the Inland Sea.

In their constant desire to indoctrinate their visitors thoroughly whenever tourism—hence profit—is at stake, the Japanese frequently compare Osaka with an Asiatic Chicago. But those of their compatriots who are more familiar with things American correct them by commenting: "The din and the smoke are there, to be sure, but the environs are delightful." Be that as it may, it is impossible to deny the smoke! At whatever time of year we have flown over the city, Osaka has always been concealed beneath a thick black cloud, and the cause became obvious once we had wandered through the streets or along her fifteen miles of canals, tottering through an absolutely incredible jungle of factory chimneys.

Once you have lived in Osaka, so they say, it is impossible to leave. But believe us, it takes courage to decide to live there. It is not that we are frightened by her more than two million inhabitants crowded in bewildering promiscuity—Japan, like the rest of the Far East, accustoms one to crowds—but once your heart and mind have been purified by the shrines of Ise, the enthusiasm with which the people of Osaka boast about their underground railway or their water chlorination plant leaves you cold. To confess this in Osaka would raise roars of laughter. The town lives for money (moreover, she manufactures it, the Empire's coinage being minted there). And this is all she lives for. On the other hand, if you applied to

The Pleasure District in Osaka

her the ironic definition of Boston—"A state of mind rather than a town"—you would meet with roars of applause from the audience. Her industrialists—cotton-weavers, steel-smelters, and manufacturers of machines or chemical products—keep their eyes glued to the graph of exports (57 % of the Japanese total), and for the most part base all their judgements on a simple but effective scale: the bank balance.

What of all the qualities that count so much elsewhere in Japan: politeness, diplomacy, breeding, and good manners? Osaka snaps her fingers at such trifles. She does not completely despise them, however. At a pinch, she regards them as possible assets, albeit far lower in the scale of values than the sole asset that carries any real weight—money. Moreover, the aim of these Japanese Babbits is to "Osakanize" Japan. In fact, this ideal forms an almost compulsory paragraph in the speeches that loudly punctuate those costly geisha dinners where the members of the local Chamber of Commerce spend their time scratching each other's backs. Tokyo is only too well aware of the situation! A number of her cafés, restaurants, etc. have already been conquered by natives of the tiny prefecture of Osaka, the smallest in size and yet the most highly populated in the archipelago. In calling her uniquely and resolutely materialistic, there is no intention of calumniating this "Japanese metropolis of commerce and industry". "And don't forget," add the local celebrities, "we possess the loveliest geisha quarters! and the finest theatres! and cinemas! and restaurants! and pleasure haunts unparalleled elsewhere!"

The Port of Kobe

Osaka Castle, from which the Tokugawa emigrated to Edo, was more fortunate than that of Nagoya, having been rebuilt (1911) in reinforced concrete. Thus it can still evoke the great deeds of an age when a well-born man, considering that money sullied anyone who touched it, entrusted his purse to a servant and never knew—nor wanted to know—how much it contained. And how could one forget Shotoku-Taishi, nicknamed the Nipponese Constantine, who appointed Buddhism as the national religion between 572 and 612? And the kind-hearted 16th emperor Nintoku-Tenno (313–99), who was so moved by the poverty of his people that he decreed a three year "fiscal holiday", and authorized his tax-collectors to resume their duties only when from the top of his palace he could see smoke rising from every hearth in Osaka. "Now I am rich!" he exclaimed (adding: "the subjects' wealth being that of the sovereign").

Being slaves to convention, and moreover having all they need on their doorsteps, the well-to-do inhabitants of Osaka sacrifice themselves to the mystic call of weekends. The business Titans rush towards the watering-towns of Wakano-ura or Takarazuka (where amusements of all kinds are available), the Ibaraki golf-links, or the baseball pitches in Koshien. Less-favoured citizens who are not against feasts for the spirit, take the train to the little feudal city of Wakayama or, better still, mingle with the millions of pilgrims who go each year to cleanse themselves of their sins in the great monastery on Koyasan, dating back to the year 816.

KOYASAN—This mountain dominates the region round Yamato where the Japanese conception of nationality slowly developed. An emperor one day donated it to a monk, Kobo-Daishi, who founded one of the first monasteries on its slopes, and was subsequently sanctified. There, in the Middle Ages, grew up one of the most colossal holy cities that ever saw the light, inhabited by 90,000 monks. Of the buildings that once housed this population, some thirty temples only have survived more or less intact, scattered amongst smooth-trunked trees beneath a veiled, grey-green light, at the whim of a hilly plateau by no means easy of access.

Koyasan is the gigantic necropolis of Japan. There is perhaps no cemetery more impressive than this immense burial ground, where the moon shines down on rows of tombs beside an avenue three miles long, bordered by ancient cedar trees.

KOBE—Wherever one goes, one is struck by the duality of Japan: "the way of the gods—the coarseness of materialism". Throughout the country the ignominy of daily life is invariably lessened by some ancient temple or hallowed spot. Kobe (871,000 inhabitants), a short distance from Osaka, escapes the rule. Her excuse is that she is of recent date—1868—when she was born of the mixed reception extended to foreign ships.

The cleanliness and hygiene of Kobe might be held up as an example. The town rambles from top to bottom of the hills, in a series of residential districts and busy streets culminating in the major port of Japan. In her stride she has absorbed villages that were themselves in the throes of extension, and even a stream, the Minatogawa, on which fierce battles were waged in the days of the dynastic struggles. Nowadays Minatogawa is a street like any other, an evening pleasure haunt flanked by restaurants, taverns, and dens where for a few yen fortune-tellers predict the future, in the midst of a mob whose sole aim seems to be idle strolling.

Hotel in Kyoto

KYOTO

REMEMBRANCE OF THINGS PAST—But why, in the name of what preconceived notion, should we waste precious days amongst the hideous sights of these modern cities, when, less than an hour from Osaka and Kobe, the calm and beauty of Kyoto is waiting to be admired? And why were we so aberrant, a moment ago, as to restrict possible excursions to Fuji and Ise? Kyoto seduces you the moment you draw near her tilled fields, where the tiniest weed would smack of sacrilege, and where the very air grows lighter and sweeter. Blue-green bamboo groves, rivers, and chattering brooks announce the approach of the town, against a backcloth of gently rolling hills dotted with pines. Then comes a series of streets flanked by houses and hotels similar to those in any other town. Yet an "indescribable something" in the air hints that this city stands out from all the others we have seen as yet. A brief stroll through the town suffices to convince us of her originality. The tiniest shop window display is a real work of art. Each exhibit is indicative of unerring taste. As in old prints, even the streets intersect harmoniously at right angles. Some are extremely narrow, and lead to canals discernible by the sound of running water and a glimpse of leafy trees brightening the banks.

Everywhere else we find the mob. But in this instance that crushing Japanese throng seems less noisy, more courteous and disciplined than elsewhere. In the side streets—veritable street-markets protected from the sun by lathing—national costume often predominates over Western dress. One could spend hours watching the calm agitation of those craftsmen who, for centuries, have been making fans by hand, or working up lacquer. Geishas fresh as porcelain, their hair sleek with camellia oil, shuffle impassively homewards on sandled feet. In front of a booth displaying funerary decorations—in a glitter of gold that adds attraction even to after-life—shaven-headed children in flowered kimonos share candy-sticks flavoured with green tea. Beyond, a bridge protected by a parapet of timeworn pine-trunks spans a stream where dyers steep their fabrics, laying their long strips of multicoloured silk out to dry on the grassy banks. On the threshold of discreetly welcoming hotels and public baths with folding doors shut tight, large sunshades of oiled paper decorated with ideograms brighten the pavements. It has rained during the night, and the vapour rising from the trees, roofs, and ground blurs the outlines, making everything seem unreal, from the buildings where wood predominates, to the seething canals, inviting us to muse beneath the shade of pines and willows.

From time to time a procession of bonzes or warriors in medieval costume holds up the traffic. Tramcars, automobiles, and rickshaws come to a standstill. The heat streams down. Oriflammes dangle from their poles. Drums beat. This timeless spectacle is so like a reproduction that, once night adds to the fantasy, the most improbable legends become admissible. In an atmosphere such as this, how easy it is to sympathize with those American officers in the Army of Occupation who refused promotion rather than leave Kyoto—a case unprecedented in the annals of military history! And how grateful we should be to the French scholar Serge Elisseev, whose personal intervention at the Pentagon during the war saved Nara and Kyoto from bombardment . . . .

In this city where Imperial might asserted itself, declined, and revived (under Meiji), where Nipponese Buddhism flourished, where art and

The Temple of Kiyomizu in Kyoto

culture found their niche, the soul rises effortlessly to a higher plane. Whether one visits the palaces, the former Imperial villas, the gold and silver pavilions commissioned by two despots who, despite their tyrannic ways, were aesthetes for all that, or any one of the 3,000 Buddhist temples or Shinto shrines, one will find the restraint of the architecture exalts the refinement of a civilization at its height. And one can only hope that the visitors who attach amused importance to the song of the nightingale (a simple alarm signal), released by walking on a certain floorboard in the Palace of Nijo, do not overlook the colonnades of cypress and pine, the green-tiled roofs, or the paintings that stand out so vividly yet discreetly against the background of gilded walls.

But beware: the atmosphere of Kyoto reacts on the organism like a drug! Europeans who went there for a week or two have been living in Kyoto for years. Whoever wants to return to the West should skim the surface without attempting to dig deep. But, if you can drag yourself out of bed early enough before the 20th-century horde of hunters of images or sensations and the pious band of Buddhists invade temples and palaces, there is nothing to prevent you from drifting into reverie, and reviving, if only ephemerally, that glorious past in which emperors, empresses, courtiers, bonzes, and monks still paraded in sumptuous costumes that would now seem to be the prerogative of dolls alone. And, when, satiated with beauty, studied elegance, and lines of supreme purity, your eyes become strained by a surfeit of exquisiteness, you have only to rest them on the picturesque charm of a Chinese garden, introduced into Japan by way of Buddhism. There, in the skilful interplay of miniature lake, rocks, cherry trees, azaleas, or irises, you will find delight and repose.

Islet in the Inland Sea

ROUND THE INLAND SEA

Nara—the "Buddhist Rome"—is quite different in appearance. The very name of the region—Yamato—of which she is the main town, dates back to the first conquerors of the archipelago. Founded in 709, and capital from 710 to 780, Nara is in fact reputed to be the oldest city in the Empire.

If the half-million inhabitants on which she prided herself at her zenith has now been reduced to 80,000, nothing within her walls hints at this decay. A 1,700-acre park—the largest in Japan—extends a welcome. Deer come out to greet us. Sacred though they may be, they are not above poking their muzzles into our pockets in greedy quest for *mochi*. Once a year, in mid-October, their horns are shorn—a ceremony the local peasants would not miss for the world.

Nara is doubtless outliving herself. Ravaged by fire time without number, her ruins testify to her ancient splendour. The spectres of courtly bookworms and noble ladies whose subtlety in love inspired poems untold still float through the shady groves. And one could wander endlessly

HIROSHIGE—*Whirlpools in the Straits of Naruto, in the Inland Sea*

between the cryptomerias, the hedgerows of wistaria blossoming mauve
in springtime, beside a lake adorned with an imposing torii—and linger
in the avenues or on the steps bordered by countless stone lanterns leading
to temples painted in startling Polynesian hues (contrasting with the
natural wood of the others)—were it not imperative to pay a visit to the
largest and oldest Buddha in the world, the Daibutsu, seated cross-legged
in the middle of a lotus in Todaiji. This colossal statue, 50 feet high, took
nine years to cast, requiring 438 tons of copper and two tons of mercury
beneath a coat of eight cwt of gold. With his gaze turned towards infinity,
and the fingers of his right hand slightly parted, he blesses everyone who
bends before him. The original (A.D. 712) having collapsed in a fire, the
present statue is not exactly true to the period, but one would hardly
notice this beneath the gloomy roof of the temple. Another statue of wood,

some eight feet high stands out, vibrant with life, beside the entrance. It is that of a priest who died about 1100 years ago and on whose knees the mothers of sick children place their infants' clothes to be sure their prayers are answered.

Far away in the forest echoes a bell that pilgrims, impatient to realize their wishes, strike with a beam swinging on a straw cord. It might well be the famous 8th-century bell weighing nearly fifty tons—the third largest in Japan. Everything in Nara was enormous, proportionate to an emergent faith and an autocracy that deemed itself unbounded.

THE INLAND SEA—The plantations we cross in returning from Nara—narrow rows of green shrubs between which peasant women with kerchiefs on their heads toil in the sun—remind us that the "tea ceremony", that communion of the being with the Almighty, was born in Kyoto. But were not Nipponese history and mythology themselves conceived in this Asiatic Mediterranean on which we are about to embark? It was by way of this maritime route that Jimmu-Tenno allegedly launched his expeditions against the Ainus of Yamato as early as the 7th century B.C., and for centuries the shores of the Inland Sea formed the setting for all Japan's military, political, and artistic activities. Now that the political centre of gravity has shifted northwards, the riverains of the Inland Sea cling all the more tenaciously to the purest traditions of the archipelago. So do the farmers and fishermen (who haul their nets to the roll of a drum, singing words so old they have lost all meaning) inhabiting the islands dotted across the generally flat surface of this 250-mile-long seaboard, bathing part of Honshu, Shikoku, and Kyushu.

With its slack waters, its islands, and islets, this shallow sea recalls certain Finnish lakes. And yet its strands and gnarled pine trees, neutral landscapes, mild climate, and islands of hard sand or granite are essentially Japanese. The voyage, broken by frequent ports of call, lasts only twenty-four hours.

The small steamship glides over the water like a swan, brushes Shodo Island (ninety miles in circumference and nearly 1,000 feet in altitude at its summit, commanding a splendid view), passes junks with esparto sails, winds between strings of islets, and finally reaches the Isle of Shikoku at Yashima where the Taira and Minamoto waged a bloody battle in the 12th century. Here we disembark.

SHIKOKU—Too little is said about Shikoku, or rather when anyone from Tokyo mentions her it is to remark casually that she goes in for fishing, produces salt, rice, and the finest handmade paper in the world. But Tokyo's feigned detachment in no wise disturbs the fervent Buddhists who annually visit one or other of the eighty-eight temples on the island, all more or less dedicated to the Buddhist saint Kobo-Daishi, whose life—though brief (794–835)—was edifying in the extreme. We, too, visited Shikoku, including Takamatsu—a large town where landscape gardening has lost none of its primitive purity—and Tokushima, to the east, where craftsmen oblivious to progress are still making such perfect marionettes that invisible strings animate not only their limbs but also their lips, tongues, and teeth! Unhappily the time was not ripe for us to witness the frenzy of those spring whirlwinds in which the sea delights in the Straits of Naruto, between Shikoku and Awaji. On the other hand, our visit to Kochi, five hours south of Takamatsu by train, was rewarded by the sight of those celebrated cocks with interminable tails—as much as twenty feet long—that play a preponderant role (often wrongly believed to be imaginary) in Japanese painting.

A few days later (Shikoku being extensive) we re-embarked on the Inland Sea to the north, by-passing Tomo, famed for her bream fisheries. Never had the sea been more pacific, "like a straw mat", as someone remarked. The very islands seemed to smile. Suddenly the poesy was disrupted by the cranes of Kure's dockyards. Nobody breathed a word. Everyone was absorbed by the thought that slightly to the north lay Hiroshima. Having partly risen from her tragic ruins, she has now dedicated herself to the cause of peace. It was a relief to sail away, and even then we could not help trembling at the thought that an error in the bomber's

The Alley of Lanterns in Nara

calculations might have destroyed the jewel of the Inland Sea, Yume-no-Ukishima (the Isle of Dreams), or Miyajima.

MIYAJIMA--an island-mountain, is concealed beneath dense pine forests. In the foreground is a huge scarlet torii, flanked by lanterns and roofed with bronze. Rising out of the sea, it bars a creek where a Shinto temple, built on piles, and several outlying temples linked by galleries, seem to float on the water at high tide, especially on moonlight nights. At the foot of the mountain, tame deer frolic along a tree-lined avenue hugging the coast, bordered by stone lanterns. The riot of colour created towards mid-autumn by the maples growing in a valley on the island is a sight even more astonishing than the temples, and more curious than the dances young girls perform there. America's Indian summer is lacklustre in comparison. Vermilions, purples, and violets battle in brilliance, mingling with gold and copper hues in an extravagant kaleidoscope toned down once again by the dark background of pines.

The Great Torii of Miyajima

Mount Aso

KYUSHU

CROSSING the straits separating Kyushu from Shikoku and Honshu, we land on the largest of the southern isles, through which Western culture was introduced into Japan. The topography of Kyushu is particularly complicated. This mountainous, volcanic region is rich in spas, the largest of which is Beppu near Oita on the Gulf of Saganoseki. The "sand-baths" there, in which the Japanese bury themselves to the neck to combat anchylosis and arthritis, are even more interesting than the attractive local flora, or the monkeys inhabiting the "sulphurous inferno" on Mount Takasaki nearby.

Some sixty miles south-west the railway actually crosses a volcanic crater, the largest in the world (eighty miles in circumference). In the centre of this incomparably fertile area rises Mount Aso, one of the most active volcanoes in Japan, which erupted in 1953, causing a number of casualties.

The Sofukuji in Nagasaki

Underground rivers feed the lakes in the lovely park of Suizenji at Kumamoto. As capital of an essentially agricultural area, Kumamoto plans to expand industrially on a large scale by mastering the torrential River Kumagawa. This "town of forests" is surrounded by innumerable beauty spots, including the Island of Amakusa where relics of Christian martyrs of feudal times are piously preserved.

NAGASAKI—In Japan, mention of the word "Christian" inevitably brings memories of Nagasaki on the other side of the Sea of Ariake, the sole port open to the West in the 16th century. It was colonized by Portuguese traders, who introduced the use of gunpowder, amongst other things. St Francis Xavier preached there, Nipponese converts undergoing the baptism of blood.

For years, to the Japanese of the hinterland, Nagasaki spelt "foreign colony". By the same token, countless Europeans pictured "Nagasaki" when referring to "Japan". Nowadays the hills around are not so much haunted by memories of Madame Butterfly or the Christian martyrs as by the last of the two atom bombs released in 1945. The fact that they killed a great many Christians, razed to the ground the Catholic church of Urakami and, almost annihilated that of Ura, the oldest in Japan, did not escape the notice of Japanese enemies of Christianity. Having constantly lost ground since Kobe, Yokohama, and Moji wrested the monopoly of foreign trade, Nagasaki, like Hiroshima, intends henceforth to devote herself to "Peace"—an ideal soon to be symbolized by a statue costing twenty million yen. Concentrating on the future, the authorities lay emphasis on her mineral resources, naval dockyards, and—being nearer Shanghai than Tokyo—the touristic value of Unzen (literally "paradise in the clouds"). This famous national park covering a 250-acre plateau—yet another former crater—2,600 feet above sea level, attracts streams of visitors each year. Despite hot springs, the air is delightfully fresh. In spring the surrounding mountains are bright with cherry blossom, followed in May by thirty-odd varieties of azalea. Winter brings the phenomenal reign of "silver down", a kind of powder frost crystallizing into strange flowers on rocks and trees.

Much further south another national park, Kirishima, encompassing no less than twenty-two mountains, lays claim to the tallest clumps of azalea in Japan (some 65 feet high). The route runs past Shimbara where in 1638 the Christians, persecuted by the Shoguns, rose in revolt, losing 40,000 men in one battle. Beyond lies Kagoshima, famed both for the beauty of her daughters and the size of her turnips! Miyazaki nearby boasts one of the earliest temples in Japan, not to mention a wood renowned for its tropical trees. Then come Arita, one of the oldest centres for ceramics; Fukuoka reputed as much for her dolls as her silks; and Moji. It would take a lifetime to exhaust Kyushu's charms, but alas, it is time to return towards Honshu and Shimonoseki.

Sand-baths

TO THE NORTH

HUGGING the coast of the Sea of Japan, after a halt at the great Temple of Izumo—a national shrine almost as important as that of Ise—and then in Matsue, Lafcadio Hearn's first stage in Japan, we reach Amanohashidate.

AMANOHASHIDATE—If we take the guides' word, the only way to admire the amazing natural dike two miles long and some 330 feet wide in places, completely barring the entrance to the small Gulf of Miyazu, is by looking at it from the heights of the village of Ejiri "with one's head between one's legs". Seen thus, it looks like an aerial bridge—hence its name, the "celestial footbridge". It is clad in a fleece of pines, beneath which runs a pathway. Carnations and camellia perfume the shores. What caprice of nature—or the gods—thus cleaved this gulf which, in part at least, is steeped in eternal peace however ferociously the sea may rage?

LAKE BIWA—It was perhaps the same divine hand that created the immense Lake Biwa (or Omi) further south which only the massive barrier of Mount Hiei would seem to have restrained from submerging the site where Kyoto was later to be built. According to Gaston Migeon, "the beauty spots round Lake Biwa have, since time immemorial, engrossed Japanese poets and painters, who extolled them time without number in paintings and poems. The eight splendours of Omi occupy as important a position in Japanese art as the 'eight beauties of Siao-Siang' in Chinese art. These eight celebrated sights and objects of pilgrimage were: the autumn moon seen from Ishiyama; a snowy evening on Hirayama; sunset at Seta; the evening bell in the Temple of Miidera; the ships returning from Yabase; a clear sky swept by the breeze in Awazu; a rainy night in Karasaki; and the wild geese coming home to roost in Kataka. The majority were to be found in the southern section of the lake, in a more confined spot where the River Setagawa used to hurl itself into a wide estuary. . . ." On this southern bank lies the small town of Otsu in the vicinity of Miidera Temple, and more particularly in that of a small headland to which clings the Karasaki pine. Well may this famous tree be described as "millenary", having been represented, already mature, in paintings dating back more than nine hundred years. It is, in fact, the triumph of Nipponese arboriculturists who won their stubborn battle against nature by forcing its branches to grow horizontally, despite its constant resistance. The weight of the boughs is supported by crutches.

It is a wonder the pine is still standing, as yet unconsumed by the fire of heaven or earth.

On the contrary, it is we who are burning—to press on hotfoot, leaving the classic To-kaido at Nagoya in favour of the Naka-sendo, or "central mountain route". From here we climb up the dark Kiso Valley to an altitude of approximately 3,300 feet. The river in its depths flows through the most pre-cipitous countryside where narrow ricefields clamber up slopes rising as far as the eye can reach, at a gradient of nearly 3 : 1. Since time immemorial its waters have been used to float the pine boles employed in building the great temples in the old cap-itals. Beyond the Torii

Lake Biwa,
from Mount Hiei

Pass—no longer haunted by the brigands of the past, who have now ceded the way to trucks that hurtle round tortuous bends along a muddy road—we descend to Matsumoto, the seat of a Daimyo named Toda, boasting an extremely beautiful feudal castle. From there we thrust as far as Nagano, home of the great Buddhist temple known as Zenkoji, the most ancient temple of the Zen sect. Then, climbing up another deep, narrow valley winding between yellow cliffs, we reach Karuizawa, a summer resort beloved of foreigners who stumbled upon it amidst the mountains.

The range is dominated by the Asama-Yama, the most imposing of the active volcanoes on the archipelago—a threatening mass 8,200 feet high, from which an occasional spiral of smoke wafts up. On its northern flank a river of lava—"the demons' cast"—is petrified, seven-and-a-half miles in length and over sixty-five feet deep in places, sculptured in fantastic blocks recalling the horrors of the 1788 catastrophe that buried fifty villages.

Like Karuizawa, the steep jagged range of the Japanese Alps (656 square miles in area) owes its popularity to the white race, represented in this instance by a British missionary, Walter Weston—the father of Japanese mountaineering—who spent four years climbing most of the peaks and exploring the gorges before retiring to London in 1896, to write an account of his expeditions. And one would be tempted to go into ecstasies over the magic of certain mountains were they not overshadowed slightly to the east, approximately in the latitude of the heights of Shiga—a skiers' paradise in wintertime—by the town that gave birth to the local proverb: "Never say *kekko* before you see Nikko. . . ."

NIKKO—Just as our lesser poets are inclined to rhyme "love" and "dove", the Japanese equally naturally associate "Nikko" and "kekko" meaning splendid, magnificent. Added to this, a hackneyed saying insists that in Nikko "all the glories of nature combine harmoniously with those of art." And indeed, no words could exaggerate the magnificence.

At the very heart of a mountainous region, in the midst of a forest—a world of its own—where evergreen trees stand stiff and straight as if straining towards the sky—long pathways follow the rise and fall of the ground amidst cryptomerias, pines, and moss, bathed in a supernatural light, amidst an atmosphere of total silence. The calm solemnity and majesty of the landscape prompted the Shogun Tokugawa Iemitsu to select Nikko, at the foot of mountains melting into the mist of this humid region like kakemono designs, to honour the memory of his grandfather, the first Shogun, Ieyasu, founder of that same Tokugawa dynasty which dominated the archipelago from 1603 to 1868. It is vain to recall the prior existence of a Shinto temple, and thereafter of a Buddhist temple in the 8th century, on this very spot, they are lost in the smoke of the past. In reality Nikko dates from the 17th century, when Iemitsu spent twenty million yen of the period (to which the 300 Daimyo, his vassals, added their contribution) on the construction of a mausoleum and temples, the conception, execution, and lavishness of which treat with due contempt the term "pettiness" that is so often applied to Japan.

Iemitsu's homage was inspired by sincere piety. History relates that he would never listen to accounts of his ancestor's life without first donning ceremonial robes, and kneeling with bowed head throughout.

Work began in 1616. In the month of May, 1617, a long procession crossed the sacred bridge shaped like a crescent moon, decorated in red lacquer enhanced by gilt ironwork, spanning the Daiya-Gawa torrent. Slowly climbing the pathways of cryptomerias, it accompanied the body of the great Shogun, previously buried in Kunozan, to its last resting-place.

The Sacred Bridge in Nikko

Each year on 17th May this imposing ceremony is commemorated with due pomp. Silks and gilt glitter between the trees, flutes and drums resound to accompany bonzes and pilgrims in their ascent to that funerary city. By way of a granite torii they reach the first floor of its terraced buildings; thence, from gate to gate, from vermilion fence to stone wall, from a five-pinnacled pagoda to an imposing torii, they pass through a first court and a second, leading to yet a third terrace defended by the horrifying statues of two guardian-kings with contorted masks— the Ni-o. This last terrace is profusely yet not over-ornamented by temples of black and red lacquer, candelabra, myriads of bronze lanterns, tanks of lustral water, small structures containing sacred scripts, a lacquered horse permanently harnessed so that the God's spirit may mount it at his whim, and those cumbersome palanquins that made the bearers puff and pant beneath their weight. Passing beneath the white Yomeimon gateway, tarnished with age, before which sculptors and architects from every country and every age bend the knee, they at last reach the holy of holies, enclosed within a wall decorated from top to bottom with high-relief representing flowers, plants, fabulous animals, and characters gilded, lacquered, and painted with so sure a sense of colour that the hues most liable to clash with one another on the contrary enhance each other, ringing out like a song of victory.

However, even this is not where the two Tokugawa Shoguns (Iemitsu having joined his ancestor in Nikko) are actually buried. They repose in sober bronze mausolea in the background, reached only by other pathways and climbing further steps. This haughty simplicity concealed behind low walls of grey granite produces perhaps an even deeper impression on the soul than the triumphal vigour of the temples, where the slightest detail proclaims the genius of that master-

The Mountains round Nikko

230

carpenter Hidari Jingoro—who may well be described as the Hokusai of sculpture, and whom Europe would have ignored had his chisel not one day given birth to the three monkey mascots, "see no evil, say no evil, hear no evil." His works, scattered between Nagoya and Kyoto, are as stupefying as da Vinci's. Our heads are awhirl by the time we leave to refresh ourself some twelve miles from Nikko on the shores of Lake Chuzenji, the overflow of which splashes over 300 feet below in a mist of

vapour that the pilgrims, clad in yellow oiled canvas, ward off as best they can with their bamboo umbrellas.

MATSUSHIMA—Many an inhabitant of Tokyo, for whom Nikko represents the far north, would end their journey here. However, having covered barely two-thirds of the archipelago, we have yet to explore the truly northern section. We shall skim through it in haste, not that there are less remarkable beauty spots here than elsewhere, far from it, but Emperors, Shoguns, Daimyo, and Samurai, whose history determines the path of tourism, have had less occasion to reap glory in the province of Fukushima within the Straits of Tsu-

garu than between Nikko and Nagasaki. Somewhat remorsefully abandoning Fukushima to her lovely mountains, curious alpine flowers, and enormous cherries, and Sendai, the intellectual centre of the north, we nonetheless break our journey in the prefecture of Miyagi at Matsushima, the last of the *Sankei*, or, literally, "the three natural wonders" of Japan (the two others being Amanohashidate and Miyajima).

But how many foreigners have so much as dreamt of spending eight hours in a train leaving from Ueno station, to lose themselves on the "isle of pines"? They have seen pine trees in plenty ever since their arrival! Yet these particular pines, and the isles where they grow, have somehow succeeded in singularizing themselves from any other island or any other pine tree. A road leads through the ricefields and groves as far as the small port of Shiogama. Suddenly, when we least expect it, we stumble upon a corner of a Bay—the Bay of Along in miniature—covering an area of approximately sixty square miles, dotted by an incoherent jumble of

The Yomeimon Gateway

nearly three hundred islands and islets of black tuff and white sand. To be sure, the Inland Sea has already familiarized us with this type of scene. The originality of Matsushima, however, lies in the fact that, battered by the sea, the rain, and the winds, these islands assume the most unconventional shapes, stretching out like needles, curving like crooks, and arching their backs bristling throughout with pines that bite into the very rock and cling to their island home like souls in Purgatory. The sight is even more astonishing in the autumn equinox, when the sky suddenly turns to lead whilst the bay glows blood-red in the blazing sun . . . .

Forty-five miles further north, we should be sure to make a pilgrimage to Hiraizumi, the historic spot where four generations of feudals established themselves in the 12th century, independent of the central authority. On this same spot illustrious Yoshitsune met his death when his brother, Minamoto no Yoritomo, the Shogun of Kamakura, swept down to reduce this last citadel of opposition, unless, as the legend runs, he succeeded in making his way to the mainland, where he reputedly recommenced his exploits under the name of Genghis Khan . . . .

All that remains of the former animation and the sumptuous palaces are the pavilions of a temple known as Chuson-ji, lost in the heart of an ancient wood, the last resting-place of four overlords whose bodies were mummified by means of a mysterious process not known to have been employed elsewhere.

In contrast, much further north again, Lake Towada, nearly 1,000 feet deep, and filling a crater that would contain Lake Chuzenji near Nikko six times over, offers a scene of mountain serenity. It is six hours north of Sendai by train, and the surrounding peaks command a view of the large island of Hokkaido shaped like a giraffe's head, on the other side of the Straits of Tsugaru.

Winter in the Hokkaido Mountains

HOKKAIDO

How is it that hardly has he disembarked in Hakodate (or hardly has he set foot on the aerodrome of Chitose, not far from Sapporo, the capital) than the traveller has the impression of being transported into another world? We shall not take it upon ourselves to explain. Evidence has, however, demonstrated that Japanese civil servants or businessmen sent from Tokyo to Hokkaido never seem to feel at home there, and appear to have only one desire, to return "to Japan". Another more significant symptom is the fact that in this archipelago where space is so confined that people tread on each other's toes, despite its 29,764 square miles (nearly twice the surface of Kyushu, or more than one-fifth of the total surface of the islands), Hokkaido contains less than one-twentieth of the Japanese population. The temperature—averaging 45° F. in Sapporo—might explain this desertion. Yet if cold currents bathe Hokkaido, hot currents counteract their influence, an icy winter being balanced by a torrid summer. Another theory is that the presence of the last of the Ainus might arouse a feeling of uneasiness in the Japanese. The battle they waged against those fearsome warriors who used to occupy the north of the Great Island is curiously similar to the struggle between American pioneers and Redskins. And yet the few thousand Ainus who have survived in this vast "reserve" are quite inoffensive—and extremely interesting from the ethnologist's point of view. The men have pale eyes and patriarchal beards; the women are tattooed with hideous moustaches and imperials as soon as they reach marriageable age; both sexes have curiously flattened arm and leg-bones, like cave-dwellers.

Who are the Ainus? No one knows precisely. The race might well descend from proto-Caucasians who emigrated across Siberia. They have retained their bows and poisoned arrows. They still hunt bears, which they worship for all that. They cultivate a curious form of art: the carving of flat wooden sticks which the men use to lift their moustaches when drinking rice wine. Thus were they at the beginning of time, and thus they remain to this day, with their costumes of motley-coloured cloth, and garlands of coarse straw wreathing their brows. The extremely rare Ainus who refused to mingle with other races now live by fishing and the cultivation of maize and a few other vegetables, near the little village of Shiraoi some twelve miles north of Noboribetsu. Their god "Kamu" encompasses the sun as well as the wind, the ocean, and the bear. In his honour, the Ainus plant long whittled sticks in front of their huts. Having emerged gentle and pacific from the bloody defeats the Japanese inflicted upon them, they now enjoy justifiable renown as marvellous story-tellers (especially when imbued with *sake*). Their extraordinarily poetic legends are centred round the bear, salmon, hunting, and, of course, the forests, mountains, and lakes of the strange land to which their victors relegated them.

Strange it is for the Japanese, but a white man, on the contrary, would feel quite at home there, the relief being such as a European or American is accustomed to. If "Japaneseness" means jagged creeks, gnarled pines, mountains flirting with the clouds, Hokkaido in relief (which, except for the volcanoes, resembles turn and turn about the Vosges and Kentucky) and in vegetation (fir trees, oaks, and beech) is clearly distinct from the rest of Japan. There are, of course, clouds of steam floating over several valleys, rising from the waters of torrents brought almost to boiling-point by the volcanoes. And then again, in several places (Jozankei, Tokachigawa, Deshikaga, Yunugu, to mention only the main ones), hot springs spurt violently from the soil.

Although intensely volcanic, other territories such as the huge "national park" of Daisetsuzan dissimulate themselves better, so to speak, in a jumble of gorges, canyons, cascades, waterways, and springs. There is, for instance,

*Summer in the
Hokkaido Mountains*

the source of the Ishikari—discovered in 1852—the longest river in Japan, which travels 250 miles before hurling itself into the Bay of Otaru. And what of the Sunkyo Gorge, where the river flows tranquilly between rocky banks forming cliffs nearly 2,000 feet high? And the lakes dotted with *marimo*—as they call that sapphire-green moss previously believed to exist only on certain Swiss lakes, and which a "law for the protection of the wonders of nature" forbids one to touch? Decidedly, the region has little in common with the three other large isles! For four or five months of the year it is clad so thickly with snow that long poles painted red and white—the colours of the Empire—are planted like tall landmarks to indicate the curves of the main roads.

As for her resources of all kinds (agricultural products, wood, fish, minerals: coal, platinum, asbestos, mercury, gold, copper, etc.), they either find outlets on the spot or fill the holds of cargo-boats leaving from ports such as Hakodate, Otaru, and Muroran for Kobe, Yokohama, or abroad. The very towns and ports have a stamp of their own. The streets and avenues are wide and straight, the buildings relatively tall and sturdy. There is a reason for these anomalies, the plans of these diverse cities—above all Sapporo—having been drawn up approximately eighty years ago by American architects. Could it be deduced therefrom that the layout of a city influences the mentality of her inhabitants? In Hokkaido one would be inclined to think so, judging by the spirit of initiative, the desire for achievement, and the ambitious projects of the population, men and women alike. And we may rest assured they will carry them out to the full.

On this encouraging note, we shall end this "lightning journey" from Tokyo to Nagasaki and from Nikko to Hokkaido, without, for all that, making any pretence to have exhausted the subject.

In this archipelago where every locality lies within sixty miles of the sea, there are countless national parks, lakes, castles, temples, islands (that of Oshima in the Bay of Tokyo, for one, where camellia oil is distilled and where young girls known as *anko*, clad in black kimonos dotted with white spots, carry their bundles and even buckets of water on their heads), that we have been force to omit, much as we should have liked to describe them. Our aim will at least have been attained if these few pages encourage the reader to pursue his study—delve more deeply into this land of Japan that must first be comprehended before one can find the key to her otherwise undecipherable inhabitants—and attempt to unveil the mysteries of landscapes from which nature, thwarted, has engendered a race of men of action, and century-long contemplation of which has turned the Japanese into a great nation of artists . . . .

WAY OF LIFE

慣習

THE JAPANESE
CHARACTER

BEFORE trying to grasp the elements forming the Japanese character, we should first recall certain historical and geographical conditions that may have influenced her psychological reactions.

THE COUNTRY—First, there are geographical factors. Japan comprises a string of islands of volcanic origin totalling 192 volcanoes (58 of which are active), constantly subjected to eruptions, and frequent earthquakes (the seismographers register 4,000 to 5,000 tremors each year), often accompanied by tidal waves. In relief, the archipelago is one of the most rugged in the world; this explains why the population is necessarily grouped round the 16 % of arable land. Again due to the extremely mountainous relief, the rivers are short and rapid, and there is thus constant danger of floods at the slightest torrential rain. Moreover, terrible typhoons generally break forth just as the rice is beginning to ripen, between late August and early October. Lastly, the fact that the houses are so densely packed together, and usually built of wood, means that fires can often destroy entire towns.

THE POPULATION—We should also like to recall a few historic facts that clarify certain aspects of the Japanese character.

Although the sea is always close at hand in Japan, in contrast to other islanders such as the British, the Japanese have always been more or less confined within their country. The sole exceptions were a handful of bold adventurers or the rare bonzes and scholars determined to make their pilgrimage to China, come what may. Organized expeditions such as Japan's repeated attempts to attack Korea, or conversely, the Mongols' efforts to invade Japan, have always ended in disaster. Thus, all things considered, until the 19th century the Japanese were far less venturesome seafarers than the Chinese.

On the other hand, when Japan was opened to the outside world in 1868 the United States, Canada, and above all, Australia, systematically restricted possible emigration within the circumference of the Pacific. Japan eventually expanded beyond her immediate periphery and occupied Formosa in 1895, Karafuto —the southern half of the Island of Sakhalin, north of Hokkaido—in 1905, Korea in 1910, the Caroline and Marshall Islands in 1919, Manchuria in 1931, and lastly an extensive area along the Chinese coastal regions as from 1936.

16th C

All these overseas territories are now lost.

For 1,500 years the nation has been stratified horizontally by a system of classes which in practice is equivalent to a caste system. Despite Western influences that have made themselves felt over the past eighty years, social traditions have maintained the Confucian hierarchy more firmly than the Japanese themselves care to admit. By upholding the Emperor—partly for reasons of immediate security—the American occupation has contributed

towards maintaining this traditional hierarchy.

Moreover, during the past fifty years, overpopulation and lack of raw materials have condemned the Japanese populace to live in the humblest conditions, if not in poverty. The sole hope of survival thus resides in enforced and continual observation of the code of relationships in regard to equals and superiors. The sole hope of rising in the social scale is by actively cultivating relations that may enable the individual to emerge from the class to which his birthright has relegated him. At the cost of immense efforts the most brilliant university scholar may cross the barrier of examinations, only to find his prowess is of no avail unless he can pull strings.

Japan is an active nation, eager to acquire anything novel, tense in the extreme, and seething within the closed vase of her narrow isles. On the other hand, it is not difficult to imagine the obstacles that would hinder large-scale "democratic" development on the model of the U.S.A. The American conceptions of severance from traditions and freedom are based on an abundance of material means and living space for each individual, which Japan could never hope to possess, or even develop.

Typical Dwelling-house

Probably more stupidities—either extravagant or deprecatory—have been written about Japan than about any other country, for two reasons. First, because the country and the people give the appearance of being easily approachable; secondly, because the Japanese avoid intense discussions with people they do not know, and, from social atavism, prefer to fall in line with their questioner's way of thinking.

IN SEARCH OF JAPANESE QUALITIES—Closer acquaintance with Japan, however, reveals the following traits—here, I leave the chair to a well-known Japanese critic who attributes twelve qualities to his compatriots—qualities which may naturally be virtues in a normal dose, or vices in an abnormal dose:

Loyalty; sense of duty and responsibility (to the extent of suicide); an optimistic (we might say fatalistic) outlook on the vicissitudes of life ("all is but a dream", in the words of the Buddhist adage); love of Nature and of contact with her; a realistic psychology ("Our energy is directed towards the solution of practical questions as they arise from day to day");

patriotism ("for us, this is practically a religion"); sense of national unity ("for centuries we have lived on our own resources"); sense of national continuity ("symbolized by the Imperial House, the Nation has retained its continuity for twenty centuries"); self-sacrifice ("effacement of one's personality has always been the philosophy of the Japanese and the basis of their education"); sense of honour ("resulting from the teaching of Bushido, or 'The Way of the Warrior'. It has at times degenerated into mere susceptibility or been deformed into rigid formalism. For all that it is preferable to callousness and indifference"); sentimentality ("the Japanese race is excitable, sensitive, emotional, quick to take umbrage, spontaneously reactive to any sign of friendship, incapable of forgetting offences and kindness alike"); a talent for detail ("this remark applies to governmental duties as well as to works of art, scientific research, or literary production"). And the critic concludes: "The Japanese are great in small things; let us hope they are not small in great things!"

The foreigner's opinion is expressed to perfection by the Harvard historian Edwin O. Reischauer: "The peoples of East Asia have consistently given a greater place in their higher culture to direct emotive response to outside stimuli and have shown far less interest than we in systems of logic. A graphic example carries far more weight with them than the neatest syllogism. Emotional expression in art or poetry is more their forte than a reasoned analysis.

" . . . . from the top to the bottom of their society, they exhibit a high artistic appreciation for what is in their own tradition and uniformly good taste in a myriad of intimate details of their daily life. There is relatively little of the dichotomy we find in our own culture between the self-conscious good taste of the self-appointed artistic minority and the bad taste and artistic vulgarity which they so deplore in others.

"The Japanese passion for natural beauty, their repeated triumphs since ancient times in the field of art, and the high level of artistic taste exhibited throughout the nation give strong evidence of their basic emotionalism, however devoid of feeling they may seem to be superficially."

SOCIAL STRUCTURE

IT is difficult, nay well-nigh impossible, for a foreign observer to formulate a more or less accurate and balanced conception of Japanese society, even if he stays in the country for some time.

The first obstacle is the language barrier, which is almost insuperable for 99.5 % of foreigners. And even when they succeed in overcoming it to a certain extent, their contacts are often limited to one particular group of Japanese—considerably augmented since the occupation—who, either by some curious inferiority complex, or by pure and simple ignorance, feign scorn for everything connected with the traditions and the very acts of their fellow-citizens. Added to this is the fact that few of these foreigners venture beyond the large cities, except for rapid excursions to well-known tourist centres or watering towns populated by well-to-do citizens like themselves. Most of them travel there by way of luxury modes of transport, either in reserved compartments on the trains, or by car, in the fastest and latest American model, which give them little or no opportunity of rubbing shoulders with "the man in the street".

Behind this façade lie immense stretches of *terra incognita*, the real country-side where over half the population lives and works. What do they do, and how do they live? Questions such as this can certainly not be solved by approaching them from the angle of the hurried tourist travelling in comfort. The only way you can reach this part of Japan is on foot—as do the Japanese themselves—or by taking those little trains and jolting buses that clamber through the maze of valleys, rugged foothills, rice plantations, and fields perched on abrupt slopes, to arrive eventually in a straggling village, the advance post on a track or road leading to a hinterland even more difficult to reach. But it is worth undertaking the effort, in order to discover the peasant at work on his little plot of land. Thankless though the soil may be, it is always tended with care. Here we change worlds, leaving behind us those monotonous, tentacular towns disfigured by the war; towns where the predominant desire is that of keeping pace with other regions, and where myriads of workers toil in factories attempting to overcome the deficit in the budget with their produce.

It is thus extraordinarily difficult to trace a coherent picture of Japanese society, which is in a constant state of exterior fluidity. It may, however, be asserted almost unhesitatingly that the years which have elapsed since 1942 have transformed the face of Japan more markedly than has the slow evolution of the preceding millenary.

THE CONSTITUTION OF 1947— Officially, all that has survived of prewar Japan is the Emperor. And even his status has been changed completely by the very first article of the new Constitution of 1947. This calls for a comparison with the former Constitution of 1889. (Quotations from the latter are mentioned in italics.)

Art. I: The Emperor shall be the symbol of the State and of the unity of the Nation, deriving his position from the will of the people with whom resides sovereign power. *(Japan is governed by a line of Emperors, unbroken since time immemorial.)*

Art. II: The Imperial Throne shall be dynastic and succeeded to in accordance with the Imperial House Law passed by the Diet. *(The Emperor is sacred and inviolable.)*

Art. III: The advice and approval of the Cabinet shall be required for all acts of the Emperor in matters of state, and the Cabinet shall be responsible therefor. *(The Emperor shall determine the organiza-*

tion of the various governmental services and the salaries of all government officials, both civil and military; he shall likewise appoint and dismiss said officials.)

Art. IV: The Emperor shall perform only such acts in matters of state as are provided for in this Constitution and he shall not have powers related to government. *(The Emperor is the Head of the Empire, and in him are concentrated the rights of sovereignty exercised in accordance with the terms of this Constitution.)*

This long quotation serves its purpose in demonstrating the importance of the changes in regard to the Emperor's person. For the first time he appeared in the eyes of the law not as the descendant of the gods (he had himself refuted his divine origin, in his message to the nation of 1st January, 1946), but as a mere symbol of his country. We should, however, hasten to add that for many of the ordinary folk, the Emperor has preserved quasi-divine prestige. After the war, certain bold spirits, Japanese and foreign alike, wondered what would be the outcome of a referendum in favour of maintaining the Emperor in power. Some estimates set the figure at 92 %.

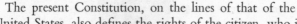

The present Constitution, on the lines of that of the United States, also defines the rights of the citizen, who is to be respected as an individual, having the right to life, freedom, and happiness. All citizens are equal in the eyes of the law, regardless of sex, race, or creed. Suffrage is universal. Freedom of conscience, thought, religion, assembly, speech, press, and all other forms of expression is guaranteed. Equality of sexes and the rights of marriage partners is established. Freedom of labour is assured, the workers having the right to organize themselves, hold discussions, and act collectively. Torture and cruelty are prohibited. No one shall be obliged to testify against himself.

Finally, the attributes of legislative and executive powers are clearly defined: the Diet is the supreme organ of State power; it alone is empowered to establish laws. Laws become valid on being passed by the two Houses. Executive power is in the hands of the Cabinet. The Prime Minister and the members of the government must all be civilians.

We consider it of interest to cite separately and *in extenso* Chapter II

HISHIKAWA MORONOBU—*Palace Scene*

—unique in the world—composed solely of Article IX: "Aspiring sincerely to an international peace based on justice and order, the Japanese people forever renounce war as a sovereign right of the nation and the threat or use of force as a means of settling international disputes.

"In order to accomplish the aim of the preceding paragraph, land, sea, and air forces, as well as other war potential, will never be maintained. The right of belligerency of the state will not be recognized."

Thus was the apparatus all set to launch the ship of State on the high seas of democracy, with its currents, eddies, and tempests broken by becalmings.

POSTWAR JAPAN—Apart from the loss of territories abroad, one of the most remarkable changes brought about by defeat was the definitive elimination of the military bureaucracy that formed a state within the State; when one thinks, for instance, that until 1945 the ministers of the armed forces

—all of whom were themselves generals or admirals in the regular forces—had direct access to the Emperor. There is little chance of this bureaucracy ever regaining its bygone influence, not so much because it was discredited by its insensate acts during the last war, but above all because of the radical change in the methods of attack resulting from the perfection of atom and hydrogen bombs.

As for the civilian bureaucracy, it emerged from the fray almost unscathed, trailing in its wake a number of postwar ministers and parliamentarians. Even the great financial trusts—the famous Zaibatsu—are slowly taking shape again, surreptitiously supported by certain statesmen.

But the most definite overall result of the war, defeat, and subsequent occupation, was to strike a fatal blow at the entire system of respect for authority and unconditional subservience to superiors—a system that had been decanted and codified throughout the centuries, and formed the basis of relationships between individuals. This system was pyramidal in aspect, with the Emperor at the summit, clearly detached from his fellow-citizens by his status as descendant of the Sun Goddess. Below him were the military, segregated from the people also. They derived their prestige from their title as defenders of the "Land of the Gods", and the fact that every soldier who died for his country immediately joined the cohort of *Kami* or superiors who protected the Empire together with the Spirits of defunct emperors. Lastly came the nation as a whole, forming the basis and the pillar upholding the Imperial system, by traditional observance of the five Confucian virtues inculcated in children from their earliest youth both at school and at home, whereby the authority of the master or the father should never be disputed.

Now, in one fell swoop the new Constitution of 1947 completely disrupted the delicate mechanism of this millenary order. From one day to the next, it accorded the individual a freedom no one had even dreamed of in the past. Religious respect for the Emperor was suppressed, the military vanished.... but on the family level the *pater familiae* survived as an enforced reminder of a bygone age. By rescinding the father's absolute rights over his children, suppressing the hierarchy established between children—from the eldest to the youngest—and liberating women from submission to the males of the family, the Constitution merely legalized tendencies that had been developing rapidly over the past thirty years, particularly between 1920 and 1930.

Transport in Days Gone By . . . . (HIROSHIGE—*Porters, on the Tokaido, at Mishima*)

The intense industrialization of modern Japan, the development of new techniques in business, banking, laboratory research, radio, television, and a thousand and one other forms of activity all tended to detach—and subsequently liberate—youth from the stranglehold of tradition. Paradoxically, the war made its own contribution by liberating women, through compelling them to shoulder responsibilities and accomplish tasks hitherto reserved for men.

Workers' unions—whose action had until the end of the war been hampered or systematically channelled into "Patriotic Societies"—suddenly developed, protected by law. This abrupt expansion was not devoid of clashes, often of a brutal nature. In fact, a distinct evolution is visibly taking place and, strangely enough, it is following the pattern of the French or Italian trade union movements rather than that of the American labour unions.

The various elections have stressed the permanence of conservative elements (75 % in 1952). The weight of rural electors makes itself felt in this figure.

Emperor Hirohito in Ritual Costume

RURAL AREAS—It should not be forgotten that 60% of the country's population is rural. Now of all the Japanese, it was the peasants who suffered least from the war, being relatively sheltered from air raids and near sources of food supply. On the other hand, it was their families who lost the most men in the war. In addition, they were living in a traditional atmosphere where numerous traces of the feudal system still survived. Over 65% of the peasants cultivated land that did not belong to them, and was, in fact, distributed in accordance with an extremely severe allotment system that often deprived them of more than half their harvest, and indebted them for life.

A hope of independence was offered to them in the form of a whole series of postwar laws intended on the one hand to free the peasants of their debts, and on the other to dispossess the landed proprietors of their estates which were sold on credit to the labourers who actually farmed it. This plan—which left only about seven-and-a-half acres to the former landowners in the three large islands of Honshu, Shikoku, and Kyushu, and thirty acres in Hokkaido—was enthusiastically acclaimed by everybody.

For all that, there is a land "famine" in Japan, 95 % of the 6,200,000 farms cultivating only five acres on an average. The peasants are saved from complete poverty by a long-standing system of co-operatives, which enable them to acquire farming equipment, fertilizers, and other products, cheaply, on credit. On the other hand, it should not be forgotten that the peasants are all the more lacking in dynamism and individual-mindedness because their plots of land are so very small.

It is thus not surprising that they are far from shaking off the hold of the former landed proprietors and small tradespeople, who form an extremely influential block from the political and economic point of view. In their ranks one encounters a number of military men who have lost their situations as a result of purges and the suppression of the army.

Peasants at Work

SURVIVAL OF ANCIENT CUSTOMS
AND TRADITIONS

THE foreign observer should watch his step in summarily qualifying the customs of peoples not born beneath the sign of the Cross as "superstitions". In the West, dread of the number thirteen, of spilt salt, or of opening an umbrella indoors, is classified under the heading of "superstitions" in the same way that in Japan an unlucky meaning is attached to the numbers nineteen, thirty-three, or forty-two—actually based on puns (in Japanese the word for nineteen is *juku*, which in turn may mean "repeated sorrows"; thirty-three, pronounced three-three or *san-zan*, may signify "unescapable misfortunes"; forty-two, pronounced four-two or *shi-ni*, is a homonym for the word "death").

SOOTHSAYING—It is impossible to overlook the importance of the role soothsaying in all its forms plays in Japanese life. Most of the techniques are of Chinese origin. The old method related in the *Kojiki*, which consists of interpreting the cracks on the surface of a deer's shoulder-blades placed on a burning fire, is strictly identical to the Chinese practice of examining a tortoiseshell that has been exposed to fire.

In Japan you come across soothsayers and fortune-tellers—*eki-sha*—not only round the temples, where the passers-by are naturally at their mercy, but almost everywhere you go: in parks and fairgrounds, on street corners, and even in the recesses between houses. They work mainly at night, and their equipment invariably consists of a small table containing a candle (or occasionally a pocket torch) and a magnifying-glass for studying the lines of the hand *(teso)* or the face *(ninso)*. Certain soothsayers are equipped for more thorough—and needless to say, more costly—investigations. They begin by spreading out fanwise in their palms a bundle of fifty thin sticks of polished reed, raising their hands to the level of their faces. Closing their eyes, then inhaling and exhaling the air vigorously through their nostrils, they suddenly separate the sticks into two smaller bundles, one of which they count. The calculations enable them to decipher the subject's future. Another method involves eight wooden plaques engraved with long and short lines, combinations of which give valuable indications as to what lies in store.

THE ZODIAC—Lastly, there is a kind of compass or map in the form of a circle, indicating twelve directions *(hogaku)* governed by the twelve animals of the Zodiac, namely, turning clockwise: to the north, the rat *(ne,* an abbreviation of *nezumi)*; to the north-north-east, the ox *(ushi)*; east-north-east, the tiger *(tora)*; east, the hare *(u,* an abbreviation of *usagi)*; east-south-east, the dragon *(tatsu)*; south-south-east, the snake *(mi,* a special pronunciation of *hebi)*; south, the horse *(uma)*; south-south-west the sheep *(hitsuji)*; west-south-west, the monkey *(saru)*; west, the cock *(tori)*; west-north-west, the dog *(inu)*; and north-north-west, the boar *(i,* an abbreviation of *inoshishi)*.

The animals of the Zodiac play a big role in Japanese life. Until quite recently they used to indicate the time of day and night, two hours at a time. At midnight there was the rat, at two o'clock in the morning the ox, at four o'clock the tiger, and so on. In ancient tales or classical drama the expression "at the hour of the ox" often foreshadowed some dire action such as a secret tryst or vengeance.

The days of the month and the years are likewise indicated by these twelve animals. The year 1955, for instance, was the year of the sheep and 1956 that of the monkey. This accounts for the frequent recurrence of the animal motif in paintings, on fans, kimonos, and a wide variety of other objects. Many children born in

Studying the
Lines of the Hand

1955 bear a name in which one of the characters is that of the "sheep".

Chinese and Japanese traditions have woven such a tissue of symbolism round these animals that it will be a long time before their influence is removed from popular beliefs, not to mention art and literature. The rat, for example, has become the inseparable companion of Daikoku, the God of Fortune, and for a good reason, since the latter is almost always represented leaning on two balls of rice, the supreme attributes of prosperity. The Japanese also say that if a house is infested with rats, that is a sign of prosperity, and the absence of rats is an omen of imminent calamity.

THE OX, or rather buffalo, is a most highly venerated beast in Japan, as elsewhere in the Far East, being invaluable in farming where everything is done by hand. On account of its calm and dignified gait, it is also the sage's favourite mount. In fact, they are often depicted together in classical paintings. A large number of statues of oxen is to be found in Shinto temples dedicated to the manes of the celebrated Prime Minister and eminent poet of the 9th century, Sugawara no Michizane, who became the God of Calligraphy and the patron saint of students. The hour of the ox was selected by women about to avenge themselves on a fickle

Greetings Card
in the Year of the Horse

256

lover. Custom required the vindicator to venture at dead of night into a temple, with the tripod of an upturned brazier crowning her head and a lighted candle attached to each of the three legs. In her left hand she held an effigy of the lover, made of straw, and in the right a hammer; a mirror dangled on her bosom; as for the nails, they were held between the teeth. On reaching the temple, she selected the most hallowed tree and nailed the effigy to it with a nail for each of the four limbs and a fifth nail for the heart. Her visit to the temple had to be repeated each night thereafter until the death of the person

HARUNOBU—*The Year of the Ox*

on whom she was avenging herself. On more than one occasion in remote shrines we have ourselves come across old trees where these nails were rusting away, as the last testimonies to ancient vengeances.

THE TIGER is the king of animals in China as in India. The white tiger is supposed to have reached the age of five hundred years, and be able to live about a thousand years. In paintings it is often represented in the midst of bamboos. The reason for this is that in India the tiger's most dangerous foe is the elephant, from whom it can escape only by slithering into a clump of bamboo shoots, where its enemy never ventures. The tiger symbolizes the force of the Buddhist faith, which is capable of penetrating the most inextricable "jungle of sin".

THE HARE—the fourth animal in the Zodiac—is a character to be respected. It is mentioned in the Shinto legends of the *Kojiki*. In Chinese and Japanese folklore, the hare is closely associated with the moon; the origin of the legend is probably to be found in the Hindu Jataka. Be this as it may, in China the hare is represented pounding drugs in a mortar, in order to extract an elixir of long life. In Japan the hare pounds rice dough for making *mochi*: circular girdle-cakes symbolizing either the moon or the round mirror of Amaterasu, the Sun Goddess. We might mention in passing that, according to the soothsayers, anyone born in the year of the hare is unlikely to meet with good fortune on the day of the tiger.

THE DRAGON is the most important mythical beast in the whole of the Far East. The conventional form in which it is portrayed originated in China. It generally has an elongated head, bristly and grimacing; wide fangs beneath a snout with two long antennae protruding above it; stag's horns at the rear of the skull; and a scaly body with a jagged crest surmounting its back. Its four feet are tipped with three, four, or five claws, according to its size. In paintings it is represented hurtling itself from the skies through a blanket of storm-clouds, with jaws agape and claws outstretched; its body may be black, green, red, white, or yellow. According to folklore, there are four species of dragons: the guardian of the heavens, the dragon that creates rain, the terrestial dragon that stems the flow of rivers, and lastly the dragon of the treasures concealed in the earth.

THE SNAKE is associated with Benten, the Japanese Venus—the Goddess of the Sea, and of Love or Beauty (Benten, like Daikoku whom we mentioned in connexion with the rat, belongs to the host of seven gods of happiness). The usual Japanese word for "snake" is *hebi*; but in the group of the Zodiac it is called *mi*. One of its other ancient names is *ja* which, in combination with other characters, gives its name to the Japanese three-stringed guitar—*samisen*—derived from the ancient word *jamisen*, because its sound-box was originally made of snakeskin. The umbrella made of oiled paper mounted on slats of bamboo is called *janome* because in shape it resembles a "snake's eye".

THE HORSE is a relatively ancient inhabitant of Japan, and certainly of China. In both countries, it used to be customary to bury a horse with its master if the latter were an emperor or a high-ranking official, so that it might serve him as steed in the world beyond. Emperor Kotoku-Tenno discontinued this custom in 646. By then, it was already three centuries since the tradition of burying the servants of princely houses with their masters had died out. Subsequently, the nobles adopted the custom of offering horses to the Shinto temples. Not being in a position to imitate them, the common people acquired the habit of bearing "images of horses" to the shrines. This explains why to this day all the votive offerings in the form of plaques, whether decorated with a horse or some other motif, are called *ema*, or "horse's image". Temples of any importance include a special building for these images, known as the *ema-do*, after the name of the votive offerings—sometimes of great value—that are suspended in them.

As for the eighth animal of the Zodiac, there is not much to be said about it. Popular imagery represents it in the guise of a goat, although its name, *hitsuji*, means sheep. There was a certain amount of confusion

HARUNOBU—*The Year of the Cock*

259

between the two species—both of which were rare in Japan until a relatively late date—at the time when the Chinese calendar was adopted, during the T'ang era in the 8th century.

THE MONKEY, on the other hand, is well known in Japan, where it still infests certain wild mountains. It is frequently depicted in painting and sculpture. Everyone knows the famous group of three monkeys sculptured for the mausoleum of Tokugawa Ieyasu erected in the 17th century in Nikko: the monkey who hears no evil, the one that sees no evil, and the one that says no evil. As a sidelight on the Pacific War, we might add in passing that these three monkeys were used as patriotic "slogans" to stress the dangers of espionage! The monkey figures in numerous folk tales. In

the Shinto pantheon, it is associated with the God of Highways, Saruta-hiko; it is also the messenger of one other important god, Okuni-nushi-no-mikoto, the patron saint of sailors. People born in the year of the monkey are supposed to inherit its manual skill. On the other hand, the year of the monkey is bad for marriages, due to the association of the noun *saru*, meaning monkey, with the verb *saru*, to leave.

THE COCK plays an important role in Japanese mythology. When the myriads of gods attempted, by singing and shouting, to make the Sun Goddess Amaterasu emerge from the grotto where she had shut herself out of spite, the cock participated so brilliantly in the din that the goddess eventually emerged from her retreat.

Badger,
at the Entrance to a Restaurant

This explains why there are always sacred cocks at large in the great Imperial Temple of Ise dedicated to Amaterasu. The porticos leading to Shinto shrines are known as *torii*, or perches, reputedly in memory of these sacred cocks. The cock is the symbol of courage in China and Japan alike. Whilst on the subject of cocks, we might mention one extraordinary breed that has been in existence for 150 years and, by skilful cross-breeding, has developed a remarkably long tail made of five to eight feathers, some of which are as much as twenty-five feet in length!

THE DOG—As befits man's most loyal companion, the dog enjoys a good reputation. In folklore, it is always performing services for mankind. The dog is often represented in the form of a brightly coloured papier-mâché toy. When placed near a child, this toy is supposed to protect it; when suspended over the child's head, it prevents it from crying and having bad dreams; when placed beside a woman in labour, it lightens her ordeal. For this same reason, a pregnant woman chooses "the day of the dog" for wearing her first maternity belt.

THE BOAR—the last animal in the Zodiac—is the symbol of courage and temerity. In the Shinto pantheon, the God of War, Usa Hachiman, is occasionally depicted mounted on a boar. There still exists an ancient belief whereby whoever eats *mochi* made on the day of the boar, at the hour of the boar (between 9.00 and 11.00 p.m.) is protected from every illness.

THE FOX—There is one animal that does not have a place in the Zodiac, but which nonetheless plays an essential role in the traditions and folklore of Japan: this is the fox, or rather Master Fox—*kitsune-sama*—as its name indicates. In the beginning, it was appointed messenger of an important Shinto divinity, Toyo-Uke-hime, the Goddess of Food, who boasts a shrine in Ise right beside that of the Sun Goddess. But through the course of the centuries, worship of the fox became concentrated in the innumerable temples of Inari, all derived from the one founded in the year 711 at Fushimi, now the southern suburb of Kyoto. Every Shinto temple of any importance contains within its precincts a shrine consecrated to Inari; in fact, they are even to be found nestling against Buddhist temples. These Inari shrines are easily recognizable, being invariably preceded by one or more torii painted vermilion. Moreover, the approaches to such temples are always guarded by countless statues of foxes, facing each other in pairs, squatting on their hindquarters. One of these holds a key—that of the rice granary—in his mouth, and the other a ball representing the spirit of the Goddess of Food.

In the minds of the masses, the fox has come to personify the God of Food. This belief is illustrated by the nature of the offerings which—with the exception of rice—consist of foodstuffs made with fat or oil, for which the animal has a particularly soft spot. Folklore abounds in tales portraying the omnipotence of the fox. One of its main attributes is supposedly the power of creating mirages, and transforming itself at will into any object or being whatsoever. If it lives to the age of fifty, it may assume the guise of a woman; at one hundred years of age, that of an enchanting maiden who plays all sorts of abominable tricks on menfolk; at the age of a thousand it becomes the great celestial fox with golden fur and nine tails, who has discovered all the secrets of nature. The fox again is blamed for many a case of hysteria or bedevilment *(kitsune-tsuki)*. In the Izumo region on the north coast, to this day certain families are alleged to be possessed of a supernatural power *(kitsune-mochi)* acquired from the fox.

LEGENDARY BEASTS—Other animals are messengers of the gods, and revered as such, for example: the pigeon, in the numerous temples of Hachiman; the pheasant in Kita; the black falcon in Atago; the stag in the Kasuga of Nara, Kashima, and Itsukushima (or the Island of Miyajima); the monkey in the Kasuga again and in Kiyoshi; the rat, in temples dedicated to fortune; the boar in Atago; the tortoise in Matsuo and Hikami-yama; the eel in the Temple of Mishima.

HOKUSAI
Japanese Tortoise and Eel

The wolf, which has almost vanished today, is an object of worship in remote and mountainous districts, where it is invoked to help mankind protect the harvest from pillaging by other wild beasts. As for the crow, it is the messenger of the gods in the Temples of Suwa, Hiyoshi, and above all Kumano, where it was said to have acted as guide to the first Emperor of Japan, Jimmu-Tenno, when the latter went astray in the mountains. On the other hand, this bird is inclined to be unpopular, for when it caws on the roof that is a sign of death in the house; and when crows assemble in flocks in the fields to caw at nightfall, they herald calamity for the region.

HIROSHIGE—*Cranes Flying over the Inland Sea near Wakano-ura*

The badger also plays an important role in folklore. Whilst it, too, plays tricks on human-beings, it is by no means as wicked as the fox. One of its occupations consists of drumming on its stomach at full moon. The entrance to many a restaurant is guarded by a model of a badger, with a

263

flask of *sake* swinging from one paw, a wide straw hat on its head, and a portly abdomen—a symbol of prosperity in the Far East. In popular speech the expression *"furu-danuki"*—old badger—is often used to denominate a crafty man.

The cat—*neko*—was apparently unknown in Japan until the Emperor Ichijo-Tenno introduced it by way of China in the 10th century. It brought with it the burden of a murky past, being credited with the malefic power of transforming itself into a woman after putting one to death. But its evil reputation would appear to date back even further, for—so the legend runs—when all the animals gathered round Buddha's deathbed, the snake and the cat alone failed to show any signs of emotion. The scorn in which the cat is held is expressed in the saying: *"neko-ni koban"*, meaning literally "coins to a cat". This animal was never utilized in ancient art, with the exception of the famous "sleeping cat" *(nemuri-neko)* sculptured for the mausoleum of Nikko in the 17th century by the great artist Hidari Jingoro. In modern times it would appear to have retrieved its popularity, the doorways of small restaurants and bars being frequently ornamented with porcelain models of cats, invariably represented with one paw raised (usually the left), to beckon passers-by. Cats with fur of white, black, and brown *(mike-neko)*, are particularly appreciated for the solidity of their skins which are used as sound-boxes for samisens—the three-string Japanese guitar; they are also in great demand as mascots for seafarers.

The stork—*tsuru*—which is confused throughout Asia with the crane, and the tortoise—*kame*—are probably the most highly cherished animals in Japan, and the ones most frequently utilized in Japanese decorative art, both of them being considered the perfect emblems of long life and happiness. In China the stork is the patriarch of the birds and the messenger of the Taoist gods. On reaching the age of 600 years, it can live on water alone—or so the legend would have it. As for the tortoise, it appears in the most ancient legends of India and China. The origin of Chinese characters is attributed to a study of the lines on its shell; moreover, soothsayers still use tortoiseshells to decipher the signs of the future. At the age of 500 years, the tortoise is covered in a long cloak of aquatic plants. One of the seven divinities of happiness, Fukurokuju—the God of Longevity—always has either a tortoise or a stork at his side. In addition, the good wishes offered on the occasion of a marriage often include the following proverb: *"Tsuru sen-nen, kame man-nen"*, meaning: "A thousand years for the stork, ten thousand for the tortoise."

The nightingale—*ugisu*—and the cuckoo—*hoto-togisu*—are beloved of the poets. The song of the nightingale, "*Ho-o-kekyo ....kekyo!*" reminds the Japanese of the name of the famous Buddhist sutra, the *hokke-kyo*. As for the cuckoo that speeds across the sky at dawn, it is looked upon as the messenger of the Kingdom of Shadows.

Butterflies — *chocho* — are regarded in Japan as the spirits of the living and the dead at one and the same time. Their presence heralds either the advent of a visitor, or the death of a friend or relation. On the other hand, in the exchange of drinking-bowls that takes place during the wedding ceremony, the long handle of the *sake* ladle is adorned with two butterflies, the emblems of a happy union. The Shinto Goddess of Food, Toyo-Uke-hime, wears a butterfly in her hair as a symbol of femi-

HIROSHIGE—*Mandarin Ducks*

265

ninity. By the same token, the horse is the symbol of masculine strength.

The firefly—*hotaru*—is the friend of impecunious students. Classical and folk literature alike abound in tales of young people reading by the light of these insects enclosed in a cage. At Ishiyama on the edge of Lake Biwa there is a solitary spot known as Firefly Valley, the very name of which has lured innumerable melancholic lovers to commit suicide there together, despairing of their thwarted passion.

The mandarin duck—*oshidori*—is the symbol of perfect happiness, since the male and female always swim side by side. Its name is often used to designate a tenderly united couple. Lafcadio Hearn relates the following pathetic story: A poor peasant by the name of Sonjo one day caught sight of a pair of ducks swimming at Akanuma and, feeling hungry, he killed one of them and ate it. The following night he was awakened by an apparition of a beautiful young woman who weepingly said to him: "Next time you pass by Akanuma, you will see something." Without any further explanation, she vanished as abruptly as she had appeared. Wandering beside the water one day, Sonjo saw a solitary duck swimming there. Suddenly it drove its beak into its breast, and expired. Stricken with remorse, Sonjo shaved his head and took the cowl.

The carp—*koi*—is respected in China and Japan as the emblem of perseverance that overcomes every obstacle. Chinese tales relate that certain fish swim up the Yellow River and attempt to cross the dread rapids of Lung-Men, the Dragon's Gate. The carp that succeed are alleged to become dragons themselves. On the occasion of the boys' festival on the fifth day of the fifth month, it is the custom to fly enormous carps of paper or cloth from immense bamboo poles, where they flutter vigorously in the breeze, symbolizing the courage that the male child of the household will have to display throughout life.

FROM THE PHOENIX TO THE SIREN—The catfish—*namazu*—introduces us to the wealth of folklore woven round more or less mythical creatures. Superstition maintains that the islands of Japan lie on the back of a gigantic *namazu*, and that the abrupt movements of its body are the cause of the earthquakes.

Apart from the four divine animals endowed with supernatural power —the tiger (occasionally replaced by a kind of griffon with horses' hoofs), the phoenix, the tortoise, and the dragon—the mythical creatures most

Koi-nobori for the Boys' Festival

frequently described in folklore and popular art are the *tengu* and the *kappa*. The *tengu* haunts the wild mountains. It has a flattened head with an enormous beak or a very long nose, eyes flashing like lightning, a squat, winged body, and limbs terminating in claws. Although the *tengu* plays tricks on mankind, it also helps those who have to take refuge in the depths of the mountains. The *kappa* is an amphibious creature haunting the rivers and lakes. It has a round head crowned with long, tousled hair, a childlike, prognathous face, and a bluish complexion; its back is covered with a tortoiseshell, whilst its feet are webbed and prolonged by sharp claws. It attacks men, and above all children, while bathing, and is held responsible for inexplicable cases of drowning.

As befits an insular country, Japan boasts a whole host of legends about the *ningyo*, a kind of mermaid. A constantly recurring theme is that of a dead siren whose body, washed up on the shore, was the omen of calamity.

In order to chase away evil dreams, the Japanese place under their pillows a piece of paper with a picture of the *baku*, or with only the name written on it. This extraordinarily shaped beast is somewhat like the tapir in appear-

ance. According to folkloric traditions, it is capable of crushing iron or stones with its jaws, and needless to say the most terrifying dreams are powerless to resist it.

To conclude our study of animals we should mention those strange stone "lions" that are found in front of Shinto temples. Depending on their shape, they are known either as *kara-shishi*, Chinese lions, or *koma-inu*, Korean dogs, which gives a clear indication of their origin. In ancient China it was customary to place these stone lions on guard outside the entrances to residences or tombs.

THE SEVEN GODS OF HAPPINESS—Schichi-Fuku-Jin—whose temples are to be found throughout Japan, represent an extremely tardy popular personalization of numerous religious currents that developed in Japan: primitive Shintoism, Chinese Taoism, and Hindu Buddhism. At this stage it is impossible to fathom their respective contributions, and still less the origin of the seven gods. The two most popular ones, Daikoku and Ebisu, appear to be slightly more Japanese than the five others, in which Hindu and Chinese influences are mingled. Be this as it may, no reference to this group of divinities has been traced prior to the 17th century. History relates that the Shogun Tokugawa Iemitsu one day had a discussion with the wise bonze Tenkai, in the course of which the latter assured him that the seven cardinal graces were: longevity, fortune, popularity, candour, amiability, dignity, and magnanimity. Subsequently, Tenkai commissioned an artist of the great Kano family to paint a picture on this theme. Such was allegedly the origin of the popular representations and literature regard-

HOKUSAI—*Hotei*

268

ing the Seven Gods of Happiness. We shall describe them in the approximate order of their popularity in Japan.

Daikoku, representing fortune, rests—as already mentioned—on two balls of rice; on his back he bears the sack of riches and in his hand he holds the mallet that procures precious metals. Ebisu, the personification of candour, is

HOKUSAI—*Daikoku*

also one of the pre-eminent fetishes in this country where—in addition to rice—the basic food is fish, for he holds a fishing-rod in one hand and an enormous bream *(tai)* under his left arm. Ebisu is thus the patron saint of fishmongers and small traders. He is even entitled to a festival of his own, Ebisu-ko, celebrated throughout the country on 20th October. Hotei, the symbol of magnanimity, is as plump and jovial as the other two. He is clad in a monastic gown opening to reveal an extensive stomach, and holds a fan—the mark of authority—in his hand. He is usually seated, propped against an enormous treasure sack that has the magic power of remaining full to the brim however much one delves inside it. Benten, personifying amiability, is the sole feminine character in the group. She allegedly corresponds to Sarasvati, the Hindu Goddess of Beauty, Music, and Eloquence. She is represented in the guise of a beautiful woman, kneeling and playing the *biwa*, a four-stringed Japanese lute. Her head is crowned with a diadem adorned with snakes, hence her legendary reputation for jealousy. Benten's temples are always situated on islands, the most famous being at Enoshima, near Kamakura, at Itsukushima (or Miyajima), and at Bentenjima, near Lake Biwa. Fukurokuju is the symbol of popularity, being reputedly capable of accomplishing as much good as the six other gods together. His name is also a sure guarantee of well-being, since it signifies: happiness *(fuku)*, wealth *(roku)*, and longevity *(ju)*. Some claim he is the Chinese philosopher Lao-tse. He is always accompanied by a stork, the bird that can live a thousand years. This god is rather comical in appearance in that, whilst he is portrayed in the guise of a dignified old man with a long white beard, he has a bald head shaped like a sugar-loaf, as big as the rest of his body. Jurojin is the God of Longevity. He has occasionally been confused with the preceding god, being also represented as an old man. This divinity is probably the Japanese version of the Chinese God of the Pole Star. He holds the sage's dragon-headed staff, from which hangs the scroll on which all the knowledge of the world is inscribed. Beside him stands the large black stag that has lived to the age of two thousand years. Bishamon is the image of dignity. He is probably derived from a Hindu god, Vaisravana, who has become one of the four guardians to be found in every Buddhist temple in Japan. He is depicted in the guise of a warrior clad in Chinese fashion and shod with flabby boots. With his left hand he leans on a long halberd with which he protects Buddhism, symbolized by a sacred pagoda held in his right hand and raised to shoulder-level.

The "treasure-ship"—*takara-bune*—that sails into port on the first of the year, is inseparably linked with the Seven Gods of Happiness. It is on sale everywhere at that period and, according to tradition, if you place a picture of this ship under your pillow on the night of 2nd January you are sure to have happy dreams. This mascot is popularly represented in a variety of forms. Sometimes it is boarded by the seven gods. Or else it contains, in whole or in part, the twenty-one "precious-objects"—*takara-mono*—of which the main ones are: the key to the rice granary, the inexhaustible purse, the lucky raincoat, the scroll of precious scriptures, the mallet of fortune, bales of brocade, an oblong coin, the pearl that fulfills desires, the anchor of security, the coral that protects one against unlucky influences, the fairies' feather-dress, sweet-smelling cloves, a weight implying prosperous transactions, the fruit of the lucky tree *(tachibana)*, and the wide hat made of rushes that renders the wearer invisible.

In between houses, at crossroads, in the middle of the woods or mountains, one often comes across the effigy of a young bonze with a pilgrim's staff in his hand. Some of these statues are sheltered in an alcove, others are exposed to the elements. They represent Jizo, the most kind-hearted and likable of all the gods in this country where divinities abound. Originally

OKUMURA MASANOBU—*Jizo Helping to Plant Out Rice*

he was the Hindu Ksiti-garbha, who became the saviour of people in danger, and above all of dead children. Statues of Jizo are frequently adorned with bibs, bearing the name of a child and offered by a mother who was worried about her infant's health. It is also the custom for certain statues of Jizo to be covered with small stones, recalling the Buddhist belief whereby after their death children run the risk of being seized on the river-banks in the world beyond and compelled to pile up stones until they are high enough to reach Paradise. These offerings of stones are destined to help the children in their task.

NATURE—In a country as mountainous as Japan, it is not surprising to find stones and rocks round which cults dating back to the distant past are centred. Such stones—long or round as the case may be—are still seen standing in the countryside and even in towns, at crossroads or on street corners, and are probably relics of ancient Phallic cults.

271

There are also "living stones"—*iki-ishi*—generally of the same shape as those mentioned above, which have the power of giving birth to other stones. Hence the belief that contact with these stones may make a woman fertile; also the custom of attempting to hit the top of porticos or the great lanterns in front of temples with these stones, in order to win the favour of the gods.

It is easy to understand that in an atmosphere such as this, where legends and traditions have kept the belief in so many divine beings and deified objects so intensely alive, the Japanese should be constantly in quest of ways and means of reconciling themselves with their divinities.

Jizo

IN THE TEMPLES—It is interesting to note that in addition to offering prayers to Shinto or Buddhist gods, visitors to temples rarely leave without having their fortune told. There are two methods of procedure: either, in special cases, by requesting a priest to invoke the gods on one's behalf; or, more frequently, by shaking an oblong box found in front of every shrine, and extracting from the opening provided for that purpose one of the fifty or hundred small sticks it contains. Each of these sticks is inscribed with a number. At the entrance to the temple, in exchange for a coin an attendant or acolyte standing beside a chest of numbered pigeon-holes hands the inquirer the written oracle—*o-mikuji*—corresponding to the number drawn. The paper first mentions whether the oracle is favourable or unfavourable, then continues with advice on business, journeys, the direction in which one should travel, threats of illness, lost objects, and unexpected encounters. On the same paper, good or bad luck may depend on the age or sex of the inquirer. In the event that the oracle is generally unfavourable, the visitor has a chance of getting out of the fix simply by ridding himself of the paper; but it cannot be thrown anywhere: it must be attached to the trees or palings round the shrines.

Another widespread custom is to bring back a charm—*o-mamori*—from the temple, usually in the form of a piece of wood or cardboard engraved with the name of a god or shrine. Dependent on its size, it is worn on one's person or placed in the house in a traditional spot. This desire for charms often serves as a pretext for long journeys or pilgrimages to temples particularly renowned for the efficiency of their protection. The most popular are the Temples of Kishibojin or Jizo for children, Hachiman for soldiers, Suitengu for sailors, Kumano for longevity, Fudo against accidents, Mitsumine against thieves, Inari for merchants. In the house, these charms are placed as the case may be on the entrance door, in the kitchen, in rooms or outbuildings that the inmates particularly want to protect, or lastly, on the altar of the household gods that one finds in the majority of households. Apart from gifts of money to temples, offerings consist mainly of fruit, vegetables, and *mochi*. They also include branches of the sacred tree of Shinto, the *sakaki*. In certain special cases and on the occasion of great festivals, Kagura dances are performed in the shrine by consecrated maidens known as *miko*—"children of the gods". These dances, like the reading of *norito*—invocations and acts of grace to the Shinto gods—always recall the legendary incident whereby Amaterasu shut herself in a grotto. Another extremely frequent offering consists of a small rectangular or pentagonal board known as an *ema*, on the back of which is inscribed the date, name, and age of the donor, and sometimes a special request on his behalf. Throughout the centuries an infinite number of motifs recurs, but the most customary are: a horse—*uma* (from which the object derives its name); people praying; an ox; a pair of foxes; the beasts of the Zodiac; a part of the sick body—particularly the hands or feet—or something suggestive of the disease; a graphic representation of a vow or desire; the description of an accident or some dramatic episode; or simply a list of people wishing to place themselves under the protection of the gods.

How to know one's Fortune ....

273

ARCHITECTURE

In 1890 Basil Hall Chamberlain, with thoughts of the Parthenon and Salisbury Cathedral, wrote: "The Japanese genius touches perfection in small things. No other nation ever understood half so well how to make a cup, a tray, even a kettle—a thing of beauty, how to transform a little knob of ivory into a microcosm of quaint humour, how to express a fugitive thought in half-a-dozen dashes of the pencil. The massive, the spacious, the grand, is less congenial to their mental attitude. Hence they achieve less success in architecture than in the other arts. The prospect of a Japanese city from a height is monotonous. Not a tower, not a dome, not a minaret, nothing aspiring heavenward, save in rare cases a painted pagoda half-hidden amidst the trees which it barely tops—nothing but long, low lines of thatch and tiles, even the Buddhist temple roofs being but moderately raised above the rest, and even their curves being only quaint and graceful, nowise imposing."

This description is still valid up to a point, despite the addition of immense modern buildings—department stores, factories, offices, hotels—as much as ten or eleven storeys high. Foreign travellers are often struck by the monotony—not to say depression—of the overpopulated, tentacular towns. But it should not be forgotten that Japan was terribly disfigured by systematic fires and air raids throughout the last war, from which only Kyoto, Nara, and two or three smaller towns emerged intact, and that rebuilding has been carried out with makeshift materials.

Harmony of Natural Setting and Materials—One factor to be constantly borne in mind is that architectural efforts are conditioned and limited by geographic considerations. Walled by steep slopes, driven back into narrow valleys and the rare plains bordering the sea, at the mercy of earthquakes, typhoons, and floods, the Japanese have worked wonders with the terrain and the simple building materials at their disposal. The very nature of the mountainous relief has made it impossible—or at least too costly—to open quarries sufficiently large to permit extensive building in stone. This material was necessarily reserved for the mighty walls of moats and the foundations of castles. As a result, Japan is perhaps the only civilized country never to have known fortified towns. On the other hand, our age of reinforced concrete is witnessing an onslaught of new buildings—limited in height, of course, on account of earthquakes—worthy to rank with those of the most modern towns. Apart from this recent introduction of concrete, materials have been limited to wood, bamboo, reeds, straw, earth, and sand.

It is difficult for anyone who has never visited Japan to imagine the degree of elegance and balance attained by the use of these extremely simple materials. It is even more difficult to furnish an adequate description. But before going any further we should delve into the past, in order to place the Japanese dwelling in its historic perspective.

In the protohistoric era there existed a primitive type of hut, built on a space hollowed out of the soil. The framework—originally round in shape—consisted of a series of unpeeled tree-trunks planted slantwise in the earth and joining at the ridge, where they were held in place by withes made of lianas and branches of wild wistaria. The roof was made of thick layers of rush or bark sloping right down to the soil, with an exterior gutter scooped out at the base to drain away rain water. The shrines for Shinto

Buildings in Tokyo

spirits, like the homes of high-ranking officials, were more elaborate. They consisted of rectangular structures built on piles and further heightened by walls, as yet very simple in design, made of woven rushes or logs. The roof terminated in a long round ridge-beam, held in place by the furthest beams of the pinions, which jutted out like two pairs of horns. From the front, the entire roof was shaped like a very wide-mouthed hour-glass. The ancient style noble homes and temples may be reconstructed quite accurately thanks to small-scale terracotta models found in tombstones dating from the first centuries A.D. This primitive form has been preserved in all its purity in certain great shrines—those of Ise, Atsuta in Nagoya, Izumo, Kashiwara, or Meiji and Yasukuni in Tokyo for instance—as well as the roofs of certain peasant houses such as those in the Kyoto region.

THE VARIOUS STYLES—Owing to the constant changes of residence at each new accession, the development of architecture was retarded until 712, when the capital was stabilized in Nara for a time. The massive influx of the T'ang civilization from China was reflected in the building of numerous Buddhist temples, the architecture of which in turn influenced that of the Shinto temples and stately homes.

In the subsequent Heian era (8th to 12th century), the temples became more pleasant in appearance, influenced by the development of the Jodo sect—and in a way opposed to the severe grandeur imposed by the mystic Tendai and Shingon sects. The gracefulness of the period was expressed in immense palaces comprising rectangular buildings linked by galleries and forming a unit closed on three sides and opening to the south. Within lay a garden round an irregularly shaped lake dotted with rocks in imitation of islands, to break the monotony.

The latter style, named *shinden-zukuri*, underwent an evolution during the Kamakura period (1186–1392), when residences for the warrior classes began to develop. Buildings in this new style—*buke-zukuri*—were no longer spread out, all the rooms being grouped beneath one roof or row of roofs. Housetops were covered with thatch or strips of cypress bark in thick layers, tiles being reserved for temples and castles.

Introduction of the *shoin-zukuri* style in the Muromachi era (1393–1572) saw the development and subsequent stylization of most of the basic elements of the Japanese house as we now know it. First of all, towards the end of the 15th century *tatami* began to take the place of planks adorned with cushions. Then the entrance doorway, or *genkan*, came into use. It consisted of two parts, the exterior being made of beaten earth or flagstones protected by an overhanging roof, the interior made of wood and elevated. This provided a convenient place for removing one's footwear before entering the passages beyond. During this same period, the use of sliding screens between rooms became increasingly widespread. These *fusuma*, as they were called, consisted of thick white paper stretched across an interior framework of light wood, and decorated with paintings. Lastly came the *tokonoma*, a wide alcove designed to highlight some rare object or painting hung on the wall in the background. If space permitted this alcove was flanked by sets of shelves of varying height and length, known as *chigai-dana*.

Zen Buddhism, with its discipline of detachment from material contingencies that had been developing since the 13th century, was to maintain the tendency towards simplicity and unadorned elegance in the arrangement and decoration of rooms. It should not be forgotten that Zen is still at the

HIROSHIGE—*House-building near Yoshida Bridge*

root of such wonderful demonstrations of harmony and equilibrium between man and nature as the tea ceremony, floral decoration, and landscape gardening.

HARMONY OF PROPORTIONS—Never having utilized stone as a building medium proper, Japanese architecture is oblivious of the problems of vaults, flying buttresses, or stonework in general. Stability is achieved by distributing the weight of the roof on the elements of the framework, which in turn are balanced on a few vertical pillars supported by wide, flat stones placed flush with the soil. The walls are merely screens filling the gaps between pillars and indicating the exterior or interior limits of a section of habitable space.

Even the most *blasé* observer cannot fail to be impressed by the pleasant proportions of Japanese roofs which blend perfectly with the surrounding countryside. The outline of their slopes, in harmony with the hills and mountains, is much less arched, more balanced, and less blatant than that of Chinese roofs. The grey-blue hue of the tiles and the infinite variety of

Typical Japanese Interior

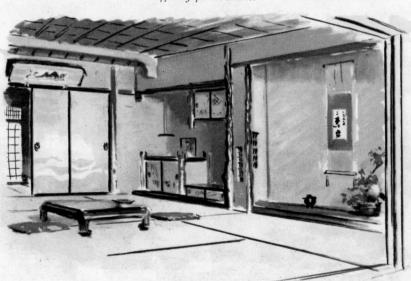

browns offered by thatch, rush, or cypress bark harmonize with the Japanese landscape, where greens and browns predominate. On account of the rather rainy climate and the fragility of the partition material, the roof projects quite a long way beyond the building, but it is so calculated as to allow the winter sun to penetrate right into the middle of the rooms, which are generally oriented towards the south. For the same reason, there are no flat roofs, apart from those on reinforced concrete buildings in towns.

"Kura"—Fireproof Building

CARPENTRY—Throughout the centuries the Japanese have developed an extraordinary liking for unstained wood, which one does not come across in any other country. To be convinced of this, one has only to observe the way a carpenter planes and polishes a single piece of wood for hours on end. In sawing up wood intended for building, a master-carpenter worthy of the name meticulously takes into account the "back" and the "front" of a trunk. In regard to trees that have grown in the plains, the part exposed to the sun and boasting the most vigorous branches is the "back", whilst the part exposed to the shade, and thus of inferior quality, is the "front". As for trees grown on the mountainside, the "back" is the part facing the open air, and the "front" is the one facing the slope. Nor does a carpenter ever forget that each piece of wood has a "top" and a "bottom", the first being nearer the bark and the second nearer the core. All these details are important, since wood tends to curve towards the "top"; moreover, on account of the sliding doors it is necessary to calculate exactly the play in both the upper and lower frameworks, to make sure the panels glide with ease.

ORIENTATION—In the whole of the Far East, the health and prosperity of the family depend on the careful construction and orientation of their home. Although faithful to their innate taste for simplicity of line, the Japanese have been profoundly influenced by Chinese traditions in regard to good or ill-omened "directions". Thus, according to ancient works, the ideal site for a house should have: on the left—to the east—a river, symbolizing the "green dragon"; on the right—to the west—a long road, the "white tiger"; opposite—to the south—a pond, suggesting a phoenix; and lastly, behind—to the north—a hill, representing a tortoise in the coils of a snake. These animals are the symbols of the Buddhist divinities protecting the four points of the compass. Tradition emphasizes that the perfect solution is to live in a house with sloping ground in front and a hill behind. On the other hand, it is dangerous to be at the summit of a hill with slopes on all sides.

Thus before beginning to build a house, one should first draw a plan, taking care that the centre lies at the intersection of two imaginary lines drawn obliquely from north-east to south-west and from north-west to south-east. The north-east is called *ki-mon*, or the devil's gateway; one should therefore take care not to build anything impure in that corner. The south-east is the *chi-mon*,

A Village in the North

gateway to the earth, or *fu-mon*, gateway to the wind. The north-west is the *ten-mon*, gateway to the sky, where one should dig the well and build the *kura*, a square white building, with narrow windows, and fireproof,

281

owing to the thickness of its walls, in which the household valuables are stored. The south-west, between the gateways of heaven and earth, is the *jin-mon*—man's gateway. Such customs may be considered mere superstitions, but it is a fact that they are often based on careful observation of atmospheric currents and climatic conditions demanding protection against the winds and storms from Siberia and Manchuria. This explains why, since ancient times, the emperors have always faced southwards, and the entrances to temples have always been oriented towards the south, apart from a few rare exceptions when the terrain made this impossible. The importance attached to "directions" is such that when illness frequently recurs in a house, the occupants often have recourse to a soothsayer to find out how to modify the orientation and disposition of the rooms.

CONSTRUCTION—Once the plan has been finally drawn up, four immense bamboos, complete with branches, are erected at the corners of the site, and linked by long narrow cords of woven rice straw, decorated with strips of white paper cut out in ritual fashion. These very simple decorations recall the *shimenawa* that are stretched across Shinto temples and porticos, and from which the *gohei* hang. They would seem to be reminiscent of objects utilized to indicate ancient spots that were hallowed or "taboo". Be that as it may, Shinto tradition regards them as essential accessories of the cult, since they recall the legendary episode of the cord stretched across the grotto where the Sun Goddess, Amaterasu, hid herself one day, and the strips of cloth hung on the *sakaki*, or sacred tree, to lure the goddess out of hiding.

But let us return to our house. A Shinto priest has been asked to bless the plot. A temporary altar, in the form of a light rush framework, has been erected right in the centre and adorned with *sake* bowls and branches of sakaki, decorated with gohei. After reading a *norito* to please the gods, the priest blesses the four points of the compass by rapidly shaking a branch of sakaki three times. Everything is now ready for the work to commence.

There is neither cellar nor foundations. The soil is simply levelled to the required dimensions, and compressed slightly. Then, on the spot where the few master-pillars are to be erected, large flat unhewn stones are driven very lightly into the soil. Meanwhile the carpenters have bevelled and polished the pillars, which are generally square and hewn as near the core as possible. These are then erected on the stones, and held in place at the top and foot by long poles, normally square or rectangular, or occasionally round, finished with dovetails or mortises. We now have a rectangle solidly balanced laterally and vertically. In the meantime, parts of the framework of the roof—such as the triangular elements forming the gables—have been assembled on the ground. If the units are too heavy, they are dismantled and then placed in position on the framework mentioned above; but as often as

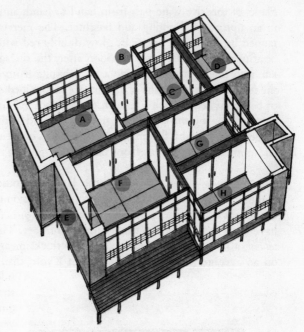

PLAN OF A JAPANESE HOUSE
A–*Bedroom*. B–*Entrance*. C–*Pantry*.
D–*Kitchen*. E–*Tokonoma*. F–*Sitting-room*. G–*Bedroom*. H–*Bedroom*

not the roof is hoisted up as is, and attached to the framework by tenons and mortises. The long beam forming the ridge is then set in place, and the skeleton of the building is thus completed.

This is the signal for a ritual festival to celebrate the "erection of the ridge", or *mune-age*. At nightfall, when the day's work is over, a great blaze of chips and wood-shavings is kept going in the very centre of the house under construction. Around it, on makeshift seats made from future elements of the framework, sit the master-carpenters and their assistants —in order of importance—clad in smocks of coarse blue or black cotton, with the name of their firm on the facings and in large characters on the back. The feast is offered by the builder, who never forgets the *sake*.

Flasks of this rice wine pass from hand to hand, and bowls are exchanged in an uproar of shouting and laughter. The merrymakers' faces, already tanned by life in the open air, glow doubly red with the reflection of the bonfire and heat of the spirits. Soon after, the singsong begins, continuing late into the night, to provide a brief respite from a life of toil in which the finest traditions of the craftsman are maintained. We have recollections of being invited to such a feast that took place in Kamakura one day when we were passing through the region. At the end of the festivities one of the carpenters—with his feet in the shavings and a bowl in his hand—declaimed and mimed an entire play from the classical puppet theatre repertoire!

THE INTERIOR—The interior of the Japanese house is the most perfect combination of daintiness and balance, the precision of proportion between the height and width of the rooms resulting from century-old canons that have been put to the test time without number. The basic measure is the *tatami*, a mat approximately two inches thick, measuring 6 feet by 3 feet on an average (being slightly larger in Kyoto than Tokyo). The reverse side is made of crude rice straw, woven to the required size, on which a very fine mat of woven rushes is stretched. The two longer sides are bordered by cotton or linen braid about one inch wide, usually black, dark blue, or brown in colour, contrasting pleasantly in line and tone with the yellowish-green mats. The size of a room is expressed in numbers of mats. The most usual dimensions are six, eight,

Façade of Dwelling-house

When the shoji are open, the sun streams in . . . .

or ten mats, whilst the exactly square rooms where the tea ceremony takes place measure four mats and a half. The *tsubo*, a unit for measuring plots of ground, represents the surface of two mats.

General use of *tatami* in the 15th century brought about a near-revolution. It was this that made the Japanese adopt their unique fashion of kneeling with their loins resting on their tucked-in feet. Their clothing was changed: whereas it previously consisted of two parts, for men and women alike it became simplified to a single long gown with floating sleeves—the kimono—wrapping from left to right. Even Japanese gardens, which developed after the 14th century, are designed in such a manner that the best way of admiring and understanding them is in a kneeling position. Last but not least, in a country that has become as over-populated as present-day Japan, the *tatami* serves an infinite variety of purposes. Any room whatsoever may be immediately converted into a dining-room by placing a low, light table and a few cushions in it, and the table may subsequently be pushed back against the wall, in the passage, to be replaced by rows of padded mattresses taken out of cupboards concealed in the screens. We ourselves have occasionally shared rooms such as this with as many people as there were mats.

The *tokonoma*, or alcove, raised about four inches higher than the mats, is generally a little over three feet deep and six to nine feet wide. It is the only decorated spot in a room, and one may well imagine how a single object—whether a painting or a vase of flowers—is set off to best advantage by the surrounding space. As for the height of the rooms, it averages about eight feet.

We have already mentioned the interior partitions—*fusuma*—between the rooms, sliding sideways on grooves in the upper and lower beams between the pillars. These partitions are nearly always four in number. *Fusuma* also serve to conceal spaces intentionally left alongside the walls, to contain bedding, cushions, and other objects that might otherwise clutter the rooms.

The external walls of the rooms leading to passages or directly out into the open air consist of squares of white paper stretched and glued to a light wooden trellis. Although translucent, these *shoji*—as they are called— filter a gentle, subdued light into the room, harmonizing with the warm tones of the wood, the white or cream-coloured *fusuma*, and the yellowish mats.

The walls, four or five inches thick, are built round a framework of narrow strips of bamboo-cane criss-crossed and held together with straw cords, thickly coated with several layers of earth tempered with finely chopped rice straw. The entire surface is then whitewashed or plastered. The inner side is often covered with a darker coat composed of sand or clay to which a seaweed compound has been added as a binding material.

WOODWORK—But it is in woodwork that the ingenuity and sense of refinement of the Japanese really comes to the fore. The scope ranges from the largest wooden building in the world—the cathedral, some 200 feet high, housing the great Buddha of Nara—to the minutest toothpick or a tiny *netsuke* on which an entire scene has been carved in the space of an inch or two. The supreme achievement of the Japanese is his house, in which the majority of elements are held together by the cut-joint method, without the help of nails. The best buildings are made of cedar, cypress, cryptomeria, or pine wood. This apparently fragile material was used for

A Garden

all the ancient temples that have
been towering over the region
of Nara for the past 1,300 years.
In order to enhance certain
details, the wood used for the
tokonoma, the ceilings, and the
upper part of the *fusuma* is
planed, polished, or rubbed
with sand, so as to bring out a
curious grain, a sinuous vein, or even a mere knot. In some cases, the
roundness or the curve of a trunk is retained; in others, a panel is flattened
by an irregular—and seemingly casual—stroke of the adze, in order to
reveal a delicate filigree of veins. And above all, it should be emphasized
that, as in so many other objects, the wood used in housebuilding is never
painted or varnished, and every attempt is made to preserve a natural
appearance.

VENTILATION—The most frequent criticism put forward by foreigners
sensitive to chilliness, or accustomed to rooms enclosed within thick walls
with narrow openings, is that the Japanese house is ill-protected against

the cold. The answer to this is that when it is not hot, the climate is still mild and relatively damp during the major part of the year. Hence the advantage of using wood, paper, and straw, which absorb a large proportion of this humidity.

GARDENS—The Japanese garden represents one of the finest creations of mankind and one of the most satisfying, having made Nature its ally. From childhood our Western eyes are formed—not to say deformed—by a conception of nature expressed in the most rigorous way imaginable by classical flower-beds in which the plants and trees—curved, clipped and transformed into animals or other set shapes—have nothing plant-like about them.

We should at least grant the Japanese that, although some people find them weird and grotesquely twisted, their trees are trees for all that, such as one might find on any windswept slope, and not imitations of peacocks. When the Japanese adorns his garden with a rock, it is merely to resemble a distant mountain, an island or a stone polished by a torrent, and not, as in China or elsewhere, some monstrous beast bristling with horns or claws. When he uses flowers, it is simply to introduce a dash of unexpected colour, such as one finds in nature in the corner of a wood or beside a brook, and not to create a blinding red or yellow mass.

Enclosed within the stifling prison of his islands fraught with tortured mountains, the Japanese has freed himself with one fell stroke. Whilst he has left his imprint on the landscape, he has also enlisted its aid. In the Ryuan-ji or "Temple where the Dragon Reposes", girt by the delightful 500-year-old Zen garden on the outskirts of Kyoto, the Japanese has expressed infinity and eternity in a flat space limited to 1,900 square feet. There, in two tombs of coarse-grained white sand and fifteen irregular stones of which only fourteen are visible at a glance, the philosopher-gardener has succeeded in illustrating this eternal thought:

"The Universe, a grain of sand; a crystal drop, the Sea."

FLORAL ART

IKEBANA, the art of "Live Flowers", is practised in every walk of life in Japan. It lies within the reach of peasants and aesthetes alike. As a refinement to feminine education, it is even taught to women factory workers during their leisure hours. In our time as many as twenty thousand professors of the art of making bouquets have been counted in Tokyo alone.

Landscape gardening, which the Japanese have brought to a fine art, is discussed at greater length elsewhere. At this stage, suffice it to say that since the Middle Ages they have demonstrated their deep love of plants by strictly adhering to complicated rules of aesthetics in garden design. Whilst trees occupy the place of honour, a gardener can put as much skill into arranging rocks and flowers as a painter in setting out the paints on his palette.

The natural consequence of this open-air art is that of floral decoration. This again is subjected to a rigorous and impressive ceremonial that originated in Buddhist temples, where bonzes used to represent the synthesis of a landscape by arranging immense sheaves of branches and flowers in

tiers, to form what was known as a *Rikka*, on the occasion of festivals or commemoration services in temples and palaces. These floral works were reproduced in the 17th and 18th centuries by painters whose albums and scrolls bore annotations indicating the place, date, and donor of the *Rikka* in question.

The extremely numerous styles of arranging flowers and adapting them to ornament houses are divided into schools. These are all derived from a fundamental school, the Ikenobo, established in the Rokkakudo Temple in Kyoto, which awards the necessary certificates to professionals.

The aim of Ikebana is to create something which reconstructs the vital impulse of plant growth. All the stems must be joined at a single point making a perfectly balanced line. Crossing of branches is strictly forbidden.

The bouquet forms a triangle, made up of three slender sheaves of unequal length. The highest one symbolizes the sky, the middle sheaf Man, and the lowest one, the Earth. The arrangement is based on an extremely limited quantity of stems or branches: always an odd number, and most frequently three or five. The main concern is to follow proportions in keeping with those in nature, with their infinite variations.

One must thus avoid symmetry, yet at the same time obey the rules of harmony which forbid the separation of the iris from its leaves, for instance, or the use of such and such a plant out of season.

It is preferable to use flowers in bud, always with their own foliage.

The selection and pruning of branches, and the art of attaching them in flower-holders, requires long practice. The sole equipment consists of a pair of scissors with short blades and long handles, a knife, and possibly a small saw for the very big branches.

The technique of flower-holders—twigs, wooden pipes, lead spikes, or heavy lead rings—must first be acquired before one can hope to attain the precision essential to the purity of line and the harmony of such arrangements.

Modern schools, known as Moribana, utilize mixed bunches of flowers from abroad, and play with their varied hues. The

resultant bouquets, arranged in bowls placed on a table, form a three-dimensional effect that may be admired from all sides. The classical linear schools, on the other hand, design two-dimensional arabesques against a naked wall.

Ikebana calls for a wide variety of containers adapted to the character of the plants they are to display. Custom has successfully adopted bronze vessels, baskets, hanging vases, and chinaware to this end.

Even in decorating the home, symbolism may be sought. For instance, you would not place the same type of bouquet near a seascape as near a view of Mount Fuji. One may honour a saint by choosing his favourite flowers, and even compose a floral poem to extol the season or some happy event.

In Japan you will not find enormous bouquets in various rooms throughout the house, as in Western countries. The refined arrangement of a handful of flowers is reserved for the alcove—*tokonoma*—in the main room, where they are set off to best advantage. Isolated on a stand in the niche of honour, the bouquet becomes a presence, an eloquent poem. The visitor bows to it as he enters the room, even before greeting the master of the house.

DAILY FARE

RICE—In speaking of Japanese food, one immediately thinks of rice. In the earliest chronicles, Japan is in fact often called "Land of the lush plain of ears of rice", and consumption of this cereal has been said to date back to the Stone Age. Here, as in China, it is one of the five essential crops, together with wheat, barley, millet, and beans. Rice (and *sake*) are essential components of the sacred offerings at all ritual Shinto ceremonies or festivals. We should add that it is the origin of two of the most ancient national festivals: Kan-name-sai and Nii-name-sai. The sovereign himself cultivates a ricefield within the precincts of his palace, whilst the empress raises silkworms, thus setting their country the example of the essential labours of man and woman.

A few grains of rice are permanently offered on the *Kami-dana*, or Shinto altar to the household gods, to be found in the majority of homes. *Sekihan*, or red rice—so coloured through being cooked with red beans (*azuki*)—is invariably eaten to commemorate happy events, and certain families still observe the custom of preparing this dish on the 1st and 15th of each month. The famous round girdle-cakes known as *mochi* are also an established element of holiday fare.

It is customary to throw a handful of rice at random in a room where a child has suddenly woken up crying in the middle of the night. Such is doubtless the origin of the ceremony of scattering beans to drive away the evil spirits, that takes place in Shinto temples and homes on the occasion of the Setsubun festival, on the 3rd February.

It should be added that rice represents approximately three-quarters of the daily fare. Prior to the war, it constituted only 60 %. This increased consumption is a source of concern for dieticians, since the last quarter of a century has seen an increase in the use of machine-polished rice (*kaku-mai* or whitened rice), a treatment that removes not only the husk but also the germ. Now, it is in this germ that the precious vitamin B_1 is to be found (a deficiency of which is the chief cause of beriberi, a disease only too frequent in this country). Fortunately for some time now the authorities have been waging a campaign in favour of a return to unrefined rice or a mixture of this cereal with barley, prepared separately.

Rice should be cooked in a sufficient quantity of water so that by the

Eating Raw Fish

end of an hour over a moderate heat the grains have absorbed all the water, without adhering to each other. It is then dressed in numerous ways. The usual manner of serving it is by seasoning it with salted slices of turnip, cucumber, or pickled plums. At the end of the meal many Japanese like to pour hot tea on their remaining bowl of rice, in order to absorb the last grains more quickly and quench their thirst at the same time. This is known as *cha-zuke*. The mixture may be made tastier by adding a piece of fish, gratings of dried bonito, or a leaf of roasted seaweed. In summer, when heat deadens the appetite, *cha-zuke* is the pleasantest way of forcing oneself to eat and slaking one's thirst at the same time.

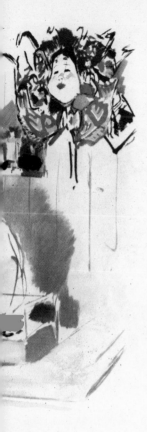

The most practical recipe for a cold meal or picnic lunch is *sushi*. It is prepared with rice to which vinegar and salt are added immediately after cooking. *Nigiri-zushi*, or pressed rice—particularly popular in Tokyo—is made by slicing-up rectangular blocks of rice and garnishing them with slivers of raw or cooked fish, boiled cuttle-fish, octopus, small lobsters, or other seafood; an even simpler formula consists of a riceball with a salted plum in the centre. To make *maki-zushi*, you place a handful of rice on a leaf of seaweed, garnish it with fish cut lengthwise and various finely chopped vegetables (the most common being *kampyo*, a kind of edible gourd, boiled and cut in strips), and roll all the ingredients into a fat sausage ready for slicing. As for *Inari-zushi*—Inari's *sushi*—it is composed of a riceball garnished with sesame seeds and lotus bulbs *(renkon)*, boiled and diced, coated with a paste made of fried beans *(abura-age)* and is the favourite dish of the fox, the messenger of the harvest god, Inari.

Then there is the whole gamut of *domburi*, consisting of large bowls of rice garnished with scrambled eggs *(tamago-domburi)*, or a mixture of scrambled eggs and pieces of boiled chicken *(oyako-domburi)*, skewered eels steeped in *shoyu* and braised *(unagi-domburi)*, and lastly, pieces of beef cooked with vegetables *(niku-domburi)*.

TRADITIONAL DISHES—In addition to rice, the staple food, we should now like to give the reader a general idea of specifically national dishes. In ancient times, like their fellow-men all over the world, the Japanese lived mainly on the produce of hunting and fishing and a few cultivated plants; apparently they did not eat beef or horsemeat, as the beasts concerned were rare and reserved for heavy labour. In the Nara era when Buddhism flourished, consumption of meat was practically prohibited, whereas agriculture—the cultivation of rice, barley, millet, sorghum, and beans—was encouraged. The majority of present-day dishes, such as *sashimi*—raw fish cut into moderately fine strips and steeped in a *shoyu* and horseradish sauce—date from the subsequent Heian era. Other popular dishes include *yaki-mono*—fish grilled over the embers; *ni-mono*—boiled vegetables or fish; *shiru-mono*—soup prepared with fermented bean paste and fish stock; *mushi-mono*—braised fish; *sushi*, described above; and lastly, Italian-type pastes including a kind of noodle *(udon)* and two kinds of vermicelli: *somen*, made of corn, and *soba*, made of buckwheat, prepared with thin fish stock.

CONDIMENTS—Another essential element of Japanese cooking is *miso*—soya bean paste. From the nutritive point of view, rice and Japanese *miso* have often been compared with Western bread and butter. *Miso* keeps indefinitely; it is used not only in making thick soups known as *miso-shiru*, but also in the preparation of all condiments of the pickle variety, instead of vinegar.

These condiments, or *tsuke-mono*, are in constant use. The most frequently utilized ingredient is *daikon*, a kind of horseradish a foot or more in length; next come egg-plant, cabbage, cucumber, and all sorts of other vegetables, with the exception of potatoes. Another popular condiment is *ume-boshi*—dried and salted plums. One of these, swallowed with boiling tea, is said to be able to cure any kind of intestinal disturbance or chill.

We have kept the most important condiment, inseparable from Japanese cooking—*shoyu*—until last. It is a liquid basically composed of soya beans, corn or barley, salt, and water. The corn is roasted and ground. After being boiled for three or four hours in huge, hermetically sealed cauldrons, the soya beans are

Greengrocer in Tokyo

left overnight. Next, the roasted corn powder is added, followed by malt
and salt water. The mixture is then left to ferment for a few days, being
stirred from time to time. It is subsequently pressed and strained, and the

finished product is then preserved in bottles or small kegs and distributed.

SEAFOOD—In an insular country like Japan, where the coasts are long and jagged and every inch of territory lies within sixty miles of the sea, fish and seafood of all kinds play a major role in daily fare. The great variety

available is partly due to the presence of both hot and cold marine currents.

Seafood is often eaten raw, salted, or dried naturally in the sun and the sea breeze. According to the way it is prepared, it is classified either as *yaki-zakana*—grilled fish (*sakana* means fish), or as *ni-zakana*—fish cooked with *shoyu*, sugar, or sweet *sake* (*mirin*), and then seasoned with various sauces, always with *shoyu* or fish stock as a basis, flavoured with grated horseradish, ginger, or simply a few drops of lemon and salt. *Su-no-mono* consists of pieces of fish, either raw or boiled, steeped in vinegar; it is particularly popular with *sake*.

Sashimi—raw fish—may be cut in various shapes, but always in thin slices. The most common fish are: bream (*tai*), tunny-fish (*maguro*), bonito (*katsuo*), sole (*hirame*), carp (*koi*), and molluscs; rarer varieties include shark (*same*), whale (*kujira*), and shellfish. These diverse types of raw fish are usually taken with *shoyu* sauce, seasoned with mustard or horse-radish.

The gamut of dried sea produce includes cuttle-fish (*ika*), sardines (*iwashi*), all sorts of small fish and various types of seaweed, of which the most common species are *nori*, a kind of sea moss, and *kombu*, a type of sea-tang.

We should also mention *kamaboko*, a fish paste sold in the form of sausages with a firm, whitish filling, cut into round slices; and *katsuo-bushi*, or bonito cut into four, boiled, and dried for weeks, until it looks and feels just like pieces of fossilized wood. Every household has a special plane for cutting slivers of this dried fish, as used

Façade of a Restaurant, by Night

in preparing soups and stock, which is used for preparing noodles or vermicelli, various vegetables, and the majority of sauces where *shoyu* is not employed.

VEGETABLES AND FRUIT—These are very varied, and often picturesque to a Westerner's eyes, providing an infinite variety of fancy ways of garnishing fish and meat dishes. In addition to mushrooms—some of which look like curious velvet flowers—seaweed, and bamboo shoots, traditional vegetables such as carrots, onions, potatoes, etc. are used, not to mention lotus, iris or lily bulbs, and the flowers and leaves of small chrysanthemums.

Japanese prints have familiarized us with spring landscapes, bright with orchards in bloom. The blossoming of the peach trees has inspired poets since time immemorial; but there are many other fruit trees, ranging from apple trees to mandarine-orange shrubs, that give their character to the northern valleys or the southern hills. We might mention *nashi*, a very juicy pear resembling an apple. There are delicious strawberries, and melons, a particular favourite for banquets and parties being a special variety known as the meron.

SUKIYAKI AND TEMPURA—Two dishes especially popular with foreigners—*sukiyaki* and *tempura*—are considered luxuries by the Japanese. The commonest type of *sukiyaki* is made primarily with beef. The first step is to chop into tiny pieces a wide variety of vegetables—with the exception of potatoes—on one plate, and carve very fine slices of beef on another. Requiring constant attention, *sukiyaki* is prepared in front of the guests, who sit round a circular table with a charcoal brazier in the centre. A bowl containing a beaten raw egg is set in front of each guest. A greased pot is placed on the brazier, and the vegetables heaped on it. After a few minutes, when they have released a certain amount of liquid, a few slices of meat are added, and the mixture is sprinkled first with *shoyu*, then with one or two spoonfuls of sugar, and finally with half-a-glass of *sake*. Each guest dips the pieces of meat and vegetables in the raw egg. Any other kind of meat may be utilized—chicken, rabbit, pork, mutton, duck, pheasant, and even boar. *Sukiyaki* is also made with oysters and mussels.

Tempura is a dish consisting of fried fish, shellfish, and vegetables, thought to date back no more than 200 years. Like *sukiyaki*, it is generally prepared in front of the guests, who dip their steaming fritters in a bowl of fish soup seasoned with grated horseradish.

The culinary picture we have just painted would be incomplete if, for the sake of exoticism, we omitted to mention that the Japanese are also fond of dishes prepared —more or less—in Western style.

BEVERAGES–The national drink is tea—*cha* or *o-cha* —which is made with a plant from the camellia family. It was introduced into Japan in the 8th or 9th century, at the time when the adoption of Buddhism established close relations between China and the archipelago. The cultivation of tea gradually developed, until in time it became the national beverage. There are various ways of preparing the leaf, but it is never torrefied, and for foreigners Japanese tea means "green tea". It is always drunk without milk or sugar. The

UTAMARO
Women Pounding Rice

finest tea is made with chalky water, which is also the best type of water for making *sake*—spirits distilled from fermented rice. Japan also produces quite good beer, though on the light side.

And now a word about mealtimes for the average Japanese. In the morning he makes a substantial breakfast of rice, eggs, *nori*, and *miso* soup; at noon, a snack of noodles (*soba* or *udon*), *domburi*, or *sushi;* and lastly, the main meal at about six o'clock in the evening. Invitations are always for the latter, once the working-day is over.

MEALTIME ETIQUETTE—A number of things are "not done". For instance, the Japanese never drink tea made the day before, and it would be a heinous insult to offer it to a guest because in feudal times it was customary to serve the previous day's tea to criminals, on the execution ground. One should also scrupulously avoid throwing hot water on cold, as this is the way water for washing a corpse is prepared. Lastly, one should never pass food from chopstick to chopstick, this being the way in which relations pass to one another the pieces of bone withdrawn from the crematorium to be placed in a funerary urn.

On the occasion of a banquet or any somewhat formal party, beginning from the tokonoma to which the guests of honour turn their backs, the order of priority is as follows: the first seat to the left, then the first seat to the right, and so on, alternately; the host sits at the bottom of the table, nearest the spot from which the dishes and drinks arrive. The seat in front of the tokonoma has long been considered the safest, being generally the sole spot in the room with a complete wall behind it, and thus sheltered from possible attack from the rear.

Salt is considered a purifying element and a protection against evil spirits. Several small pyramids of salt are often to be seen at the entrance to restaurants, shops, geisha houses, and even private homes. In certain traditionalist families, the mistress of the house scatters a pinch of salt in the doorway after the departure of an unwelcome guest. It is also customary for the famous giant wrestlers known as *sumo-tori* to throw salt at random into the arena before beginning a fight, and between rounds. Then again, it is advisable to purify oneself with salt on returning from a burial or a visit to a dead person. For similar reasons, many peasants, and even cityfolk, clean their teeth with salt.

On moving into a new home, an ancient tradition demands that one offers packets of *soba* to one's two immediate neighbours and to the three houses opposite. This is derived from the fact that the homonym of soba means "close by". Moreover, it also represents the figure 5, regarded as a good omen.

For a wedding, a birth, or any other happy event, one offers a few pieces of dried bonito, another custom originating from a pun, in that fish prepared in this way—*katsuo-bushi*—implies *katsuo* meaning victory and *bushi*, warrior.

Whilst on the subject of presents, the word "tip" is often translated by *cha-dai*, the price of tea, recalling the days when pilgrims and passing travellers made this a pretext for donating money to temples that lodged and fed them free of charge. Money must always be wrapped in paper when handed to anyone. By the same token, after being wrapped in the usual way gifts are then done up in a *furoshiki*—a silk or cotton square that is extremely useful for

Picking Tea

carrying parcels. In many a tavern or restaurant, on paying his bill the guest receives a small souvenir carefully wrapped, generally consisting of a bath-towel bearing the name of the house, or some locally manufactured object.

THE TEA CEREMONY

GREEN tea, reduced to an impalpable powder and beaten with a bamboo whisk until slightly frothy, was originally used by bonzes to stimulate them in their meditations. It was also found to have medicinal qualities.

In the 15th century Shuko —Master of Ceremonies at the court of the Shogun Yoshimasa in Kyoto—inaugurated the first tea rites by having a small building, exclusively reserved for the "teas" that the head of state offered to his courtiers and distinguished guests, erected on a hillside remote from the centre of the town. This *Ginkakuji* or "Silver Pavilion"—so-named because it was decorated inside with silver leaf—has been preserved to this day, and is still open to visitors.

Certain rites connected with tea-tasting apparently originated in the encounters that used to be manœuvred between feudal adversaries with a view to reconciliation. The lords were obliged to leave their arms at the door, and the long preparations entailed by the ceremony gave them time to appease their warlike mood.

These meetings gradually began to resemble those societies where brilliant men exchange aesthetic views, whilst the host flaunts to his guests the luxury of his art collections.

In the 16th century Rikyu, Tea-Master to General Toyotomi Hideyoshi, drew up the formula and laid down the rules of etiquette for *Cha-no-yu*, meaning literally hot water for tea. He purified the spirit of the ceremony, and restored a basic simplicity that is valid to this day.

These rites are immutable. Only a few details vary here and there in accordance with the tendencies of the schools that grew up as a consequence of Rikyu's teaching, or even according to region. However, in the main the ceremony is identical.

A rustic hut or a small room measuring four mats and a half was selected in preference to palace reception rooms.

The ideal setting is a small pavilion, built in the garden and generally composed of two rooms: an anteroom, and the tearoom proper or *cha-shitsu*, near the pantry which plays a major role.

The pathway leading to it and the little garden surrounding it should be designed by a landscape gardener and—whatever their dimensions—should be a finished composition complete with rocks, trees, a brook, etc.

The guests wait in this garden until they hear the gong announcing that the host is ready to receive them. Having washed their hands and rinsed their mouths, they enter the pavilion by way of an opening so narrow that one has to crawl through it on one's hands and knees. The reason for this is first, lest they might have a sword concealed beneath their robes, and second, because they should leave their pride outside.

The room is bare, with the exception of the tokonoma alcove which is adorned with a precious kakemono. On entering the room, the first act of each guest is to go over and bow to this work of art, in admiration.

Meanwhile the tea-master or host has arranged the brazier on the ground. He subsequently brings in a small jar of fresh water, then the bamboo ladle and the bowl-washer, and finally the bowl complete with bamboo whisk and spatula, and the tea-caddy.

Using the spatula, he puts the green tea powder in the bottom of the

bowl, pours hot water on to it, and beats the preparation with the whisk made of bamboo switches. When the mixture is entirely covered with green froth, the bowl is offered to the guest of honour who tastes a sip of it and then passes the vessel to the next guest. The last one is supposed to finish the beverage entirely.

The utensils are then handed to the guests, to be admired. In actual fact, the tea bowl, the bamboo spoon, and all the ritual implements are often extremely old, and the associations attached to them enhance their value.

A refined meal, prepared and served by the host himself, precedes the tea rites. But simple gatherings for tea, strong or weak as the case may be, accompanied by pastries, may take place at any hour of the day or night. A fall of snow, a moonlight night, the arrival of a friend, some memorable date—or simply the desire to show connoisseurs an *objet d'art*—may serve as a pretext. When drinking weak tea, it is customary to offer one bowl per person.

Contemplation is still the order of the day, the guests communing with each other in an atmosphere of mutual benevolence and a levelling spirit.

This purely spiritual ceremony of aesthetic enjoyment confers on the Japanese the worship of simplicity, together with respect for true beauty and sympathy with Nature. It develops self-control, a noble attitude, and the gift for essential gestures. The feeling of passing time links the participators with eternity.

In the feudal era, Cha-no-yu appeased warlike passions and mettlesome spirits. Nowadays it brings home to the Japanese the true meaning of their civilization.

DOCTORS AND HEALERS

THE question of food leads us to discuss medicaments. Before going any further, we should first point out that Japan possesses an abundant network of extremely modern hospitals, where doctors are trained in the latest methods of tracking down and combatting disease. For all that, there still exists an exceedingly active and strictly local technique of healing, and a pharmacopoeia often of Chinese origin.

As early as the 8th century, the Imperial House founded a medical school in its new capital of Nara where, amongst other things, the teaching included the techniques of acupuncture, cauterization with *mokusa*, and massage. In addition, a school of pharmacy was housed in an annex.

In the Shoso-in, a collection of precious objects attached to the Todaiji and situated behind the building of the great Buddha of Nara, one may still see innumerable receptacles containing plants, herbs, seeds, and medicinal powders which have been preserved for over 1,200 years and some of which, so the specialists say, still have curative properties.

Acupuncture treatment *(hari-kyo)* has developed an extremely advanced study of 660 "sensitive points", controlling the nerves and muscles of the human body. Needles made of gold, silver, or platinum, of ten different sharpnesses, averaging about two inches in length, are driven into these points to a varying depth and at a varying frequency. This treatment is recommended for nervous disorders, spasms, paralysis, congestion, or inflammation.

Treatment by *mokusa* (a contraction of *moe-gusa*—burnt herb)—is similarly based on this study of the 660 "sensitive points" of the body, the most current being along the spine and under the knees. A pinch of artemisia leaves *(yomogi)*, dried and reduced to powder, is applied to the skin and burnt with the tip of an incense stick. This treatment is recommended in cases of fainting, rheumatism, neuralgia, general fatigue, or intestinal disorders. The pangs of childbirth are also said to be relieved by applying *mokusa* to the little toe of the right foot. In olden times, children used to be punished by having this painful *mokusa* treatment inflicted upon them. There still exists a curious custom whereby one can drive away a guest who is undesirable or who outstays his welcome: it consists of secretly burning artemisia beneath the clogs he has left in the entrance.

As for masseurs, or *amma*, they are legion. Many of them are blind men who earn their living in this way. They may sometimes be seen quite late into the evening, groping their way through the town with a stick and announcing their arrival with two plaintive notes played on reed pipes.

There is also a species of peddler, of both sexes, who comes from the remote township of Toyama on the Sea of Japan, and wanders in spring-time from town to town, selling pills to cure disorders of the stomach

TORII KIYOMASU—*The Actor Ichikawa Ebizo in the Role of a Patent Medicine Vendor*

"Inro"—Medicine Box
(18th century)

(*dokudeshi*: counter-poison). These peddlers have a curious sales technique that consists of entrusting their clients with boxes or sachets containing an adequate supply for the coming year, and collecting payment when they pass by again the following spring.

Numerous methods are recommended for getting rid of a cold. The most current is to "sweat it out", a formula that presents no difficulty considering the high temperature of Japanese baths. Apart from hot *sake*, occasionally with the yolk of an egg added, an infusion of ginger, orange peel, or grated horseradish is recommended. In olden days it was customary to order a bowl of burning noodles, to be eaten whilst immersed to the neck in the public baths.

In every town one may still come across ancient chemists' shops which advertise their presence by means of enormous wooden signs mellowed by time, and a collection of show-bottles displaying curious objects, generally calcined. In actual fact, the contents are the remains of animals—monkeys, snakes, molluscs, insects, and bones of every species—pulverized to produce a potion consisting of calcium, magnesium, alkali, or natural acids. Monkey-skulls are good for headaches; bats for baldness; falcons for the skin; sparrows' feet and claws for colds; whole sparrows for rheumatism; owls' ashes for sore throats. A mixture of sparrow and goldfish is used to cure fever, and crab-meat for beriberi. Rats, sunflower stalks, or cakes of beeswax are equally effective against lumbago. Cures for tuberculosis consist of either the ashes of a black snake, or a decoction made of snakeskins or silkworm cocoons. A sure way of winning a maiden's favour is by sprinkling her with the powder of calcined lizards, since these little creatures are reputedly always found in inseparable pairs.

Other noteworthy old wives' remedies include the following: for seasickness, a pinch of sulphur on the navel; for toothache, the ash of pine needles; for bad dreams, a diet strictly confined to sweet potatoes; for boils, a poultice of butterflies steeped in sesame oil; for diarrhoea, a decoction of peony roots; for a hangover, a boiling hot infusion of cloves; for inflammation of the ears, an application of juice extracted from dead grasshoppers.

Firefly ointment assures immunity against all sorts of misfortunes; it even stops thieves from entering a house occupied by someone who has made use of it. Bears' gall-bladders and oil from giant toads possess rare properties for curing all kinds of stomach disorders. Ginseng root—especially the Korean variety—is the supreme wonder drug, said to have the power of prolonging life. Throughout the Far East, it is often credited with aphrodisiac properties, as are grilled snake, or soup made of soft-shelled fresh-water tortoises known as suppons, which, incidentally, has a delicious flavour.

Masseur

WOMEN AND CHILDREN

FIFTY years ago, Lafcadio Hearn wrote: "The most wonderful aesthetic products of Japan are not its ivories, nor its bronzes, nor its porcelains, nor its swords, nor any of its marvels in metal or lacquer—but its women." A great deal of ink has flowed on the subject of Japanese women, and when short of ideas passing journalists invariably fall back on this seemingly easy theme. Our sole intent at this juncture is to make a humble attempt to reinstate women in their rightful—and highly important—place in the social framework.

In ancient society Japanese women played a brilliant role. From the 9th to the 11th century, for instance, the court saw a golden age of remarkable poetesses, such as Ono-no-Komachi, Murasaki-Shikibu, Lady Tachibana, and Sei-Shonagon. If women wove, spun, and dyed material, they also busied themselves with art, literature, and music. Mixing freely with the men, they were as lively and brilliant as their sisters of future generations were reserved and shy.

In the mid-13th century the nobleman Abutsumi wrote the following wise advice to his daughter, a lady at court: "Education of women need not extend beyond writing, painting, music, incense, history, novels, and poetry (quite a considerable programme in itself!). A woman should attempt to charm with her heart and mind rather than with her beauty and her talents. Esteem it unimportant to have many friends; a few, well chosen, suffice. In exchanging gifts, be neither too ardent nor too cold, neither too insistent nor too reserved. Remember that you will be judged by your friends. Court life may be pleasurable in the extreme, but it also has its share of trials, often demanding uncommon moral courage. Whether or not you love spring flowers and autumn maples, never forget to contemplate the frostbitten winter plants. Naught could more eloquently express the vanity of this world. Our life is but a fleeting dream. Study the doctrine of Buddha with care, and let not the sorrows of this world perturb or torment you."

On the other hand, in the year 500 B.C. Confucius wrote: "Men and women should never sit in the same room after the age of seven." The Buddhists added: "Woman is a creature with an angelic appearance, masking a diabolical spirit in the depths of her being." The Japanese critic who quoted these words hastened to add that at about the same epoch in the West Socrates wrote: "Woman is the source of all evil; her love is more fearful than man's hatred."

WOMANLY DUTIES—From the 14th to the 16th century, civil wars relegated woman to an inferior rank. Subsequently, the great Confucianist exponents of the 17th century codified her role. It was then that Kaibara Ekken drafted his *Onna Daigaku*—"Greater Learning for Women". They should

UTAMARO—*A Celebrated "Beauty" of the Day*

observe the "three main precepts of obedience": obeying their parents in their youth; their husband throughout their marital life; their children in their old age. Ekken singles out "five moral diseases" in women: disobedience, anger and hatred, backbiting, envy, and stupidity. In order to have a better understanding of Japanese women, we feel it worthwhile to quote certain salient passages of this remarkable document which formed the basis of feminine education for over 250 years.

From the outset Ekken warns us: "In view of the fact that on reaching womanhood a girl is destined to enter a new home and live in subservience to her father-in-law, it is obviously more important for her than for a boy to accept her parents' teaching reverently." And he goes on to say: "In a woman, a virtuous heart is more precious than a lovely face.... The sole qualities befitting a woman are gentle submissiveness, chastity, charity, and serenity." From early childhood a woman should observe the demarcation line between the sexes and exercise restraint even in her relations with her brothers and husband.

Ekken then enumerates the "eight reasons for divorce": disobedience to one's parents-in-law, lack of progeny, lascivity, jealousy, leprosy or other repugnant diseases, untimely chattering, disturbing the atmosphere of the home, accusation of theft. He once again stresses the fact that a woman should submit to her parents-in-law, "even if they feel the need to hate or despise you."

A long chapter is devoted to wifely duties: "She must consider her husband as her sole lord, serving him adoringly. Until her death, a woman's primary duty is obedience .... She must regard her husband as Paradise itself and spend her time devising ways of ceding to him, thus escaping the punishment of Heaven. She should not even dream of jealousy. She should be the first to rise and the last to retire; occupy her day with spinning, weaving, and sewing; drink tea and *sake* in moderation only; she should not enjoy drama and ballads, avoiding public places and even visits to temples until the age of forty. At New Year and during the five Festivals, she should visit her husband's parents before her own. She must not go anywhere without her husband's permission .... A married woman should treat her servants with due circumspection, disdain to listen to their chattering, and always direct them firmly yet with understanding."

The last chapter deals with the "five frailties of woman" mentioned above, "Stupidity" being the mother of the other four. Ekken labours upon the fact that Woman "is so stupid by nature that she is in duty bound to beware of herself constantly, and obey her husband." And the work concludes thus: "If women act according to the precepts we have laid down, her conjugal relations can but be harmonious and continuous, and her home a scene of peace and concord."

It is only fair to add that this rigid code found its exact counterpart in the equally rigid laws of Bushido—the Way of the Warrior—and the sumptuary Tokugawa edicts that meticulously regulated men's lives from the 17th century. The immense strides towards emancipating women made in the past fifty years, and above all since 1945, will be all the

UTAMARO—*Sewing*

more appreciated if we mention that the grandmother, if not the mother, of every modern Japanese girl was raised according to these principles.

EDUCATION OF GIRLS—If the *Onna Daigaku* is no longer followed to the letter, and if 99 % of the girls of today have not read a line of it, their education nonetheless tends to prepare them to be flexible and disciplined, and subsequently helps them to develop resignation to their lot in their attitude towards their husband and in-laws.

In addition to general schooling, Japanese girls take countless varieties of lessons in deportment. They learn, for instance, how to greet people—a detail that indicates a person's breeding from the outset. Handshaking is still not customary in Japan. The correct way to greet someone encountered out-of-doors is to stand with your feet together bending the top half of your body about 45°, keeping your hands flat on your thighs with your elbows glued to your body. Indoors, the classical form of greeting is to kneel on the mats with your arms slightly curved and your hands flat on your thighs. The most ceremonial manner is to place your hands flat on the mats in front of your knees, either parallel with them or at a wide angle, and bend slightly until your brow touches the back of your hands.

There are also several ways of walking on the mats, opening and closing *fusuma*, carrying a tray, etc. and setting it in front of a guest, holding a fan, tying a bow, and carrying *furoshiki*. Moreover, the slightest gesture is accompanied by long-established ritual sayings.

However, the most favoured accomplishments are floral arrangement and the tea ceremony, two forms of aesthetic refinement expressing the dual trait of Japanese genius—love of detail combined with simplicity—in arts that call for complete renouncement of individual emotion and adherence to the strictest rules.

Whereas in times gone by *Cha-no-yu* was practised by warriors in search of peace, nowadays it is often studied by young girls as one of the numerous exercises to prepare them for future ordeals in their family-in-law.

MARRIAGE—This quite naturally leads us to marriage, which assumes the utmost importance in a Japanese girl's life. Love matches or free choice of partner are still exceptional. The family cell has been so strongly moulded throughout the centuries that it has survived all the political upheavals and foreign influences.

On the young man's side, the family cannot be over-cautious in selecting the woman who is to become not only the wife of their son or grandson, but above all the mother of the children who will perpetuate their name, and the matron who is to preserve the cult of the household gods and the memory of the dead. In addition to these primordial duties, she must at all times be ready to serve, assist, or tend any member of her husband's family. The scission with her own people is so complete that in certain

OKUMURA MASANOBU—*Maid Dressing her Mistress's Hair*

areas it is customary to celebrate a funeral ceremony for the bride-to-be in the home she is about to leave.

In order to lessen the risks of error and save the two families from committing themselves too deeply from the outset, the preliminary negotiations for finding a bride or groom are entrusted to an intermediary, generally middle-aged, known as the *nakodo*.

The first question to be tackled is that of the social status, tastes, health, position in the family (elder or younger son or daughter, father living or dead—in the latter case, the responsibilities will be all the heavier, etc.). It is also essential to obtain details of the surname, first name, and date of birth. In fact, the Japanese often go so far as to consult a soothsayer who specializes in examining the respective positions of the future bride or groom, according to the stars and the points of the Zodiac; not to mention the number of "outlines" in the characters with which the surnames and

317

first names are written (the ciphers for the latter are varyingly auspicious in accordance with a long-established list).

Certain deep-rooted superstitions must also be taken into consideration, such as the belief that a girl born in the year of the "fire-horse"—*hinoe-uma*—"will burn her husband", i.e., bring about his death and ruin his family. Fortunately this recurs only once every sixty years; the last was in 1905.

Once the *nakodo* has assembled all the favourable elements and obtained

UTAMARO—*Spring-cleaning*

the tentative agreement of both families, a day is set for a meeting between the future bride and groom— under joint supervision. This interview, enabling the young couple to observe each other and perhaps even exchange a few words, is known as *mi-ai*. It often takes place in the *nakodo's* home or in a public place such as a temple, park, or theatre.

Assuming both families are satisfied with this first

Wedding Present

encounter, an exchange of presents—*yuino*—corresponding to an official betrothal, takes place. Thereafter, neither of the parties may retract from the marriage. Certain rural and traditionalist families still observe the old custom whereby only the groom's family sends gifts. Elsewhere, the bride's family in turn sends gifts equivalent to half those she has received: clothes, *tai* (the lucky fish), *sake*, *surume* (cuttle-fish dried and pressed), linen material, fans, all of which symbolize long life and happiness. Nowadays there is a tendency to simplify matters by simply exchanging a sum of money representing the value of the gifts, wrapped in ritual paper.

Then a propitious day is set for the wedding. Three days previously, the bride's belongings are transferred in great pomp to her new home, as the wife should arrive equipped with everything she is to need for the rest of her life. This includes *tansu*—cupboards and chests full of kimonos, gowns, and other articles of clothing; *futon*—mattresses and eiderdowns; a table, and a dressing-table. It may also comprise a musical instrument— either a *koto* or a *samisen;* a set of kitchen utensils, etc.

The marriage ceremony, *yome-iri*—entry of the bride *(shugen)*—used to take place in the evening. This tradition is still respected in certain country districts, and the long procession winding slowly through the village streets, preceded by lanterns and headed by the betrothed in her magnificent attire, is a wonderful sight. Occasionally the bride has to suffer affronts, a

Bridal Headdress

symbolic preparation for the future trials of life. In some cases she is spattered with water, earth, or mud. In others children beat her with cords or long bamboo switches; or again, she has to overcome an obstacle or cross a barrier two or three feet high, and it is no easy matter to accomplish this gracefully in such cumbersome clothes.

Nowadays the ceremony usually takes place in the morning or afternoon, in a Shinto temple. The two families line up on either side of the room, with the bridal pair facing the altar at the far end. Behind them stand the matchmaker and his wife. After reading a *norito*, the white-clad priest then turns towards the congregation, purifying and exorcizing them by thrice shaking at them a sacred wand adorned with paper streamers cut in ritual patterns. The *nakodo* then steps towards the altar and reads a kind of oath of fidelity, in the name of the bride and groom. Then, to the strains of sacred *gagaku* music, two *miko* advance towards the couple. These young girls attached to the service of the temple wear white linen kimonos tucked into long red skirts with stiff pleats, of the same material; their hair, which is never cut, is gathered at the nape of the neck with a ribbon, and flows down their backs. One of them carries three white goblets of fragile earthenware; the other holds a kind of long-handled ladle of gilt metal decorated with butterflies, containing *sake*. The first and smallest goblet is presented to the groom and filled with three dashes of spirits; he drinks it in three sips. The *miko* then passes this same goblet to the bride, and the same movements are repeated. The second slightly larger goblet is presented first to the bride, then to the groom, the third and largest being offered first to the groom, then to the bride. This exchange of goblets thrice repeated—*san-san-ku-do*—marks the central point of the ceremony. The *miko* then offer each of the guests a goblet in honour of the bridal pair.

The wedding kimono is generally of very heavy black silk ornamented with the family "blazon" on the back, sleeves, and breast. The sleeves are extremely long, dangling to the ankles, whilst the hem of the garment trails on the ground for about a foot. The edges of the sleeves and of the kimono itself are richly adorned with motifs of gold, silver, and other colours representing the symbols of long life: pine trees, bamboos, plum trees, or storks. As for the sumptuous sash of heavy brocade known as an *obi*, this is fastened high at the back, in imitation of butterfly's wings, another symbol of happiness. The bride's headgear consists of a tall wig with "ear-phones" known as *taka-shimada*, round which a band of red and white silk, the *tsuno-kakushi* or "horn-hider" is fixed, to remind the wife she should never give way to jealousy, a sentiment represented by horns in Japanese tradition.

The ceremony is followed by a banquet at which the families have the opportunity of becoming better acquainted. The bride then changes her ceremonial kimono and obi for a simpler variety, a gift from her husband. After the love-feast, tradition demands that the couple be led to the bridal chamber by the *nakodo* and his wife, and that they again exchange goblets thrice.

A few days later—usually on the third day after the wedding—the young couple call on the bride's parents. This ritual visit is known as *sato-gaeri*, the "return home".

The lower classes, however, simplify the marriage cere-

The Bride with her Friends

mony. Moreover, wartime and postwar upheavals, and the ensuing new laws have encouraged the younger generation to emancipate themselves and insist on being allowed to "live their own lives". For all that, the ancient social system still survives, and it will be a long time before young Japanese obtain the right to choose their partner freely.

THE GEISHA—In a study of Japanese womanhood, we shall no doubt be expected to mention the geisha. We shall devote only a few lines to the subject since, despite everything that has been written, they are nonetheless an outdated survival of the 18th century. The word was coined in the mid-18th century. Originally established in the famous Yoshiwara district near Edo, the geishas kept pace with urban development, spreading to Fukagawa, Yanagibashi, Kyobashi, Horiecho, and finally Shimbashi. In Kyoto they are to be found in the celebrated Gion quarter, and their renown has spread abroad by way of prints.

In olden days a geisha's apprenticeship began even before the age of ten, but under current labour laws she cannot now begin until she is sixteen. The young girl undergoes long training in special schools where she learns various arts such as singing, dancing, music, the art of preparing flowers and tea, the way to present objects, behave in society, etc.

The apprentice is tied by a five- to ten-year contract to a "headquarters" directed by a former geisha, who subsidizes her boarder's numerous expenses, to be subsequently reimbursed by a sum withheld from her earnings throughout the duration of the contract. There, the young *hangyoku* (or *maiko*, in Kyoto), is placed under the protection of an established geisha, who teaches her the secrets of the profession and later, in the course of a special ceremony—somewhat similar to the wedding ceremony—confers on her a pseudonym comprising part of her own name. She also helps her protégée along the road by introducing her to her favourite clients.

The latter are rich businessmen or high-ranking officials who spend immense sums to recompense the services of these fascinating entertainers, who are always clad in the most luxurious and dazzling kimonos, and skilled in the art of charming men. Geishas have, in fact, found their niche in a society where man reigns supreme, and all important invitations and more or less delicate discussions always take place outside the home and even the office.

Geishas

In our era of ultra-modernization and new-rich vulgarity, the geisha has become a luxury article, threatened by the countless "taxi-girls" who frequent bars and cafés where the joys of alcohol and feminine company may be obtained at a lower rate.

At this stage, we should perhaps add a word about the kimono, which sentimental travellers would hate to see disappear. We do not believe it will ever die out completely, but there is no denying that this mode of attire has become extremely costly, that it calls for numerous accessories, takes a long time to put on, and lastly, was made for life on mats, in an era when women seldom left their homes, never working in offices or shops, or having to run for the bus or tram.

For the modern girl, the kimono is only too often symbolic of the subservience she has observed in the attitude of her mother or grandmother towards the males of the household. One can therefore hardly blame her for wanting to use Western-type clothes, giving her at least a feeling of physical freedom. Happily for the traditional garment, recent years have seen a radical simplification in the cut of kimonos and in the way of tying the indispensable obi.

CHILDREN—It might be said that the first celebration for a Japanese takes place four months before his birth; he is then supposed to have received his soul *(tamashi)* in his mother's womb. This calls for a ceremony whereby with his left hand the father passes the maternity belt *(yuwata-obi)* to the mother, who takes it in her right hand. The maternal grandmother or sister of the pregnant woman then helps her to wind it round her body; it consists of a band of natural silk about eight feet long. As mentioned before, this ceremony normally takes place on the day of the dog, an animal reputed to give birth with ease.

The birth of a boy or girl provides yet another pretext for friends and relations to visit the happy household with gifts in the form of baby linen, lengths of silk, toys, boxes of cakes or *katsuo-bushi*—dried bonito—a symbol of happiness.

The birth of twins used to be considered shameful, on the assumption that this could happen only to animals. The parents therefore gave them particularly propitious names, to enable the twins to overcome future calamities arising from this unfortunate hazard of birth.

On the evening of the seventh day of his life the baby is presented to

UTAMARO—*The Teasing Mother*

the family and friends; this is the O-shichi-ya festival, which begins with
the preparation of *mochi* and *sakihan*. The infant then receives his first
presents, similar to those described above. This is also the day on which
his name is announced. For girls, it is often the name of a flower, plant, or
other item connected with nature: Plum *(Ume)*, Chrysanthemum *(Kiku)*,
Lily *(Yuri)*, Pine *(Matsu)*, Bamboo *(Take)*, Snow *(Yuki)*, Green *(Midori)*,

Spring *(Haru)*, Autumn *(Aki)*; or again, a name implying a feminine virtue: Purity *(Sei* or *Kiyo)*, Comfort *(Yasu)*, Bounty *(Yoshi)*. Formerly, the honorific prefix "O" was added to the first name—a custom still retained by geishas *(O-Kiku*: Miss Chrysanthemum). Since the Meiji era, it is customary to add the suffix *"ko"* to all feminine names *(Umeko*: Miss Plum).

On the thirty-first day after the birth of a boy and the thirty-second after that of a girl comes the *miya-mairi* ceremony, consisting of a visit to the (Shinto) temple protecting the district or the family. Clad in a kimono of fine black silk stamped with the family blazon on the back, sleeves, and breast, and with the cords lightly knotted round the neck of the grand-

Shichi-go-san Festival

mother or some other relative who is carrying it, the baby goes in great pomp to visit the ancestral spirits; it cannot be taken by its mother, who is still impure in the eyes of the gods. The priest leads the group to the inner altar, where he reads a *norito*, and then thrice shakes a *gohei* over the infant's head to drive away evil influences and invoke the blessing of the gods. Once the ceremony is over, the baby is presented to the friends and relations, and a further exchange of gifts takes place. The person carrying it distributes bags of glucose sweets, a token of the meal the infant is supposed to share with its guests. In return it is showered with toys—in the form of gaudily painted and stumpy papier-mâché dogs known as *inuhariko*—symbolizing future strength and health.

The baby is the tyrant-king—or queen—of every household, and the family panders to its every whim. One advantage of Japanese mats is that children can crawl all over the house without getting dirty. Infants are often seen strapped to women's backs, or to the back of an elder brother or sister. From the age of two they begin to run about outside on little

wooden sandals fastening round the ankles.

Meanwhile, on reaching the age of 120 days they participate with a group of relations in the "festival of the first food", or *tabezome*. A small table covered with brightly coloured miniature dishes and bowls is set in front of the child. The mother or grandmother takes it on her knees and pretends to feed it. In actual fact, only a few grains of well-cooked rice are slipped into its mouth —a symbolic feeding to indicate that the infant has once and for all set foot in life. This festival is also the occasion when the mother reappears in public for the first time after her confinement and thanks the guests for their past kindnesses.

The 15th of November following the child's third birthday is the first big festival in which it officially appears in public. This is the *Shichi-go-san* (7–5–3), when children of these ages are taken on a solemn visit to their patron temple, the *Uji-Gami*, to strengthen their links with the gods, the above numbers being regarded as lucky. Moreover, the age of three is considered as the transition from babyhood to conscious childhood. In ancient times there were only two festivals: at the age of three for boys, when they were clad for the first time in a kind of bell-shaped skirt with stiff pleats—a miniature *hakama*—and when, in noble families, they were intro-

duced to the vassals and domestic staff; and the age of seven for girls, when they received their first obi.

Nowadays *Shichi-go-san* is a festival for boys and girls alike. They are dressed in bright kimonos or sometimes disguised as little samurai, sailors, or soldiers. Booths swarm round the temples, selling biscuits, sweetmeats, cakes, toys, and talismans symbolizing lucky elements. For boys there is Kintoki, the child who was reared in the woods and renowned for his strength, or the big spotted dog with heavy jowls, also a symbol of might. For girls there is the pair of dolls representing the elderly couple Jo with his rake and Uba with her broom, implying a long and happy marriage to come. There are also bamboo branches laden with ritual trinkets: precious coral, the dice

of good fortune, the mallet of the rice-god Daikoku, and the straw cloak that makes one invisible in time of danger.

Another holiday exclusively for children takes place all over the country in August, beside the little local shrines dedicated to Jizo. This celebration, known as *Jizo-bon*, approximately coincides with the Japanese Festival for the Dead. In Japan this is an occasion for rejoicing, echoing with the happy shrieks of excited children. In a preselected house open to all and sundry for the occasion, or beneath a tent, an altar is erected, lit by countless lanterns and laden with offerings of fruit and flowers. Processions are organized for the children, as well as other amusements in keeping with their age, such as story-telling, puppet-shows, or conjuring tricks. On all sides groups of children are to be seen with their parents, clad in *yukata*—light summer kimonos of white cotton decorated with blue motifs.

DOLL FESTIVAL—There is one fête for girls alone, the doll festival or

Dairibina: The Emperor and Empress

Hina Matsuri, on the 3rd of March. Adoption of the Gregorian calendar has upset the date and significance of many Japanese holidays. The 3rd of March, for instance, according to the old lunar calendar, was the occasion when the peasants fêted the first fine days. It was the signal to purify the household and its occupants, and prepare for the essential tasks of rice-growing. Everyone made clumsy paper dolls, to which the misfortunes and sicknesses of the family were transferred before throwing them in a nearby river. Such was the origin of *Hina Matsuri*. The first dolls of ancient Japan were not toys but representations of gods or human beings. The Japanese word for doll, *ningyo*, is written with two characters meaning "human being" and "image". The original *ningyo* were, in fact, charms to protect one against sickness, calamities, insects, and other evil influences. In the country rudimentary dolls of woven straw are still to be seen in doorways, at the entrance to villages, or in a corner of the fields. During certain festivals—particularly the famous *Gion-matsuri* of Kyoto in mid-July— some of the carnival chariots are decorated with huge dolls, a survival of ancient rites.

Moreover, since the 12th century noble families have developed the custom of commissioning series of "Court dolls"—*Dairibina*—representing the Emperor, the Empress and their Court. After the 14th century the dolls became increasingly beautiful, and in the 17th century every class of society adopted the custom of erecting a series of shelves in the tokonoma, where the dolls and their accessories were arranged. Nowadays they are left there throughout the month of March.

There are four types of dolls: the simplest, reminiscent of the ancient cult, are made of paper; they may also be of wood or terracotta, some more precious examples even having faces and hands of delicately lacquered wood and garments of rich silk and brocade.

Fifteen dolls complete the series. On the highest shelf two *Dairibina* larger than the others sit in state, representing the Emperor and Empress; on the second shelf are three *kanjo*, or ladies-in-waiting, with five musicians in the third row, and lastly, on the lowest shelf, two pages and three guards. Lacquered dinner-services in miniature are laid out on tiny tables in front of the Imperial dolls. Other objects of daily use are spread out round the platform, such as chests, dressing-tables, braziers, palanquins, etc., generally of finely decorated lacquer.

The peach festival on 3rd March is also called *Momo-no-sekku*, when the shelves where the dolls are ranged are decorated with sprigs of peach blossom, symbolizing happiness in marriage. The shape and velvetiness of the peach suggest the qualities characteristic of women: gentleness, grace, and serenity. We should add that the dolls and their accessories are taken carefully with the rest of the young girl's trousseau when she gets married.

The dolls we have described are not made to be handled, but there are other varieties for small girls to play with. In the country they are very simple toys made of barley straw—*mugiwara*—which, being more pliable than corn, is used for all kinds of woven objects. Other more elegant dolls are sold in the towns.

BOYS' FESTIVAL–Boys have their fête on 5th May,

Children's Tournament.
Lacquered 18th-century Tray

UTAMARO—*Kintoki being Suckled by Yama-uba*

known as Tango-no-sekku. This is the time of year when the insects swoop down on the fields. In days gone by the farmers used to fly banners on bamboo poles to frighten them away, and place warrior dolls with grimacing faces in the fields, as scarecrows.

Every household containing one or more boys erects a tall bamboo pole from which they fly enormous cloth or paper carps known as *Koinobori*. Blowing into their gaping jaws, the breeze swells and animates the fish, which symbolize Man's struggle against the current of life. Warriors with grimacing masks, clad in ancient armour, are placed in the alcove, as in the doll festival. Occasionally they are replaced by an effigy of Kintoki, the child-Hercules who was reared in the woods and, so the legend runs, used to wrestle with wild beasts. Other symbolic attributes are scattered around, in the form of horses, war banners, lances, halberds, sabres, etc. In many homes they are kept on display all through May.

GAMES—Little Japanese girls, like their sisters all the world over, play at tea-parties, hopscotch, hide-and-seek. They also skip; and at this point we

Children Playing

should like to describe a curious way in which they use the skipping-rope—a pastime for girls only. Two of them hold the rope, gradually raising it above the ground. The third little girl does not have to jump over it, but simply catch the rope with the tip of her foot, pirouetting her entire body.

The manual skill and delicate touch of the Japanese is proverbial. For children this is channelled into all kinds of games of folding paper—*origami*—and cutouts—*kirigami*. These are current pastimes in kindergartens and primary schools, and magazines for women or children devote pages to the subject. Multicoloured paper for this purpose, generally about four inches square, is sold by the packet in all stationers and toyshops.

EDUCATION—Japanese children grow up cradled in affection which often borders on doting. They are seldom punished, and never beaten. Whenever they fly into tantrums, some member of the family always rushes to console them with sweets and generally pander to them. Psychologists are perturbed by their lack of initiative, which they often attribute to the fact that at the slightest sign of boredom, fatigue, or irritation mothers suckle their children—even after the age of three or four—or carry them in their arms or on their backs.

Towards the age of four children are taken to the *yochi-en*—kindergarten—where they amuse themselves like their fellows all over the world. It is interesting to note that drawing with coloured crayons and watercolour paints are favourite pastimes both in kindergartens and primary schools.

The educational system, which has been revised since 1947, prescribes a pyramidal arrangement, different from the complicated prewar system of vertical compartments gradually separating pupils beyond primary school. The present plan calls for the American-type "6–3–3–4" system, i.e. six years of primary school; three of middle school, three of high school, and lastly four years of university.

The tragedy is that there are too few primary schools, all of which are overcrowded because the mass of children increases by a million per year. The situation becomes worse as the pupils rise to higher grades. One can no longer talk of transitional examinations, as each of them is competitive in which 40 to 60 % of the candidates are eliminated. Yet Japan has the lowest illiteracy rate in the world: .5 to 1 %. The sole road to success in so overpopulated a space is to reach the highest possible scholastic level. But even for university graduates it is often difficult to find employment.

This all goes to explain the general impression of tension overriding Japanese youth. To the worries of study are added the constant shocks of a society in the throes of evolution, where the drama of changing generations and that of the normal struggle for life become extraordinarily

At the Bookseller's

acute. Hence the high percentage of suicides, both individual and collective. Hence the nervousness and anxiety characterizing relationships between young people of both sexes. Many a young love is blighted when it comes to marriage, as this question is settled not by the couple concerned but by their families, as emphasized above.

At this juncture we feel it advisable to make a digression in regard to the extremely ramified and complicated character of relationships between human-beings in Japan, in the type of society that has developed through the centuries and still survives to a great extent. These explanations will help to clarify certain social constraints that appear aggravating, if not incomprehensible, to foreign observers.

We are referring to the system commonly known as *oyabun-kobun* (parents-children), of which the strongest form of expression is the relationship between groups descending from a common ancestor, clan, or family. Within this assembly other groups are formed on a hierarchical scale according to whether they descend from elder or younger branches. This explains why a young Japanese not only owes obedience and support to his parents, but also has to observe similar rules of conduct towards other members of groups more or less closely connected with his family. These obligations pursue him throughout his life, and marriage adds to them.

In these circumstances, it is quite impossible for him to create an "independent home". In any case, the lack of space in Japan sooner or later obliges the young couple to take in relations, close or distant, if the latter are not living with them from the outset. Should they later enjoy relative wealth, this merely adds to their responsibilities, as they then have to help an ever-increasing number of people connected with their family.

Through *oyabun-kobun*—extended to any business or industrial undertaking—superiors have obligations to their inferiors and the latter, in turn, must implicitly back up the former. With the sudden development of workers' unions since the last war, elements of dissension, highly complicated and hard to settle by official arbitration, have grafted themselves on to the traditional employer-employee relationships. In accordance with the above-mentioned system, in times of crisis—whether family or national—the groups strengthen their ties and automatically uphold each other. By the same token, the Emperor's status has not changed in most people's minds, since he is now considered not as an ordinary sovereign, nor even a god incarnate, but as a kind of "Supreme Father" to every Japanese.

TRADES AND CRAFTS

BASING themselves on over-hasty observations and official statistics often tinged with propaganda, some of the most well-meaning writers have described Japan as a country where heavy industry dominated the economy as a whole. Whilst such views were not entirely unfounded, especially in prewar days, they reflect only one side of the picture: the industry that enabled this country, devoid of raw materials of any kind, to resist the American colossus so long, being for the most part centred round the Empire's overseas possessions, mainly in Manchuria.

The Japanese archipelago was—and is once again now that it is confined to its original surface—an essentially agricultural country, and a land of craftsmen and artisans. And the country's drama lies in the very fact that her agriculture, her crafts, and even her fisheries do not and never will suffice to keep her alive. Willy-nilly, small trade has to sacrifice its place to large-scale factories, the sole form of industrialization capable of producing enough for export, which in turn makes possible the importation of essential goods.

Now in the present state of affairs, agriculture, crafts, and small trade simply serve to absorb excess manpower. The resultant semi-unemployment explains the apparently low figure of officially declared unemployed; and this, in fact, is the gravest consequence of Japan's overpopulation. National income is thus widely distributed, but by the same token the individual income is dangerously low. Hence the survival—nowadays paradoxical—of crafts which, picturesque though they may be, operate on a very low rate of production and are, into the bargain, characterized by an exaggerated form of division of labour.

AGRICULTURE—One might imagine that in a country as modernized as Japan, agriculture would be mechanized. In actual fact, this is far from the case, mechanization being absolutely out of the question. Even the use of draft animals is impossible, due to the rugged contours of the country. Only when one has seen ricefields sometimes barely 6 feet wide, rising in tiers 3 feet above one another up the slopes of a narrow valley, can one realize that the human machine is the only one capable of accepting so thankless a task. The altitude, the abruptness of the slopes, and above all the lack of water, form the sole insuperable barriers: springs or torrents are captured and tamed from the outset, and their precious waters trickle step by step down the gigantic stairway. And, to the rhythm of the seasons, the peasants—men and women alike—toil on the steps, hoeing the soil, thinning out young plants, and splashing in muddy water up to the knees to reap the waving rice with the sickle. Then—and this is not the least of the peasants' trials—the sheaves have to be carried as far as the road, where they are hung out to dry on scaffolds, forming a golden wall all along the wayside in autumn. Finally the harvest is brought in on hand-drawn carts—or ox-drawn wagons in less rugged regions—and threshed. The straw is heaped in tall cylindrical sheaves built up round tree-trunks, introducing a picturesque note into the rural landscape.

However, a "void" rainy season, or on the contrary an over-abundant one, or again a typhoon trailing catastrophic floods in its wake, are enough to ruin the harvest, and thereby the precarious life of the peasant, if not that of the country as a whole, as was the case in 1953 when the scourge assumed national proportions. Neither too much water nor too little; such is the be-all and end-all of Japan's whole existence. This too explains the bitterness of the quarrels over the distribution of the waters. Since time immemorial unjustified deviation of an irrigation canal has always been one of the offences most severely punished both by custom and by law. Folklore abounds

338

Ricefield in the Plain

in tales about the misfortunes befalling anyone guilty of such a crime.
Wherever the climate permits, a row of mulberry bushes is planted
along the dike marking the boundary of each field, to make sure not an

inch of ground is wasted. The leaves serve as food for silkworms, which Japanese peasants have been breeding since ancient times to supplement their revenue. This relatively easy and profitable task befits the women better than hard toil in the fields. In the old days they used to spin the silk themselves. Latterly, small but more modern spinning mills have provided employment for young girls who worked there for a year or two—just long enough to build up a dowry. Unfortunately this little industry is now seriously threatened by the growing demand for artificial textiles, and the two million or so workers who used to make a living from the silk trade in one way or another will shortly swell the ranks of the unemployed waiting to be absorbed into an already overcrowded industry.

FISHING—The above applies mainly to the "mountain villages". In addition, there are the "seaside villages", Japan being composed solely of mountain and sea, apart from a few narrow coastal plains which are rapidly being overrun by the monstrous expansion of urban areas. These "seaside villages" combine fishing and farming. The ricefields are quite as steep as those inland, but there they are cultivated almost entirely by women, the men devoting all their time to the sea, an even harsher calling. Their task is quite as important as rice-growing, since Japan lives almost exclusively on rice and fish: she alone consumes approximately one quarter of the fish caught throughout the world. The fishermen, however, have benefitted from modernization more than the farmers: the majority of boats—those used for deep-sea fishing at least—are motorized, and throughout the night the little ports echo relentlessly with the noisy backfiring of overworked engines, the Japanese being champions at tinkering with things mechanical. In the small hours the fishermen may be seen bringing in heavy cargoes of tunny-fish and superb pink bream—the delight of *sashimi* enthusiasts—not to mention countless other fish less appreciated but more plentiful and better suited to the modest purse of the average Japanese.

The fishermen have many another source of income, such as little octopus and cuttle-fish which are popular items of daily fare. Then again, the children gather huge quantities of shellfish and molluscs on the beach. Whilst the oysters are second-rate, there are other delicious varieties such as *sasae*, a kind of murex. Enoshima is renowned for this delicacy, cooked in the shell. Along certain coastlines diving-girls may still be seen hunting fish with a harpoon or diving for shellfish, often in extremely deep waters.

On the other hand, the famous "pearl fishergirls" from the Bay of Ise hardly ever operate now except for tourists and amateur photographers, such primitive methods being no longer adequate for large-scale pearl-oyster culture, as introduced by Mr Mikimoto. It is obviously more rational to raise a catch laden with oysters than to hunt for them one by one in the depths of the sea!

The beaches, especially round Chiba on the Bay of Tokyo, present another curious sight in the form of seaweed fields. Sea-moss, or a type of miniature seaweed, is cultivated in these fields, marked off by wattle fences submerged in the sea some two or three score yards from the shore. It is subsequently piled up and dried right on the beach, producing those dark green leaves known as *nori* which the Japanese eat in great quantities with rice or in soup. Cultivation of seaweed is one of the major activities of a fisherman's wife. Another of her manifold tasks is the complicated preparation of those tiny fish an inch or two long that are placed by the thousand on the wattles, to dry in the sun. Once dry, they are reduced to powder for mixing with rice or soup, or coated with a sticky jacket of caramelled sugar and crunched with a glass of *sake*.

Mutual help and social solidarity are even more indispensable in coastal villages than in the mountains. The men devote their spare time to collective tasks such as the construction of boats, building wooden walls along the shore to protect the houses from typhoons or tidal waves, and making fishing tackle. On

Drying Parasols

the beach one often sees busy groups directed by the carpenter, fitting the hull of a new ship or twisting interminable ropes. It is only through such communal efforts that these poor villages, continually decimated by the sea and in constant peril of its waves, have succeeded in surviving and relentlessly fulfilling their role as victuallers of the nation.

PEASANT CRAFTS—The fisherman's life is a hard one, with little time for leisure: summer and winter alike, the demand for fresh fish has to be satisfied. The activities of the mountain peasant on the other hand, are purely seasonal, dependent on the cycle of rice-growing and cultivation of secondary crops. Winter—especially in the high valleys where villages are sometimes snowbound for six months of the year—condemns him to enforced seclusion, but not idleness. The land is carved up so severely that even in the best years it barely yields enough to keep the wolf from the door. He therefore goes in for a thousand-and-one minor crafts which, though not particularly remunerative, provide him with a little fish to flavour his rice.

With inexpensive raw materials, such as wood and bamboo, available on the

Carpenters

342

spot, he manufactures countless ingenious trifles, amusing or useful as the case may be, extremely cheap but invariably in exquisite taste. One of the best-known is the *kokeshi*, a small wooden doll turned on a lathe and painted, similar to our skittles. Over the past few years there has been a tremendous boom in the *kokeshi* industry. What was once a sturdy, inexpensive toy has now become an *objet d'art*, highly sought after by tourists and collectors. What was once a clumsy doll with features summarily sketched in Indian ink has assumed the most varied forms, loosened up, and shaken itself free from the rigidity of the medium employed. The most heterogeneous types have thus been created, representing legendary characters, theatrical heroes, mother and child, soba-vendors, etc. In short, the most imaginative ideas have been introduced into an art which, by its very nature, tended to be stereotyped. Unhappily the peasants who used to manufacture these toys during the winter lull are seriously threatened by competition from large-scale industry, which manages to reduce the cost of output still further. More serious still is the fact that these mass-produced goods are often in the worst of taste.

The only claim to artistry in the manufacture of soles for *geta* lies in the quality of the wood employed, but the trade is of great importance from the economic point of view in a country where leather is scarce and costly. Japanese clogs are less complicated than the European variety, consisting simply of a rectangular sole mounted on two vertical slats, carved out of a single block of wood. Needless to say, wood is also used for manufacturing other everyday objects such as trays, chopsticks, boxes, and small pieces of furniture, most of which originate from the workshops of these peasant-craftsmen.

Bamboo also offers countless possibilities in the form of baskets, wattle fences, vases, pieces of furniture, lamps, and innumerable other items. Cut into fine but extremely stout strips, it is also used for the framework of parasols and fans. In front of houses along the wayside, objects such as these are often seen stretched out to dry in the sun.

All these little industries were gradually dying out. But in recent years they have grown in popularity and taken on a new lease of life, thanks to the efficient intervention of men of taste who devote every moment to tracking down, supervising, and reviving local crafts. After studying all the techniques, they reindoctrinate the peasants in forgotten crafts, and find outlets for their work by creating a snob movement in favour of

Tatami-maker

folkloric art. Rich Japanese and foreign tourists have reached the pitch of offering ransom prices for these objects which no one would even look at a few years back.

ARTS AND CRAFTS—The artisans—more correctly described as artists in the case of Japan—have likewise reaped the benefit of these efforts. For purely economic reasons, industrial competition has long supplanted them in the

manufacture of everyday objects, but handicrafts of an artistic nature—although threatened for a while—have at last weathered the storm and emerged more flourishing than ever.

Of all the minor arts of Japan, pottery is probably the one most appreciated by foreigners. It goes without saying that we are referring to genuine pottery and authentic art, and not to that ghastly chinaware known as "Japanese art" with which only too many Western houses are decorated—representing portly gilded "Buddhas", vases bedaubed with atrocious pink cherry trees or hideous geishas, overladen *satsuma* that no self-respecting Japanese would deign to own—bought as souvenirs in one of those so-called "Oriental art" shops which are as remote from art as they are from the Orient. On the contrary, we should like to describe that heavy pottery, intentionally crude in appearance, skilfully irregular in outline, coloured in carefully studied and inimitable shades. There is a tale of an ancient potter who devoted ten years of his life and his entire fortune to the quest of a hue glimpsed for a moment on an over-ripe persimmon in the setting sun. To this day, his emulators are legion; the renown of some has spread beyond the frontiers of Japan, and certain young European and American potters come expressly to study in their school.

Their secret lies in the preservation of technical traditions allied with constant research for new ideas. If they still work according to methods established over the centuries, with rudimentary lathes and tools, using wood-heated ovens, none of the latest artistic movements of the West escapes their attention, and they successfully combine the two sources of inspiration. For all that, their production is strictly Japanese, providing a further illustration of this country's astonishing powers of assimilation and adaptation.

The art of lacquerwork has undergone a similar evolution. Although for a while it strayed into the field of multicoloured lacquers—calling for technical acrobatics but betraying a lack of taste—it has now returned to its traditional sobriety, scorning polychrome and various inlaid material.

Primarily Japanese lacquerwork serves a utilitarian purpose, and whilst there is no denying the taste of the worthy craftsmen who manufacture the trays and bowls in daily use, they are apt to be lacking in imagination. But here again, in addition to these craftsmen we find a number of great artists who have succeeded in rejuvenating their art in contact with the West.

Lacquerwork is a complex art: in addition to his technical skill proper, the lacquerer has to have a sculptor's touch and an artist's eye. The form of the object counts as much as, if not more than, the pattern in the general effect. The artist thus has to be as sure of his chisel as his paintbrush. But the wood-carving is relatively easy compared with the application of the lacquer itself which is put on gradually, in a series of hardly perceptible retouches, sometimes at intervals of several days. Since the colour changes as the lacquer dries or is exposed to the sun, from the outset one has to have a precise idea of the shade to be achieved. It is, in fact, a long and exacting work of patience, demanding slow and meticulous preparation.

At Kamakura near Tokyo, a special technique known as *Kamakura-bori* or Kamakura sculpture is still employed. Such lacquers are covered with a coating of a uniform colour, ranging from bright red to dark brown. In this case the pattern is carved in the wood before lacquering. The craftsmen have set up shop on the outskirts of the great Temple of Hachiman where they sell their own goods, and they may thus be seen at work, crouching on mats in the raised section of their booths.

Another artistic handicraft is the manufacture of "Kyoto dolls". These are not toys, but ornamental dolls, inspired by ancient prints or characters from classical drama. On a slender framework of wire bound with narrow bands, rich costumes of precious silk are meticulously draped and sewn in the most graceful attitudes. A sculptured, painted head with carefully arranged hair completes the astonishing illusion of life created by these charming little figures. And before the strollers' dazzled eyes windows full of dolls revive the unreal world of Harunobu and Utamaro.

THE CRAFTSMEN—Where should one draw the shifting line between arts and crafts? Is the sculptor of lanterns, Buddhist statues, and funerary steles an artisan or an artist? And what of the bamboo and paper lantern-maker, the fan painter, the country weaver, the poster artist, and calligrapher? One can only conclude that in such cases the qualification depends on the man himself rather than the craft.

Even the humblest and least gifted of these little craftsmen is not entirely oblivious to aesthetic considerations, and one is often surprised by the artistic worth of an inexpensive fan or some humble, uncouth Jizo adorning a crossroads. A clumsy rice bowl in a village shop is often richer in pure beauty than certain pretentious, costly articles displayed in the modern art department of a large store. Although the economist may congratulate himself on the progressive disappearance of these crafts in favour of more profitable industrial production, one cannot help regretting the more or less imminent loss of this undeniable asset, introducing beauty into the daily life of a people.

Two unassuming craftsmen—the carpenter and the tatami-maker—cooperate in their various ways in creating that masterpiece of harmony, the Japanese house.

So much has been said elsewhere about housebuilding that it is unnecessary to dwell on the subject here. However, I should like to relate an anecdote illustrating the extent to which Japanese houses differ from our own. One of our friends had rented a villa beside the sea for the summer. On entering his new home, he noticed that the door at the end of the veranda was jammed and refused to slide. He sent for a carpenter and asked him to plane the door. The craftsman lengthily studied the case, scratched his head, exclaiming *"Chotto matte kudasai...."*—"Just a moment, please"—and went off. He returned half-an-hour later with an assistant carrying a truck-jack. The carpenter then slipped this under the side of the house, raised it, placed a wedge beneath the middle pillar.... and the door slid.

Out-of-doors the carpenter is generally recognizable by his blue cotton tunic cut in the old-fashioned style, with a large character—the emblem of the firm employing him—imprinted on the back. Facetious residents once made a journalist believe that these men were former Samurai, and that the mark was their blazon. This brought forth an extravagant article on the arrogance of this caste which, though

ruined, carried the pride of its rank to the extent of wearing its armorial bearings even when performing the most menial tasks.

The tatami-maker operates in a workshop opening on to the street, and it is wonderful to see the dexterity with which, on a rigid frame lined with horsehair, he weaves the slender strands of rush that give the house its rustic perfume and the floor that springy golden texture, so pleasant to bare feet.

SMALL TRADE—It is extremely difficult to draw the line between the craftsman and the tradesman. The fact that in the past craftsmen themselves used to sell their products doubtless explains the extreme specialization of small trade which is still the rule to this day.

The small tradesman himself often puts the finishing touches to the objects he retails. The shoe merchant, for instance, buys the soles of *geta* (wood) or *zori* (woven straw) and the cords from the respective specialized craftsmen, and assembles them himself to suit his clients at the time of sale.

Kimonos are sold in rolls of material which the merchant cuts and sews himself to his buyer's measurements. This also applies to many other everyday objects.

The china shops are

Lantern Painter

348

a curious sight, with their piles of plates, cups, and bowls of every size and shape, and teapots hanging from every inch of the ceiling.

The fruit-vendors lure passers-by with attractive stalls where colours are carefully blended, with the warm hues of oranges and persimmon predominating in a real feast for the eyes.

The multicoloured, tempting pastries promise subtle pleasures in store, but the wealth of cakes on display differ only in appearance, being all made of sweetened bean dough, pleasant enough, but monotonous.

Specialization even extends to restaurants, or at least the small shops that serve snacks at all hours. There are *soba-ya*, selling buckwheat noodles; *tempura-ya* where one may sample fried fish or shellfish; *sushi-ya* where rice-balls topped with a slice of raw fish are prepared in front of the clients; and *unagi-ya*, where cooks adept in the use of the fan officiate in front of the grill where eels chopped alive are being browned.

If you so wish, they will deliver their specialities to your home, and thus give strollers the surprise of seeing errand-boys weaving deftly in and out of the cars like trick cyclists, with one hand raised in the air to balance a tray piled with china bowls or lacquer boxes several storeys high.

The strolling soba-vendor and the small booths installed in the busiest streets at dusk to serve tardy prowlers or night-watchmen, are one of the most amusing elements of the capital by night.

There would be no end to it if one wanted to enumerate all the minor crafts still practised in the street, curious, wretched crafts that are gradually disappearing just as they have already vanished from more favoured countries. Japan should, however, be given credit for the fact that the most wretched craft of all—begging—is practically unknown there. This is undoubtedly due to the strong family and social ties that drive the obligation to help one another to extremes, and the fact that in Japan the blind who are destitute elsewhere traditionally pursue various professions—primarily massage and acupuncture.

To complete this picture of labour in Japan, we should add that a good half of the country's active population toils from morning to night in offices or factories similar to those all the world over, devoid of picturesqueness, and threatening in a relatively short time to devour what remains of the craftsman's freedom, spontaneity, and fertile imagination.

SPORTS

As in so many other spheres, the Japanese have adopted the sports and amusements of the West. There is no need to enlarge on the brilliant role Japanese swimmers, wrestlers, and gymnasts in general play in international sports meetings. Lawn tennis, table tennis, etc., also have their supporters and experts in Japan, but without the slightest doubt the favourite sport is baseball.

Although cycling competitions and horse racing have become increasingly popular since the end of the last war, in the main this can be attributed to the lure of financial gain rather than the call of sport, immense crowds being attracted by the system of sweepstakes.

Love of games of chance and the fascinating prospect of successful gambling have given rise to those noisy, vulgar establishments known as *pachinko* that have sprung into being since 1948. The name is derived onomatopoeically from the sound of the little balls distributed by these gambling machines in place of money. Such gains may subsequently be exchanged for cigarettes, preserves, soap, and a host of other things. *Pachinko* machines are lined up by the hundred in long rows, and crowds flock to play them.

Sumo

SUMO—According honour to whom honour is due, we should make it

350

plain that *sumo*, or ordinary wrestling, is a sport that has been practised in Japan since time immemorial. It is mentioned in the *Kojiki* (8th century), and has been patronized by the court ever since emperors were emperors.

No village fête would be complete without its wrestling match, in which even primary schoolchildren come to grips. Many a Shinto temple contains a special arena within its precincts. Nowadays these matches are often televised, and clusters of spectators assemble in front of the screens exhibited in shop windows.

Folklore has handed down a whole series of legends about the "strong men" who were endowed with extraordinary might by a god they had once assisted. There is, for instance, the tale of the man who, single-handed, raised the ridge beam of a temple under construction that a thousand men had been unable to shift. These Goliaths were the first *sumo-tori;* they practised a kind of all-in wrestling, often terminating in the death of one of the adversaries.

In our times those mountains of flesh known as *sumo-tori* do not belong to a special race, but they reach this size in height—not to mention girth—as a result of a glandular deficiency. Moreover, they often die at a relatively early age, between fifty and sixty.

The arena, a colossal wooden building, may contain as many as five thousand spectators. In front of the entrance flutter multicoloured flags announcing the names of the competitors in gigantic letters. Nearly all these names end in *yama*, meaning mountain—and this is no misnomer since these heavy, thickset giants, gifted with herculean strength, some-

Judo

times weigh more than four hundred pounds!

The ring consists of a square platform erected in the middle of the stadium, topped with a straw roof or a cloth canopy. In the centre of the square a circle is marked out with bales of straw: the main object of the game is to expel one's adversary from this circle. The public is seated on straw mats arranged in tiers round the ring. The action is governed by forty-eight rules defining twelve movements for each of the three techniques, which consist respectively of pushing, twisting, and hurling one's sparring partner over one's body. The match is won immediately one of the wrestlers touches the outside of the circle with any part of his body.

THE ART OF SABRE FIGHTING—In a country where the feudal system continued until 1868, it is not surprising that the art of sabre-fighting should have been developed to a high degree. It is known as *ken-jutsu*, the art of the sword, or *kendo*, the way of the sword.

Training is carried out with a long stick made of strips of bamboo tied very tightly together. The length of this stick—which exceeds that of a classical blade—is 4 feet 4 inches; the handle, covered in leather, is 1 foot 4 inches long, and held in both hands.

The art of fencing has mainly developed since the 12th century, when Japanese blades were tempered to a degree of perfection rarely equalled elsewhere. Bizen (Okayama) was particularly renowned for its high-quality swords.

The fencer's face is protected by a mask made of metal bars; his head is covered by a hood, falling on to the shoulders and lined with thick wadding. As for the chest and the tops of the thighs, they are shielded by a "coat of mail" made of strips of lacquered bamboo.

The aim is to make "cuts" at the head, face, arms, and trunk, and "thrusts" at the throat. Points are awarded whenever these parts of the body are hit in accordance with certain precise rules.

Judo—We have left to the end the form of sport known as *judo*, which has become extremely popular in Europe over the past few years. The origin of this art, dating back to the middle of the 17th century, is thought to be an adaptation of a form of Chinese wrestling designed for hand-to-hand fights. In that era it was known as *yawara-tori* (from the word *yawara*, meaning gentle), in order to distinguish it from sword-fencing.

Be that as it may, in 1882 Mr Jigoro Kano, an educator who subsequently became a senator, established in Tokyo a kind of training centre for both body and mind, known as the *kodo-kan*. Reviving certain *yawara-tori* techniques, he developed and codified them to produce a form of disciplined wrestling, now known by the name of *ju-jutsu* (the art of litheness), or *judo* (the way of litheness).

Sabre Contest

Size and physical strength are of little importance since, through rigid disciplining of reflexes, this form of wrestling enables one to foil the most brutal attacks and overcome one's opponent by seizing every opportunity to turn his carelessness or weak points to one's own advantage.

The wrestlers wear trousers of coarse, unbleached linen, rather tight fitting and extending to just below the knee; the body is protected by a loose jacket of the same cloth, fastening from left to right and held together at the waist by a narrow belt in white, black, violet, or one of several other colours, according to rank. There are nine grades, but the four highest, from six to nine, are primarily honorary. One may rise from one grade to the next only through arduous training and numerous combats, in which the wrestlers' physical and moral qualities are examined at length.

Training is carried out in a very meticulous fashion, under the constant supervision of qualified professors; it takes place in special rooms known as *dojo* where the floor is covered with thick straw mats. It comprises two major divisions: the first is known as *randori*, or free exercises, in which

the adversaries employ every method of stance, attack, and throwing, provided they do not hurt each other; the other division consists of *kata*, or forms, wherein the exercises are concentrated on certain special forms of attack and defence.

Judo pupils first learn the various ways of falling. Only then do they progress to the most elementary movements, the eight forms of *kuzushi* (unbalance). Then come the two most elaborate techniques: *tsukuri*, or preparation for attack, and *kake*, attack. Wrestling techniques proper comprise the various movements of the three combat possibilities: *nagewaza*, the technique of throwing; *katame-waza*, the technique of holding fast or controlling; and *atewaza*, the technique of attacking the vital points of the body.

A judo match is won immediately one of the wrestlers signifies that he wants to be released from a hold, or when the umpire considers he cannot release himself from a final clinch. In any case, the umpire is entirely free to have a combat begun all over again, or to interrupt it, since it is not a question of overwhelming, wounding, or disabling one's opponent, but of vanquishing him through elegance and purity of movement.

This is just another example of the self-control, beauty of gesture, and extreme refinement that one encounters in every phase of Japanese life.

THE TWILIGHT OF LIFE

I N the preceding chapters, we have followed the various stages in the life of a Japanese from birth to manhood, in every phase of his daily round. Before concluding, we should like to add a word on the "twilight of life"

INKYO—Since the 12th century, in relatively affluent families and in certain rural districts it is customary for the parents, after a long lifetime of toil, to abandon their business worries to the younger generation. This form of voluntary "retirement" is known as *inkyo* (literally: dwelling in the shade).

The elderly men or women are then free to devote themselves to their favourite pastimes or to fulfil hitherto unrealizable dreams such as chess-playing, the tea ceremony, cultivation of flowers, or travel and pilgrimages. In springtime and autumn in particular one often sees huge groups of old people travelling by road or rail to visit famous spots or the most renowned Shinto and Buddhist shrines.

ANNIVERSARIES—The sixty-first birthday is celebrated in a particularly ostentatious way. The reason for this is that, according to a tradition that originated in China, everyone who lives beyond a complete cycle of sixty years is supposed to be "reborn" to another cycle of life. Hence the name *honke-gaeri* (literally: return to one's origins). A family banquet is held in honour of the sexagenarian, and for this special occasion he dons a red kimono, a red bonnet and socks—the colour of baby-clothes.

The seventy-seventh birthday is significant on account of the happy meaning connected with the figure seven. Moreover, the various lines composing the Chinese character for the word "joy" resemble the characters signifying "seven-ten-seven" (the pronunciation of seventy-seven) linked together. The eighty-eighth birthday is likewise based on a pun: the Chinese character for "rice" (a precious product in the Far East, as well we know) resembles the characters "eight-ten-eight" (pronunciation of eighty-eight) superimposed.

FUNERAL CEREMONIES—Then comes the time when the Japanese sleeps his last sleep. His body is washed in hot water and clad in a garment of light cotton.

The vigil *(otsuya)* begins the following evening and lasts throughout the night. Friends and relations arrive with gifts, cakes, boxes of tea, etc. Meanwhile, a photograph of the deceased is placed on the very top of the temporary altar erected in the largest room in the house. The gifts are laid out on the shelves below, whilst a perfume-burner is placed at the foot.

A priest, usually of a Buddhist sect, recites *sutras* and burns the first pinches of incense. Each of the visitors then goes to kneel in front of the altar, burns three pinches of incense, and meditates. As elsewhere throughout the world, the vigil is an occasion for discreet celebrations, in memory of the merits of the departed.

The body is placed in a coffin, oblong in shape for the Shinto cult, and in the form of a box or barrel for Buddhists (in the latter case, the corpse is curled up inside the barrel).

The procession goes as far as the crematorium where the body and coffin are burnt simultaneously—a custom that has become generalized since the expansion of Buddhism in the 8th century. Finally, the ashes, placed in an urn or a box, are interred in the family burial ground.

In order to make sure the deceased crosses to the other side, services are held every seventh day until the forty-ninth day, by which time he is supposed to have finally crossed the space between the "two worlds".

Thereafter, offerings are made to the spirit of the deceased on the *butsu-dan* or Buddhist family altar, on the first, third, seventh, and thirteenth anniversaries of his death.

MODERN
JAPAN

現代日本

INFORMATION AND EDUCATION MEDIA

E VERY morning at about half past five before going to school a small boy laden with newspapers, which he counts as he runs along, clatters your letterbox. For Tokyo, this is the signal to waken. The housewives get up and push away the wooden screens; the men kneel on the mats, drinking their first bowl of tea and reading the papers.

DAILY PAPERS—In our house eight newspapers are delivered each morning. Not counting my three English-language editions, that makes five papers for a family of five Japanese adults. This is approximately the average for Tokyo and very little more than that for Japan as a whole, numbering over 45 million adults out of a total population of 89 million.

And there are thousands of small boys like the one in our street who run through the town at break of day each morning, passing the milkboys, the vendors of morning soup, the dustmen, the early pedlars, and the casual labourers hastening to catch the first underground train in order to wait outside the labour exchange for a "job by the day".

Whatever the weather, and whatever their lessons and homework, all over the country youngsters trot by with copies of some of the most widely circulated newspapers in the world under their arms. Each day they distribute 186 daily papers, the total printing of which runs into 35 million copies. From the far Siberian north of Hokkaido to the tropical south of Kyushu, the list is headed by the *Asahi*, the *Mainichi*, and often the *Yomiuri*, which are perhaps the three largest newspapers in the world.

The *Asahi* boasts a circulation of 6,000,000 in the morning and 2,700,000 in the evening; the *Mainichi* runs into 4,500,000 in the morning and 2,900,000 in the evening, whilst the *Yomiuri* has a run of 3,000,000 in the morning and 1,600,000 in the evening. And in addition to these enormous printings, a dozen other papers exceed a million readers. The three largest provincial dailies—the *Hokkaido Shimbun* of Sapporo, the *Chubu Nippon* of Nagoya, and the *Nishi Nippon* of Fukuoka (Kyushu) each print over two million copies daily.

In the underground each morning, everyone is absorbed in a newspaper. In the evening rush-hour at about five o'clock in Tokyo, the passengers read the *Tokyo Shimbun*, a cultural daily exceeding a million in circulation. At about 10.00 in the evening revellers mellow with *sake*, on their way back from gay parties, indulge in lighter literature in the form of the *Naigai Times*, or some other popular-style daily, each of which has a printing of . . . . 200,000.

PERIODICALS—In addition to this flow of daily papers, there is an even greater avalanche of weeklies and other periodicals. Each month 2,500 periodicals are published, five or six of which boast a literary standing on a par with *The London Magazine*. One of them, the *Bungei Shunju* —"Spring and Autumn of Literature"—prints about half-a-million. The Japanese seem to live for literature; between clients, even the bootblacks often immerse themselves in monthly papers of the first water.

One has the impression that in this immense, overpopulated city of Tokyo, where, barely separated from each other by the slender walls of their houses or simply by fusuma, eight million men and women live serried together; eight million pairs of eyes are roving incessantly from top to bottom of the tiny lines of elegant characters, each of which to our Western eyes seems to have a magic life of its own.

BIRTH OF THE PRESS—Whilst the history of the "news industry" as a whole goes back a hundred years, it really began to boom only half-a-century ago. Its birth may perhaps be traced back to the day when Motoyama, the new director of the *Osaka Mainichi*—the Osakan daily—had an observatory built on the roof of his building, from which a telescope was permanently directed at the "enemy", the *Osaka Asahi*, or "Osaka Rising Sun". And there he perched, with one eye glued on his objective, dreaming of the

The Asahi Building in Tokyo

day when he would hear the streets of Osaka resound with cries of "*Mainichi-Asahi*" instead of the customary "*Asahi-Mainichi*".

That was in 1906 when the war with Manchuria was at its height, and the newspapers were waging a private war amongst themselves with a volley of special editions—running into approximately twenty-two per month—announced by newsboys ringing little bells. Innovations such as this increased circulation by several tens of thousands; but the *Asahi* maintained the lead.

The *Asahi* was the first to announce the record circulation of 400,000, celebrated by the purchase of a new aeroplane, the fifth in its squadron. A few months later the *Mainichi* victoriously retorted with 400,000, shortly after it had revived the popularity of the old puppet theatre in Osaka, which had long been on the wane. Osaka was no longer big enough. The two giants had practically eliminated all the secondary papers. Still vying with each other, and still side by side, they had conquered Kyoto and Kobe, Shimonoseki and Fukuoka. The immediate objective then became Nagoya

363

and Central Japan. Subsequently each in turn attained a circulation of 600,000, then 700,000 copies. They agreed to call a truce on dumping in the west and south of Japan since both the *Asahi*, as the professors' newspaper, and the *Mainichi*, as that of the tradespeople, cherished the same dream: that of attacking and conquering Tokyo where sixteen medium-sized but well-edited papers were fighting for the market.

Once again the *Asahi* was the first in the field, by reviving a small paper that was vegetating. Boycotted by its confrères and distributors alike, the tiny *Tokyo Asahi* was fast losing ground. The founder of the *Osaka Asahi*, Murayama, the son of a Samurai, then established himself in Tokyo. One day, sporting his frock-coat, top hat, and a grey tie, with a silk handkerchief adorning his breast-pocket and a silver-knobbed walking-stick in hand, he made a tour of all the newsvendors in the capital. With each vendor he was courteous in the extreme, bowing before them as profusely as if he were asking for their daughter's hand. By the end of the week, 80 % of the newsvendors were supporting the *Tokyo Asahi* which was thus resuscitated, to reach a circulation of 100,000.

Motoyama also went to Tokyo. He bought up an old newspaper, the *Tokyo Nichi Nichi*, amalgamated it with a satellite that was rapidly declining, and constructed a building in the shape of a keep to show his intention of holding fast. This was the heyday of Japanese economy. As a result of the First World War, the Westerners had practically abandoned all the Asian markets to Japanese trade. It was the era when audacity knew no bounds. It was also the time of the earthquake in Tokyo which destroyed both the capital and Yokohama in 1923. The wooden houses blazed like torches, and all the newspapers with them—or all but two, the *Tokyo Nichi Nichi* and the *Hochi*. The *Mainichi (Tokyo Nichi Nichi)* then launched a major offensive. Followed by a youth carrying a case full of gold, Motoyama in turn made a tour of the distributors throughout the ruined city, offering each of them a handful of yen to rebuild his booth and become his exclusive agent. The streets resounded with cries of *"Mainichi, Mainichi alone"*: Motoyama was nearing his aim. But the *Asahi* was being built up again.

Motoyama intensified his campaign. He lowered the price of the *Mainichi*, distributed premiums, cinema tickets, rice coupons.... (The *Mainichi* became a goldmine for the distributors, enabling them to make a living simply by selling it .... to the ragmakers.)

One year after the earthquake, the situation stabilized itself. The *Mainichi* printed 400,000, the *Asahi* some 150,000, and a number of smaller newspapers managed to hold their heads above water.

One of the latter, a paper that had borrowed the name of the former "Gossip Column"—*Yomiuri*—was bought up by Shoriki, a man in his forties who was formerly a brilliant head of the Secret Police, and a friend of the ex-Minister of the Interior who had handed in his resignation following an attempt on the life of the Emperor. To redeem himself, the policeman turned journalist, and its executive, Shoriki, had genius. A year later he was in prison, but the *Yomiuri* had a circulation of 130,000. And it continued to grow. Whilst the *Asahi* and *Mainichi* were buying up aeroplanes (one had seventeen by 1938 and the other fifteen) and organizing aerial exploits such as the Kamikaze's Tokyo–London flight in ninety-four hours and the Nihongo's world tour, the *Yomiuri* was treating Tokyo like another province, bringing out district editions.... and inaugurating coloured illustrations, games, etc. By pandering to the public, it became the accepted newspaper of Japan as a whole, firmly backed by the powers-that-be. In 1937 it was the leading newspaper of the capital, and by 1939 its circulation had reached 1,000,000.

The three giants had thus asserted themselves, and conquered Japan. They now wished to share the Far East. Through the medium of the "Information Bureau" the government reduced the number of dailies from 106 to 59, to the advantage of the larger ones, and, to reward them for kotowing to super-nationalism and distributing the news communiqués of the Domei Agency—which had become the propagator of the "holy war"—it shared the loot

Late Extra!

amongst them. The *Asahi* was granted an exclusivity for reporting in the Philippines, the *Mainichi* in Java, the *Yomiuri* in Burma and Timor.

Came war, defeat, and utter confusion. The press became so unreliable that the Emperor lost confidence in it. His declaration regarding the cessation of hostilities on the 15th August, 1945 was made by radio. Then came occupation, and the radio continued to be the favourite informational medium.

Meanwhile Japanese journalists, freed after fifteen years of tyranny at home, shook off the yoke of their former serfdom. In quest of a democratic solution, they wavered towards the left and formed powerful unions in an attempt to eliminate the influence of the onetime directors who had been stripped of their titles but not of their shares.

After a brief period of effacement, the American authorities entrusted the direction of the immense Japanese press to a former provincial newspaperman from the U.S.A. The latter brought force to bear, in order to put the *Yomiuri*, for one, on the right road. Certain publications were suspended, and the press was henceforth subjected to censorship as severe as during the war. Even the form changed: instead of the thousands of Chinese characters utilized prior to the war, a maximum of 1,850 was permitted.

So, to forget the present hard times, people listen to the radio, a network in a class of its own, broadcasting some of the finest programmes in the world.

RADIO AND TELEVISION—Whilst the press, handicapped in its movements and hostile to the people and the authorities alike, was clashing with the thousand-and-one irritations created by all-powerful "paternalism", the radio managed to give the impression that it was subjected to less outside interference than was printer's ink. Radiomen went out into the streets to glean first-hand impressions from passers-by, and each listener had the feeling he was hearing himself expound his own state of mind. The radio became cultural, and even surreptitiously resistant.

All this serves to explain the vogue it now enjoys. The relatively low price both of receivers and of the monthly tax should also be borne in mind. Although a poor country with a standard of living far lower than that of many other nations, Japan boasts a radio-set for every six inhabitants, and in urban areas, one per person (in the U.K. there is one for every four in-

Newspaper District in Tokyo

367

habitants approximately, and in the U.S.A. for almost every inhabitant).

At home there are six of us, and there are five radio-sets. The master of the house prefers historical programmes and political commentaries. His wife listens to the "quiz" sessions and the broadcasts for women in which she learns all about everything: what women's rights entitle them to, how to run the household, and general reactions to the various events of daily life. She is particularly fond of the interviews and commentaries transmitted direct from the street by roving reporters equipped with miniature recorders. As for junior, he tunes in to broadcasts of baseball matches and *sumo*—Japanese classical wrestling. The daughter favours programmes of classical music, songs, and educational broadcasts such as the "Joys of Music". Speaking for myself, I am mainly interested in the news. The only person who is not content is the maid. She is saving up to buy herself a small set of her very own, on which, throughout the livelong day, she can listen to the tangos and raucous songs of the "bandits" known as *naniwa bushi*.

In the little shopping streets of Tokyo, each tradesman has his loud-speaker constantly blaring, often tuned in to a different station from his neighbour. You have to walk twenty yards or so to find your programme again, or shut yourself up in a small café dedicated to Bach, Mozart, or Beethoven, where you may escape from the cacophony and the bleating and listen to good music.

The cafés, restaurants, department stores, and newspaper buildings have installed television sets in their windows or beneath small porches outside. Through the infernal din of the *pachinko*, loudspeakers, and taxi horns, the people flock round the screen, forcing their way in like a squadron of suicide-planes. There is a constant urge to see, know, and learn a little more. It has been demonstrated that everyone who installs a television set in his shop doubles his turnover. Moreover, the Japanese is not so much curious as eager to acquire new knowledge. To a certain extent this explains his passion for the most modern informational media.

Whilst the radio's prestige is well-established, television is still in the research stage (three transmitting stations are in existence so far); however, great efforts are being made to improve it from one day to the next. Pictures of all kinds have an amazing attraction for this visually minded people. What great strides have been made in half-a-century, and more particularly since the armistice.

EDUCATION—On the morrow of capitulation the country attempted to sort herself out. It was difficult for Japan to pull herself together again after the first total invasion in her history. Having it daily drummed into them that they had been misused by their former leaders, Japanese youth, as elsewhere, tended towards the left. The students—characterized by their square caps and tunics fastened to the neck with brass buttons —began to discover that the democracy they had inherited from defeat was merely an illusion. They wanted to be entirely free, and were suspicious of the intrigues that would one day unmask their former chiefs and restore them to power. Above all, in breaking away for the first time from the set teaching of the past, they were anxious to learn more and explore new spheres. The materialism and technical progress that the Americans introduced were not enough. To replace the dreams that used to be served up to them as the basis of their history, they yearned for greater knowledge and a universal field of learning.

In order to provide spiritual nourishment for forty million under-twenties, approximately five million of whom were students, the Americans reformed education

369

by introducing a system based on their own. Private universities then began to develop at lightning speed. Nine years after the defeat, there were already 550 throughout the country. In Tokyo alone in less than two years, in addition to three State Universities, some 140 non-governmental establishments came into being. Whatever may be the value of the diploma conferred, the young Japanese all aspire after a university title; first, to satisfy their thirst for an encyclopaedia-like knowledge; second, in order to join some student association; third, and above all, to have an additional chance of finding employment some day in a country permanently threatened by an economic slump. For all that, even today after reconstruction and the Korean boom, the number of university graduates who find a stable situation within a year of leaving college is estimated at barely 5 %.

The big universities (particularly that of Tokyo which, in student slang, is always referred to as the "Red Gate" on account of its ancient doorway, and which, by the way, has lost its title of Imperial University) are constantly besieged by thousands of young people. The same thing applies to the three largest private universities: Waseda, Keio, and Meiji. In 1954 the University of Waseda alone received 120,000 candidates for the 5,000 vacancies available. In the Keio Faculty of Political Economy, the vacancies were put up for competition, at the rate of one per thirty-seven pupils, already short-listed. A university of needlework has 50,000 students throughout Japan, of whom there are 6,000 in Tokyo alone. It reached the stage where vacancies were actually being bought, as the former rich families could not bear to think that democracy was also levelling the right to education. In fact, at its height the situation—commonly known in Japanese as the "postwar reign"—was similar to that in certain European countries after liberation, with their profiteers and adolescent misfits.

CULTURAL LIFE—Despite this atmosphere of cultural famine and dubious transactions even in artistic spheres, it was for all that the springtime of the new culture. Yet it was a spring where few books blossomed, for the old volumes had been prohibited by the military, the more recent ones by the Americans, and there had been time to prepare only summaries of future works to be used as textbooks. This explains the queues of students to be seen from six o'clock in the morning at the doors of the libraries that survived air raids and looting. And this is the most tragic and poverty-stricken sphere of all. The country as a whole contains barely 1,500 libraries, less than 300 of which possess a stock of more than 3,000 volumes. One alone—Ueno Library in Tokyo—contains nearly a million, three others exceeding half-a-million. Altogether, there are less than nine million books to be fought over by fifteen million readers. Moreover, most of them are old editions published between the 1923 earthquake and the wartime fires. In the main, there is seldom more than one copy of each title.

The great world powers have done very little for these libraries: the Americans have made a number of donations, so have the British, but the French contribution is negligible.

Disappointed by the limits to international philanthropy, the Japanese have frantically set about translating Western authors. Certain masters created translation chains, to the great advantage of all the middlemen involved in the sale of copyrights.

Direct importation of foreign books developed in proportion to the

Kyoto Town Hall

quotas set by the Exchange Control authorities: 50 % from the U.S.A., 20 % from the U.K., and barely 5 % from France. But these imported books are expensive, and Japanese students therefore continue to read in the booksellers' shops round the Kanda district, which is to Tokyo what Charing Cross Road is to London. And there again, the books are not up to date ....

In an attempt to appease this yearning for the outside world that neither books nor newspapers could satisfy, the press, the radio, and nascent television began to invite outstanding representatives of modern art. Exhibitions of Matisse, Picasso, Braque, and Rouault were organized; the masterpieces from the Louvre made the perilous journey. A number of musicians were also invited, from Yehudi Menuhin to Walter Gieseking, and Louis Armstrong to Jacques Thibaud, who met his death en route; stars such as Marian Anderson and Josephine Baker, and scores of other dancers, lecturers, and scientists. And every time, despite the high price of entry—for Japanese pockets—there was a full house; Matisse drew over 100,000 visitors in Tokyo alone; pianists filled theatres containing 4,000 people twice daily.

The young people of Japan are broken-hearted at the thought that they are at the end of the earth. Their dream is to break away, travel, and escape from those four isles. And they welcome every opportunity to make this reverie come true, if only in imaginary voyages: they read, they study, they look and listen, they queue at the doors of inadequate libraries .... and they day-dream.

AN UNSMILING ECONOMY

WHEN in 1868 Japan reopened her gates to the outside world, the Japanese gave up their habit of "separating the wheat from the chaff" (known in Japan as *mabiki*, from the ancient practice of putting a ball of tissue paper in the nostrils of newborn children regarded as surfeit). The total population, which had been maintained at about thirty million inhabitants for the past 300 years, immediately soared skyhigh. The government of the new Emperor Meiji, who dreamt of a brand new country as hard as nails, was at once confronted with the urgent and thorny problem of feeding this constantly growing population, without alienating the country's independence to imperialism, the danger of which was beginning to make itself felt.

There were only two solutions.

The first was to develop agricultural production in the four main islands of the archipelago, which are as big as two-thirds of France. Unhappily, 80 % of the soil is laterite, covered with a few inches of arable land. And how could an ever-growing population live on 16 % of cultivable soil?

The second solution was to export manufactured products, thus enabling Japan to procure foreign currency for the purchase of the necessary foodstuffs. But there again the gods were unkind. Apart from copper, there was practically nothing in her soil that could be used for international trading.

All that remained was a variant of this second solution: the creation and development of a modern industry primarily concentrated on export. Although lacking both raw materials and outlets, Japan adopted this

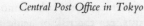

Central Post Office in Tokyo

expedient despairingly—yet enthusiastically. So enthusiastically, in fact, that, whilst for thirty years her industry provided a livelihood for the ever-increasing younger generation, she forgot the prime object of industrializing the country—to obtain, through export of finished products, the foreign exchange required for purchasing food.

For the young enthusiasts of the Meiji era, industrialization of the country became a symbol of superiority. We all know the outcome: the annexation of Formosa (1896), Korea (1911), Japanese occupation of Asian markets during the First World War which had obliged Westerners to withdraw, the subsequent annexation of Manchuria (1932), war with China, the dream of a "Greater Asia", that of world conquest .... and the ensuing collapse.

In 1945 Japan concluded her concertina-like expansion, and retreated to her 1868 frontiers. But she now numbered 72 million inhabitants. In losing her empire, she also lost three-quarters of her 1940 production capacity. All she retained was a conviction of her vocation as "the factory of Asia".

The former masters of her economy, the famous Zaibatsu—the "clans of the favoured"—or trusts, ran the risk of being purged, but the collapse of their groups would have involved Japanese economy in a serious period of confusion. Moreover, the American occupying forces were deaf to Japan's vocation as an industrial power. They dreamt of a pacific Japan, cured for ever of her schemes of aggression. But, like the governors of the Meiji era, they too were confronted with the problem of how to help the country feed herself.

As in the past, certain experts favoured the agricultural solution, which would have averted for all time the risk of Japanese industrial competition on world markets and Japan's return to the path of adventure. There was nothing to be gained in surface, every inch of worthwhile land being under cultivation already. The only answer was to increase output and develop a sense of ownership in the peasants. The agricultural reformation was consequently carried out in their favour, each family inheriting a plot of land about as large as a pocket handkerchief.

But, despite these measures which were more spectacular than effective, Japanese stomachs continued to demand an additional 200,000 tons of rice, 40,000 tons of corn, 100,000 tons of sugar, and 60,000 tons of soya annually, representing a total of $ 600,000,000 worth of imported foodstuffs.

The first harvests were bad. The "democratized" peasants ran up debts with dishonest financiers, who mortgaged their black market profits.

The sole way out was the second solution of the Meiji era —an industrial renaissance, or revival of the "risk factory". The Americans hesitated for a long while, being still keen to encourage democracy. Meanwhile, inflation spread, the black market reigned, and the virtues they were so anxious to inculcate into Japanese youth

"Tsurumi" Naval Dockyard in the Bay of Tokyo

were powerless against daily hunger. The U.S.A. granted Japan large-scale assistance, fully aware that their efforts were gratuitous, but the Japanese infant became heavier and heavier. The prisoners returned home, together with the six million emigrants that the conquest had brought to the continent. Unemployment was on the increase, the standard of living was declining and, not knowing which way to turn, the Japanese drifted at the mercy of waves of discontent. The Americans then decided to rebuild and rehabilitate Japanese industry, but they set about it with great prudence, avoiding any form of manufacture that might serve a warlike purpose. That was in 1947, and the first step was the textile industry.

The next two years were a curious period of confusion. Whilst on the one hand the government was attempting to disrupt the former cartels, on the other, in the throes of inflation, it was doing all it could to help the "good industries" which, of course, were not entirely divorced from the former groups. It was during this period that a new industrial class—the "postwar profiteers"—began to flourish, using the black market as their raw material, and taking full advantage of the confused situation.

The occupation authorities were exceptionally indulgent in regard to the banks which were merely obliged to change their names. The former groups that had grown up round development companies before the war, under the names of Mitsui, Mitsubishi, Sumitomo, Yasuda, etc., replanted themselves in a kind of mushroom-bed round the banks —which financed them—and these banks were the selfsame firms that used to be cultivated by the cartels. Mitsui gave birth to 250 "independent" firms, Mitsubishi to over 200.... For a while some people made a pretence of believing that the old cartels were broken for ever, and that Japanese economy could step off again on the right foot—a democratic foot. It looked as if the only task that remained was to reabsorb inflation. SCAP entrusted this difficult assignment to a Detroit banker, Mr Dodge.

He drew up a programme epitomized by the slogan: "Super-balanced budget", in which expenditure was reduced and taxes were increased.

But another impediment was to stem the boom in Japanese industry. Japanese products which, prior to the war, were the cheapest in the world, suddenly became the most expensive.

Paradoxical though it may seem, the high cost of Japanese goods is

Industrial Suburb of Yokohama

easily explained by the fact that Japan has to import the majority (if not all) of her basic products. Since three-quarters of the coke required for her industry comes from the U.S.A., manufacturing costs are three times as high as for American or British industry. The same thing applies to rubber and to 90 % of the ferrous minerals.

Another factor is the increasingly high cost of labour. Although very low in comparison with international standards, salaries in Japanese industry are relatively high (300 % above prewar level). Moreover, whilst there is a surfeit of manpower in the country, the output per man-hour is extremely low. By way of illustration, the extraction of a ton of coal, for instance, requires 3 Indians, 2.3 Japanese, 1.3 Frenchmen, 1 German from the Ruhr, 0.8 Englishmen, 0.4 Canadians, 0.2 Americans. As a result, although the Japanese miner is paid five times less than his American colleague, a ton of coal costs only $1.05 in manpower in the U.S.A. as against $3.64 in Japan.

Industry, in the thick of reconstruction, was well aware of its difficulties, which were aggravated by the fact that its former markets had been substantially reduced: China, who used to absorb as much as 20 % of Japan's exports and supplied 12 % of the imported products required in her industry, shut her doors to trade with the Japanese Empire. Manchuria was also closed to her, and Korea boycotted Japanese goods. Hong Kong was reluctant to act as a port of transit. South-East Asia continued to be tied by preferential Empire tariffs. India, who had long been the main buyer of cotton goods, became a competitor. Pakistan alone seemed willing to absorb Japanese products, for a certain length of time.

The future looked black. And then, suddenly, "manna" fell from heaven, in the sorry guise of the Korean War. Japanese industry went full steam ahead. The arms factories, hitherto relegated to the background, became the most in demand. The index figure of industrial production tripled and in 1950 actually exceeded the 1934 figure. The war yielded $800,000,000 per year.

The war may have saved Japan, but the livelihood it produced was purely artificial. It tied her to a single buyer, the United States, who has become responsible for two-thirds of Japanese exports and one-third of her imports of raw materials. The rebuilt industry even changed the face of a country which five years previously had been looked upon as bucolic. The produce of arms factories had become her principal export. Textiles, which had long held the lead, were relegated to third place. In order to live, Japan was in need of the boom produced by the war.

Since the Korean War came to an end, Japan has been experiencing a slump. A wave of bankruptcies is sweeping the country. Every month

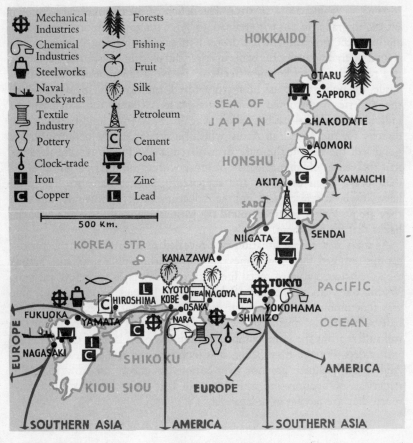

Economic Map of Japan

over 50,000 unhonoured cheques are issued, representing a total overdraft of several million pounds sterling. In 1953, out of a population of 87 million inhabitants, six million full or part-time workers were unemployed. The country is doing her best to force the doors to new markets, the major temptations still being China—which in 1953 represented 1 % of Japanese foreign trade—and rearmament.

But, taken as a whole, foreign trade represents only 8 % of the national income, as against 18 % in 1934. The deficit of the commercial balance is on the upgrade. In 1953 it attained 50 % of the total imports. Becoming alarmed, the government has decreed an austerity policy, calling for the refusal of credit—hence the bankruptcies; and blocking of salaries—resulting in a restriction of trade union freedom. To avoid the upheavals that might ensue, the police force has been reorganized, and executive power—which the Americans disrupted in an attempt to facilitate the expansion of individual freedom—has been allowed again. Apart from industries working directly for the American Army which, in occupying the country, makes good half the deficit, the only firms that manage to survive are the ones that succeed in obtaining loans—in other words, the multiple mushrooms that sprang from the great and supposedly defunct Zaibatsu. The dead have thus been resuscitated, and the Zaibatsu reformed; however, this time they are no longer grouped round the former export firms, but round the banks that finance them.

As soon as the new situation was revealed in its true light, the former groups resumed their old names, and Mitsubishi, Sumitomo, and Yasuda are as concrete a part of social life in present-day Japan as before the war. Within ten years of the end of the war, the Japanese economic machine was functioning again, thanks to its military manufactures, on the same basis as before and during the war. As far as normal trade is concerned, it still suffers from the same complaints as in the past: lack of raw materials and outlets. For the time being, it is living on the American occupation. And if the Japanese are not over-curious to know just how long this American occupation and assistance will last, they often ask "just how much they are paying in independence"

IDIOSYNCRASIES
OF JAPAN

IN 150 WORDS

AND MINOR SURPRISES IN STORE FOR TOURISTS

Harakiri—A vulgar word for *seppuku*, meaning "to cut one's stomach" (the first foreigners who found their way to Japan and brought back this expression hardly frequented high society). The operation consisted of slitting the stomach from left to right and from bottom to top, by means of a short sabre carefully wrapped in paper so that the blade protruded only about two inches. This symbolic wound seldom being sufficient to cause death, a friend, relation, or vassal then chopped off the victim's head. This form of suicide has totally disappeared nowadays. Don't make the same mistake as a certain journalist who wrote: "The young officer committed harakiri by shooting himself in the temple."

Table Manners—Never leave your chopsticks vertically in the rice as this is the way in which the offerings to the dead are arranged. By the same

Abunai: dangerous. Exclamatory: ABUNAI YO! Look out! One of those many-purpose words that every foreigner ought to know (*see also*: DAME).

Ano ne: call word, without any precise meaning, used only to attract attention. The first word the foreigner learns.

Arigato: thank you!—More politely: DO MO ARIGATO GOZAIMASHITA.

Banzai: literally—ten thousand years; equivalent to our "Long live . . . ." There are other ways of saying the same thing, such as CHIYO (a thousand generations), YACHITO (eight thousand generations).

Bashi: *see* HASHI.

Biwa: four-string viola, as used by medieval bards.

Bozu: monk. Hence: bonze.

Bugaku: court dances of Chinese origin, performed in the Palace and in certain temples.

Don't be astonished to see a hurried cyclist weaving his way through the crowd, and balancing six trays laden with steaming food, one on top of another. You'll learn he is a waiter delivering a meal for six to a private home—and you may be sure not a drop of sauce will be spilt on the way.

token, ladies, always close your kimono by folding the left flap over the right. Closing in the opposite direction is a sign of mourning.

At a dinner party, don't eat too quickly. You are there to enjoy yourself and not to gorge yourself. On the other hand, don't be afraid of over-drinking; it would take an impressive number of those little goblets of *sake* to upset a good whisky-drinker. Don't be in too much of a hurry to finish any of the tiny dishes that are set in front of you by the dozen. It would be immediately replaced, and you would be morally obliged to do justice to it. Chat, drink, joke, compose verses, sing, and, from time to time negligently dip the tip of your chopsticks in the dishes. After two hours of this sport, you will feel satisfied, and far more comfortable than after an only too copious Western or Chinese dinner. Contrary to Chinese custom, you are perfectly entitled to commence, and even empty, the

BUNRAKU: puppet theatre in Osaka (*see* JORURI).

BUSHI: warrior, knight—a term used by the Japanese where Westerners would say SAMURAI.

BUTSU: Buddha. DAIBUTSU: colossal statue of Buddha, in Kamakura and Nara.

CHA: tea; one generally says O-CHA. "CHA-NO-YU": "hot water for tea", or the Tea Ceremony. CHA-DO: The Art of Tea-making, or the ceremonial rites. CHA-WAN; tea bowl (often of great value). CHA-DAI: tea money, i.e. tip.

DAIMYO: feudal lord. DAIMYO and SAMURAI constitute the BUSHI class. Literally, "great name".

DAME: one of the most useful terms in the Japanese language, implying broken, spoilt, improper, impossible, dangerous, etc. The word with which foreigners pro-

tect themselves against the countless traps the Japanese set for the uninitiated.

DO: the road, or Way; used only in composite words. In the sense of road—TOKAIDO: the East Sea Road; SUI-DO: waterway. In the sense of Way, i.e. manner of art, with a moral tinge about it: BUSHIDO (the Way of the Warrior); CHA-DO (the Art of Tea-making); KYU-DO (archery); KA-DO (the floral Art); JUDO (the Art of litheness), etc.

DOH: pavilion of a Buddhist temple.

DOZO: be so kind as to; if you please. Used in inviting someone to help themselves, make themselves at home, come in ....

EMA: literally—painted horse. Small wooden plaque bearing a painting or calligraphy, offered to a temple as an *ex-voto*.

bowl of rice that terminates the meal, but you will rarely feel so inclined.

SHOPPING—There are plenty of large, well-laid-out stores, known as "depato" (from department store). There you will find practically everything that is on sale in establishments of this nature all the world over, plus a number of departments peculiar to the country, including a kimono floor; a "Japanese art" floor displaying ceramics, lacquerwork, dolls, bamboo objects; utensils for the tea ceremony, calligraphy, flower arrangement, etc. The small shops, on the other hand, are extremely specialized, division of labour being the golden rule, to meet the permanent surfeit of manpower. The most curious offshoot of this is the way in which tradesmen selling similar objects are grouped by street: there is thus a street where one sees nothing but radio sets in spare parts (one shop sells the cabinet,

EMAKIMONO: scroll of paintings. Illustrated manuscripts written on rolls of silk or paper several yards long. Also known as: MAKIMONO.

FURO: hot bath; generally taken in a wooden tub, lined inside with copper, and heated from underneath.

FUROSHIKI: a silk or cotton square in which packets carried by hand are wrapped. Advantageously takes the place of a handbag, briefcase, or even a small suitcase. Ladies of fashion have squares to match their kimonos.

FUSUMA: sliding partitions forming interior separations in houses; opaque and often decorated with paintings—not to be confused with SHOJI forming the outer walls and made of translucent paper.

GEISHA: literally—someone versed

in the arts. There being a surfeit of literature on the subject, we

In each district there is a watch-tower where a fireman perches untiringly day and night, ready to ring out a warning at the slightest sign of suspect smoke or the tiniest suspicious glimmer. It's often a false alarm, but prevention is better than fire . . . .

another the valves, a third the wiring, and so on); another where they sell only sweets, books, or accessories for the Buddhist cult, as the case may be.

FIRES—In olden days, fires were called the "flower of Edo". Every town in Japan has been periodically destroyed by this scourge, and the wind has only to join the fray for the fire to spread like lightning through the houses of wood and paper. Each village boasts a watch-tower complete with a bell. The firemen are remarkably well organized and equipped, and uncommonly efficient; they usually have to pander to the fire by cutting down the neighbouring houses. They are so devoted to their dangerous duty that there are hardly ever any victims, except perhaps amongst the rescuers themselves. To protect themselves against falling sparks, the latter have no need to dwell on it. We should, however, point out that

If you notice a smell of burnt flesh, you'll probably find there's a healer's dispensary nearby. Moxa (literally mokusa) is shock treatment that consists of driving wads of ground artemisia under the skin, and setting fire to them. Should you suffer from rheumatism, this is apparently just what the doctor ordered.

they are not what they are often idly thought to be . . . .

GETA: shoes basically composed of a wooden block attached to the feet by cords interlaced between the big and the second toe.

GO-: a prefix indicating that the word to which it is attached refers to the Emperor, to a god, to a person worthy of respect, or simply to the second person. O-, ON-, MI- (rarer) have the same meaning. Not to be translated by "honourable", "august", etc.

GOHEI: strips of paper offered to a god.

HAIKAI: poem of seventeen beats.

HAKAMA: kind of skirt-cum-trousers slit on one side which men wear over their kimonos. At one time adopted by bluestockings, schoolteachers, and suffragettes.

HAMA: beach; forms a component

wear helmets with neckguards, curiously reminiscent of the ancient warriors' headgear.

FIREWORKS—If fire is a constant menace, for all that it is also a source of joy when under control. The most unimportant festival, especially in summer, is a pretext for a spree of "fire flowers". All the toyshops sell "outfits for the little firework-maker", providing children with a harmless assortment of squibs, Bengal lights, and small rockets. For adults, the municipal corporation of Tokyo continues to hold its wonderful firework displays on the Sumida River, for which it has been famed since the Tokugawa era. The best way of enjoying them to this day is by going to have a drink with musicians of the fair sex, on the boats hired out by the riverside restaurants.

of various place-names, e.g. YOKO-HAMA.

HAORI: loose jacket, which, with the hakama, completes male ceremonial dress. Women wear a more brightly coloured variety.

HARAKIRI: vulgarism for SEPPUKU.

HARI: needle, acupuncture.

HASHI: literally, stick for eating, i.e. chopstick; generally referred to as O-HASHI.

HASHI: bridge. In compound words: -BASHI, e.g. NIHON-BASHI.

HIBACHI: "fire-pot"—charcoal brazier made of ceramics or wood, lined with copper—the sole means of heating in Japan.

IE: the house. To express the idea of possession: UCHI—my house, the "home"; O-TAKU—your house, the "residence".

INRO: a series of small superimposed boxes worn on a belt, containing the personal seal (IN), and various drugs or perfumes. In keen demand for collectors.

IYA: disagreeable. IYADA!: "I don't like it!", "no!"—favourite expression of the under-fives.

-JI: Sino-Japanese reading of TERA, Buddhist temple. Always a compound in the names of temples.

JIN: Sino-Japanese reading of HITO—man. Used as a component in names of nationalities: NIHON-JIN (Japanese); IGIRISU-JIN (English); FURANSU-JIN (French), etc.

JINJA: Shinto temple.

JINRIKISHA: vehicle (SHA) drawn by human (JIN) power (RIKI). Hence the English word rickshaw. Hardly ever used in Japan nowadays.

JORURI: chanted recitative accompanying Bunraku.

JUDO: the art of being lithe.

JU-JUTSU (incorrectly spelt jiu-jitsu):

TIPPING—Tips are practically unknown. Don't offer them inconsiderately, since you will run the risk of hurting the person who has rendered you a service; the way in which he feigns to ignore your gesture would make you lose face. On the other hand, if you stay in an inn, you will be expected to pay a supplement "for tea" *(cha-dai)* that may be as much as half or even the total price requested. However, this practice has almost died out, except in remote country districts, and in this case the rule of conduct will be indicated by the reasonableness of the bill. Most hotels now add a *sabisu* (service charge) of 10–20 %. In such a case, pay the price indicated, and discreetly slip a note (wrapped up) to the waitress who served your meals. But no one will ever lower himself to ask you for a tip.

PRESENTS—Never is a gift refused, on the other hand, provided it is offered

the technique of litheness; to show that a moral element was being introduced, the reformers of this sport called it JU-DO.

KABUKI: one of the three types of Japanese classical drama.

KAGURA: sacred dances of Shinto temples.

KAKEMONO: paintings or calligraphy hung in the *tokonoma*.

KAMI: Shinto divinity.

KANA: Japanese syllabic, phonetic writing; comprises two series of fifty characters: KATA-KANA, used like our italics, and HIRAGANA, or script.

KANAI: literally—"that which is inside the house", i.e. my wife.

KANJI: Chinese ideogram, as opposed to KANA.

KANNUSHI: the master (NUSHI) of the god (KAMI)—Shinto priest.

KAWA: river; in compound words:

-GAWA, e.g. SUMIDA-GAWA, the Sumida, Tokyo's river.

KIMONO: garment, gown—especially for women.

KITSUNE: fox. An animal held in dread on account of its gift of assuming various guises in order to hoodwink mankind.

KO: Sino-Japanese reading of MIZU-UMI, lake. Used as a component in the names of lakes: BIWA-KO—Lake Biwa.

KOI: carp. Symbol of long life, and strength. This explains why on 5th May, the Boys' Festival, each family hoists on a mast as many paper carps (KOI-NOBORI) as there are boys in the household. Its homonym with KOI, love, is the source of countless poetic puns.

KOKESHI: small wooden doll shaped on a lathe and painted.

KOKU: Sino-Japanese reading of

in accordance with the rules. But make it proportionate to the service rendered, or to the financial standing of the person to whom you are presenting it. Otherwise you would put him under an obligation to reciprocate, or else you would look as if you despised him. The art of gift-making is governed by extremely subtle rules, which are difficult for foreigners to grasp. Other than in exceptional cases, offer presents of little value but which show that you have selected them with taste and discrimination. If you spontaneously offer someone an object to which you are known to be attached, your gesture will be doubly appreciated. Don't be too hasty in taxing a Japanese with bad taste if he brings you one of those sumptuous horrors that Europe or America qualify as Oriental art! He will simply have assumed that you share the doubtful taste tourists are apt to show, and imagine he is making you happy.

KUNI, country. Used as a component in the names of countries: BEI-KOKU (America), EI-KOKU (England), FUKKOKU (France), I-KOKU (Italy), etc.

KOME: Rice in grains. As a plant, it is called INE; cooked, it is known as MESHI, or GO-HAN (GO being honorific); in the latter case, it also signifies meals.

KOTO: a kind of long harp with thirteen, seventeen, or nineteen strings, similar to the harpsichord. It is the most pleasant-sounding Japanese instrument to Western ears.

KUDASAI: "be so good as to"; used in forming the imperative.

KURA: fireproof strong room where objects of value are kept.

KURUMA: anything on wheels. According to era, designates the most common vehicle, formerly a

JINRIKISHA, nowadays a motorcar.

KYOGEN: comedy-farce forming an interlude between Noh plays.

Don't wax too impatient if you can't find the number you are looking for in the Japanese Telephone Directory straight away. Even for the Japanese themselves it requires earnest study and infinite patience to work their way through reference after reference until they come to the right page.

THE TELEPHONE—Of all the towns in the world, Tokyo beats the record for telephoning. It is unusual for a visitor who calls on you for more than five minutes not to be overcome by a sudden desire which propels him to ask if he may use your telephone. It is also unusual for a telephone conversation to last less than a quarter of an hour: since one never quite knows with whom one might be dealing, the most tactful and non-committal expressions have to be employed—and that takes time. In the theatre or cinema from time to time someone comes in with a paper banner, or a small luminous sign lights up, saying: "Mr So-and-so is wanted on the telephone." You will never be asked to pay for a 'phone call in a restaurant, a café, or a shop: it would be the lowest form of caddishness to refuse so natural a service. In the majority of public telephone-booths, you ask the operator to get your number for you, and she enjoins

MAGURO: tunny-fish, one of the most delicious fish eaten as *sashimi*.

MAIKO: apprentice-geisha in Kyoto —literally, "little dancing girl";

You may be curious to know why the lantern-bearer is wearing a policeman's uniform. The answer is that he is one of the many "specials" detailed to announce the imminent passage of official processions by means of these lighted signals.

in Tokyo they are called HANG-YOKU, "semi-jewel".

MATSU: pine tree, an essential element of any Japanese landscape. In love poems, evokes MATSU, to wait.

MATSURI: Shinto temple festival. HINA-MATSURI: the puppet festival—3rd March.

MI-: prefix indicating connexion with the gods, the Emperor, or an important person (*see* GO).

MI-KADO: "the sublime gate", former name for the Palace, occasionally applied to the Emperor. Although obsolete since the 15th century, this term is still used by foreigners instead of TENNO.

MI-KO: priestess, or female servant in a Shinto temple.

MIZU: cold water. Hot water is called YU.

MOKUSA: artemisia. Designates the

you not to forget to put the price of the call in the small box placed under the apparatus for this purpose. Always note numbers you may need, since, owing to the complicated system of addresses, consultation of the telephone book is a cross between a wager and a game of chance for the best-trained native of the country, even if he is employed by .... the telephone inquiry service itself.

THE EXACT TIME—The radio announces the time every fifteen minutes, trains leave and arrive to the second; whenever technical necessities so demand, the Japanese can be punctual. But in private life this race against time, which makes Western life so exhausting, is no longer justified. How can you reproach someone for arriving a quarter of an hour late, when you know he has had to travel ten miles or so in order to join you? And

treatment consisting of burning wads of this plant driven under the skin.

MON: blazon. Men and women alike wear it embroidered on their HAORI.

MONO: thing. Very frequent in compound words: MONO-GATARI: recital of things (tale, novel); KAKEMONO: thing suspended; SUI-MONO: thing drunk by supping (soup); BAKEMONO: thing that appears (ghost); KIMONO: thing one puts on, etc.

MURA: village. Frequent as a second element in a surname: KITAMURA, SHIMOMURA, TAMURA, UEMURA, etc.

MUSUKO: son, my son.

MUSUME: daughter, my daughter. This is the word the French writer Pierre Loti wrote as *mousmée*, with quite a different meaning,

foreign to the Japanese term.

NE-SAN: elder sister. Name used for calling shop-assistants or waitresses in cafés and restaurants.

NETSUKE: small carved trinket for attaching a tobacco-pouch or medicine box to one's belt.

NIHON, or NIPPON: sunrise, Japan. Japan is derived from the Chinese reading of this word: JE-PEN.

NINGYO: doll. Plays a major role in Japanese life.

NOH: first and most ancient form of classical drama.

NORITO: ritual Shinto prayer recited on certain occasions.

NOSHI: thin strip of dried *awabi* (shell) that always accompanies a gift.

OBI: belt; any kind of belt, not only the wide sash worn by women.

ODORI: dances related to KABUKI, or modern dances.

when you are really too much behind schedule, you can always fall back on the telephone, and the convenient little remark that sets everything to rights: "I am sorry to have kept you waiting." Tokyo's backbiters claim that "Kyoto time" is on an average an hour behind normal time, which is almost true, and far from unpleasant!

SURNAMES—The surname is always announced before the first name. In the past, the clan name was followed by *no*, corresponding to the nobiliary particle: Minamoto no Yoritomo means Yoritomo of the Minamoto clan. When writing in English or addressing foreigners, many Japanese have acquired the habit of beginning with the first name, in Anglo-American fashion. But as this custom is not generally followed, it results in a certain amount of confusion, foreigners who are not forewarned having no way

ONI: demon, a popular character in children's stories.

ONSEN: thermal spring, a pleasant variation of FURO.

PACHINKO: gambling-machine (a variation of a fruit-machine). Together with typhoons and earthquakes, this form of gaming is one of the worst scourges Japan has ever known.

RONIN: errant SAMURAI, made homeless by annihilation of his lord's family. Highway robber or righter of wrongs—the ideal character for drama or novels.

SA....: accompanied by a gentle scratch of the head with the right hand, is the Japanese man's reply to any rather precise question.

SAKANA: fish. In compound words: ZAKANA.

SAKURA: the Japanese cherry tree.

Beautiful flowers, but no fruit; symbol of the BUSHI.

SAMISEN: three-stringed guitar.

SAMURAI: warrior in the service of a DAIMYO. The word signifies: he who is in service, i.e. vassal, liege.

-SAMA, -SAN: polite suffix attached to a proper name; may be translated by Mr, Mrs, or Miss as the case may be.

SAN: Sino-Japanese reading for YAMA, mountain, e.g. FUJI-SAN. As a component in names of mountains, occasionally in the form ZAN, e.g. HIEI-ZAN.

SASHIMI: raw fish.

SEN: the hundredth of a yen. Now a thing of the past.

SENSEI: term of politeness used in addressing professors, doctors, lawyers, etc., as a substitute for SAN.

SEPPUKU: suicide by disembowel-

of distinguishing the surname from the first name. Throughout this volume we have therefore adopted the Japanese custom of indicating the surname before the first name. There being relatively few surnames, and an infinite variety of first names, celebrities in the spheres of history, art, and literature (both past and present) are commonly referred to by their first name, when the latter is unusual. A writer who wants to assume a pen-name as often as not contents himself with modifying his first name.

ADDRESSES—Addresses on letters begin with generalities and finish with particularities: department, town, district, street, number, name. Addresses in Tokyo are highly complicated, owing to the fact that streets have no names and houses no numbers, or numbers that are not consecutive. It is difficult, if not impossible to trace someone of whom you know only the

ment—privilege of the BUSHI.

SHIKATA GA NAI: "There's nothing one can do about it." A formula that expresses the patience of the Japanese, and emphasizes the impatience of the Westerner.

SHIMA: island. In compound words, occasionally JIMA: MIYAJIMA.

SHIMBUN: newspaper.

SHOCHIKUBAI: the three plants of good omen—SHO (MATSU), the pine tree, CHIKU (TAKE) the bamboo, and BAI (UME), the plum tree.

SHOGUN: a general. Formerly used to designate the military Regents.

SHOYU: soya sauce, the favourite seasoning of the Japanese.

SHUJIN: master, my husband.

SOBA: noodles made of buckwheat.

SUMO: professional heavy-weight wrestling.

TABI: socks with the big toe

separated, enabling one to wear GETA and ZORI.

TAI: kind of bream, one of the daintiest fish in Japan.

A crowd swarming round your taxi is a good sign that you may soon reach your destination if you are in the right district, since—the numbers not being consecutive—the only way of finding an address is by conducting an inquiry amongst the people in the neighbourhood.

address. Don't rely on taxis to get you there: the driver will expect you to show him the way.

FORMS OF GREETING—The Japanese is unfamiliar with the custom of shaking hands. When out-of-doors, he bows very low. Indoors, he kneels down and then prostrates himself until his brow touches the mat. This gesture is repeated several times, each bow being accompanied by a murmured expression of politeness. In principle, whichever of the two interlocutors holds a higher social status should give the signal to stop. But it would be most unmannerly to imply thereby that one considers oneself superior. The safest course therefore is to lean slightly to one side, in order to observe your companion; thus you are able to synchronize your movements, and at the same time safeguard your honour.

TANUKI: badger. The perfect match for the KITSUNE as far as practical jokes on mankind are concerned. In compound words DANUKI.

TATAMI: flexible mats that take the place of floor-boards in Japanese houses.

TEMPURA: fried fish, shellfish, or vegetables.

TENNO: celestial king. Usual designation of the Emperor. His own name, KINJO-TENNO-HEIKA—H. M. the present Emperor—is never uttered. A defunct emperor is designated by the name of his reign: MEIJI-TENNO, TAISHO-TENNO.

TERA: Buddhist temple.

TOKONOMA: niche in once of the walls of the room, where a KAKEMONO is hung, above a bouquet of flowers, an *objet d'art.* etc.

TORII: monumental portico leading to temples and other hallowed SHINTO spots.

TSURU-KAME: crane and tortoise, symbols of long life.

UKIYO-E: "pictures of this drifting world"—the famous prints, often depicting evil haunts, UKIYO.

UNAGI: Japanese eel—one of the daintiest dishes imaginable.

WAKA: poem of thirty-one beats, also called TANKA.

WATA: cotton-wool. Hence the English word wadding.

-YA: suffix indicating the names of trades, e.g. SOBA-YA, soba vendor; PAN-YA, baker; HON-YA, bookseller, etc.

YAMA: mountain. One should not say: FUJI-YAMA (*see* -SAN).

YEN: Japanese money. Literally: round.

POLITENESS AND CONVERSATION—You should always make a show of attentiveness whenever anyone speaks to you. All you have to do is to repeat *ha! so desa ka?* (oh, is that so?). Shades of meaning are indicated by stress, so that in these few words you can express all kinds of interjections ranging from "no kidding!" to "good heavens: is that so?" The fair sex use the more harmonious expressions: *sayo de gozaimasu ka?* (same meaning). A hearty man exclaims: *so ka?* or even *ha!*, in a very guttural voice.

If you wish to raise an objection, say *shitsurei itashimasu ga . . . .* "It is not etiquette, but . . . ." ("Forgive me for being so rude, but . . . ."). This convenient formula may also be used in taking leave of people, in an ambiguous way once again: "I apologize for leaving so soon," or "I apologize for having stayed so long."

If your host in turn retorts *shitsurei . . .*, this may imply, as one pleases:

YUKATA: light cotton kimono as worn in summer.

-ZA: suffix indicating the names of playhouses, e.g. KABUKI-ZA, BUN-RAKU-ZA. The suffix for NOH theatres is DOH, as for temples.

ZAIBATSU: "financial clans" The huge family "trusts" that used to dominate Japanese economy—MITSUI, MITSUBISHI, etc.

ZORI: shoes designed on the same principle as the GETA, but with soles of woven straw.

JAPANIZED FOREIGN EXPRESSIONS

Through necessity or snobbishness, the Japanese have introduced into their language a large number of foreign words, mainly English and French. These expressions are re-modelled to conform with the possibilities of transcription into kana,

and when retranscribed in Latin characters, as pronounced, they are very hard to recognize, especially as the most frequent ones are

If the most cordial reception gives you a pain in the back, it's simply because you have not acquired the art of crouching on your heels for a few hours at a time. After a certain amount of training, you may one day discover that those seemingly hard mats are really quite comfortable . . . .

"I apologize for giving you such a poor reception," or "I apologize for not detaining you," or again "for having detained you."

O-matase itashimashita—"I have kept you waiting, I apologize" permits anyone, anywhere, and on any pretext to keep you waiting indefinitely, especially if he has already said *chotto matte kudasai*, "wait a moment....", or the fateful word *tadaima* meaning "right away", i.e. "now" or "next week"—if it doesn't mean "never" as certain evil-minded people would have it. If you observe the rites, all you can do is to reply with a smile: *do itashimashite*—"don't mention it ...." *O-matase* has become a word of warning, such as barked out by the station loudspeaker to announce that the train is about to leave.... exactly on time: "You have taken the trouble to arrive early; if you haven't left yet, neither the station-master nor the engine driver is to blame!"

abridged if too unwieldy. A few examples will suffice:

BIRU for BIRUDINGU: building.

Thus: MARU-NO-UCHI BUILDING becomes MARU-BIRU.

TEREBI for TEREBISHION: television.

ZENESUTO for ZENERARU-SUTO-RAIKU: general strike.

INFURE for INFURESHION: inflation.

A few of the expressions derived from other languages have met with great success, for example:

ABEKU: *avec* (with) has acquired the meaning of going out with a girl friend.

AIRON: an iron.

DEPATO: a department store.

LANDEBU: rendezvous.

And more recently:

APURE-GERU: *après-guerre* (postwar) which designates recent literary, philosophical, and artistic movements, as well as the failings attributed to them: in short, the word has met with a fate similar to French existentialism.

INDEX

Ago Bay 207
Aichi 69
Akanuma 266
Amakusa, Island of 224
Amanohashidate 226, 232
Ariake, Sea of 224
Arita 225
Asakusa 161
Asama-Yama (Volcano) 228
Aso, Mount 223
Atago 262
Atami 198
Atsuta, Temple of 205, 276
Atsuta Bay 193, 205, 208
Awaji, Island of 220
Awazu 133, 226

Bentenjima 269
Beppu 223
Biwa, Lake 133, 201, 226, 227, 266,
269, 388
Bizen 91, 353

Caroline Islands 242
Chiba 341
China 51, 52, 54, 55, 73, 77, 81, 82,
88, 94, 97, 121, 192, 206, 241, 257,
258, 259, 261, 264, 266, 268, 288,
293, 301, 357, 374, 378, 379
Chitose Airport 235
Chuzenji, Lake 231, 234

Daisetsuzan National Park . . . 236
Daiya-Gawa Torrent 229
Dan-no-ura 28
Deshikaga 236
Deshima, Island of 57

Edo 29, 96, 116, 156, 161, 182, 193,
211, 322
Ejiri 226
Enoshima 196-8, 269, 340

Formosa 172, 242, 374
Fuji, Mount, see Fujisan

Fuji-Kawa, River 202
Fujisan 38, 96, 114, 182, 194, 198,
199-202, 203, 206, 213, 292, 392
Fukuoka 225, 362, 363
Fukushima 232
Fushimi 261

Gifu 204, 205
Gora 198
Goshako Bay 207

Hakodate 238
Hakone District, The 198-9
Hakone, Lake 200
Hakone-Machi 198
Haneda Airport 178
Hasama Bay 207
Heian (Heian-Kyo) 26-7, 58, 81, 106
Hiei-zan 82, 226, 227, 392
Hikamiyama 262
Hikimoto Bay 207
Hi-no-misaki, Cape 24
Hiraizumi 234
Hirayama 226
Hiroshima 32, 220, 224
Hiyoshi 263
Hodogaya 173
Hokkaido, Island of 23, 36, 172, 194,
234, 235-8, 242, 253, 361
Hong Kong 32, 378
Honshu, Island of 23, 75, 172, 174,
219, 223, 225, 252

Ibaraki 212
Ichi-no-Tani 27
India . . 73, 81, 91, 165, 257, 264, 378
Indo-China 32
Indonesia 32
Inland Sea 174, 176, 194, 208, 217-22, 263
Ise . . . 205-7, 208, 213, 226, 261, 276
Ise, Bay of 38, 206, 341
Ise-Shima 205
Ishikari, River 237

Ishiyama 226, 266
Itsukushima (Miyajima), Island of
                        82, 262, 269
Izu Peninsula 203
Izumo . . . 23, 24, 144, 226, 262, 276

Japan, Sea of 23, 172, 174, 226, 309
Japanese Alps 228
Jozankei 236

Kagoshima 56, 174, 225
Kai Province 201
Kamakura 28, 29, 56–7, 86, 109, 110,
  195, 196, 197, 269, 284, 346, 384
Karafuto 242
Karasaki 226
Karuizawa 228
Kashima 262
Kashiwara 276
Kata Bay 207
Kataka 226
Kirishima National Park 225
Kiso, River 205, 227
Kita 262
Kobe 160, 194, 208, 210–11, 212,
                    213, 224, 238, 363
Kochi 220
Korea 25, 37, 52, 75, 78, 172, 174,
        204, 206, 241, 242, 374, 378
Koshien 212
Koyasan 82, 212
Kumagawa, River 224
Kumamoto 224
Kumano 263
Kunozan 229
Kurama 65, 66–7
Kure 220
Kurihama 195
Kuril Islands 172
Kyoto 26, 58, 62, 65, 69, 81, 82, 87,
  88, 92, 96, 106, 109, 116, 126, 137,
  144, 152, 158, 182, 190, 193, 194,
  198, 208, 213–6, 219, 226, 231, 261,
  274, 284, 288, 290, 304, 322, 331,
                    363, 371, 390
Kyushu, Island of 28, 31, 56, 75, 91,
  92, 172, 174, 194, 219, 223–5, 235,
                        252, 361

Manchuria 32, 54, 172, 242, 282,
                  337, 363, 374, 378

Marshall Islands 242
Matsue 226
Matsumoto 228
Matsushima 232–4
Matsuo 262
Mie, Prefecture of 205, 207
Miho 42
Miidera 226
Minatogawa, River 212
Misaka Mountains 199
Mishima 251
Miyagi 232
Miyajima (Itsukushima), Island of
                    82, 222, 232, 393
Miyanoshita 198
Miyazaki 225
Miyazu, Gulf of 226
Moji 224, 225
Mongolia 54
Moto-Hakone 198
Motosu, Lake 202
Mount Fuji, see Fujisan
Muroran 238

Nagano 69, 228
Nagara, River 205
Nagasaki . . . 57, 94, 224–5, 232, 238
Nagoya 174, 194, 202–5, 211, 227,
                  231, 276, 362, 363
Nakasendo, The 227
Nara 23, 26, 58, 59, 62–3, 75, 76, 79,
  80, 86, 106, 122, 124, 194, 214,
  217–9, 221, 262, 274, 276, 286, 287,
                        308, 384
Naruto, Straits of 218, 220
Nikko 53, 93, 194, 228–31, 232, 234,
                  238, 260, 264
Noboribetsu 236
Numazu 198

Oita 223
Okaba 195
Okhotsk, Sea of 172
Omi, see Biwa, Lake
Osaka 31, 124, 137, 141, 142, 156,
  157, 158, 160, 162, 194, 208–12,
                  213, 362–3, 384
Oshima 238
Otaru, Bay of 237, 238
Otsu 226

Pearl Harbour 32
Philippine Islands 32, 366
Port Arthur 31

Ryukyu Islands 172

Sagami Bay 195
Sagami Province 201
Saganoseki, Gulf of 223
Sakhalin, Island of 172, 242
Sakura (Volcano) 174
Sapporo 235, 238, 362
Seiko, Lake 202
Sendai 174, 232, 234
Sengokuhara 198
Seta 226
Setagawa, River 226
Seto 91
Shikoku, Island of 108, 172, 194, 219,
                220-22, 223, 252
Shimbara 225
Shimonoseki 30, 225, 363
Shiogama 232
Shiraoi 236
Shizuoka 69
Shodo Island 220
Shoji, Lake 202
Siberia 54, 282
Singapore 32
Sumida, River 387, 388
Sunkyo Gorge 237
Suruga Bay 193
Suruga Province 201
Suwa 263

Takamatsu 220
Takarazuka 160, 212
Takasago 42
Takasaki, Mount 223

Tokachigawa 236
Tokaido, The 96, 116, 117, 173,
            193-4, 195, 198, 227, 251, 384
Tokushima 220
Tokyo 29, 60, 78, 96, 136, 145, 158,
    160, 162, 167, 171, 172, 174, 177,
    178-92, 193, 203, 211, 220, 225,
    232, 235, 238, 275, 276, 284, 289,
    295, 297, 346, 354, 361, 362, 363,
    364-5, 367, 368, 370, 371, 372, 373,
                387, 388, 390, 393
Tokyo Bay 193, 238, 341, 375
Tomo 220
Torii Pass 228
Tosa 108
Towada, Lake 234
Toyama 309
Tsugaru Channel . . . 174, 232, 234

Uji 82
Uji-Yamada 205
Unzen National Park 225
Ura 224
Urakami 224
Utsunomiya Pass 195

Wakano-ura 212, 263
Wakayama 212

Yabase 226
Yamato . . . 23, 28, 212, 217, 219
Yashima 220
Yellow Sea 172
Yokohama 172, 179, 193, 194-5, 224,
                238, 364, 377, 387
Yoshida 277
Yoshino 28
Yoshiwara 95, 161, 322
Yunugu 236

Chinzan-go gardens— (handwritten)

ACKNOWLEDGEMENTS

The Publishers would like to thank the following organizations for their permission to use the illustrations on the pages indicated—

GALERIE HUGUETTE BÉRÈS (photographer ELSER) – 313, 325, 333, and the endpapers. BIBLIOTHÈQUE NATIONALE – 30, 31, 37, 109, 115, 117, 173, 175, 186, 195, 199, 242/3, 251, 257, 259, 262, 263, 277. MUSÉE GUIMET (photographer ELSER) – 24/5, 27, 29, 38, 39, 41, 42, 43, 44, 102, 107, 110, 111, 112, 113, 114, 118, 218/9, 248/9, 265, 271, 301, 309, 310, 315, 317, 318, 332. BIJUTSU SHUPPAN SHA, TOKYO – 81. HEIBONSHA, TOKYO – 90/91. TOTO BUNKA COMPANY, LTD, TOKYO (from *Pageant of Japanese Art*) – 86, 92. F. A. BROCKHAUS, WIESBADEN (from *Die Japanische Malerei, 1953*) – 88/9. PRODUCTION DAIEI (Bellotti–Film, Rome) – 166. PRODUCTION DAIEI (Pathé–Overseas, Paris) – 168. PHOTOS BRENET – 167, 181, 206, 244, 275, 285, 320, 334, 363, 371, 373. PHOTO KEYSTONE – 252. PHOTOS MAGNUM–BISCHOF – 179, 203, 284, 341, 375. PHOTOS PAUL MOUSSET – 197, 213.

All the illustrations reproduced in the chapter on *Art* were provided by ELSER, as well as those on pages — 23, 45, 256, 268, 269, 328/9, 330/31.

Also acknowledged with thanks is the permission received from the following publishers to quote extracts from their books—

Harvard University Press, *The United States and Japan* by Edwin O. Reischauer (p. 245)

The Macmillan Company of New York, *Japan, an Attempt at Interpretation* by Lafcadio Hearn, 1924 (p. 312)

John Murray (Publishers) Limited, *Things Japanese* by Basil Hall Chamberlain (p. 274)

Drukkerij Holland N.V.—Senefelder,
Amsterdam

4/9/58 454 — Read— Bridge to the sun; 3 Bamboo

Kyoto — Kamo River
      Heian Shrine —
      V. adm. Yamagota home & garden
   * Nomura villa — finest in Japan
      Tatsumura silk Mansion —
      Sekiho Shrine (Moss gardens)
      Ryōan—Ji Temple (Stone garden)

Nara
      — Park
      To-daiji Temple (Daibutsu)
      Kasuga — 1000 lanterns

Kyoto — shin KYOGOKu Alley
         （新京極）

china Tachikichi
bags — Yamamoto
country style restaurant — JUNIDAN-YA
      (MIZU-DAKI   Gion-Kyota   (12 steps)

SILK STORE — ORIDONO